A SOUND OF STRANGERS

Musical culture, acculturation,
and the post-Civil War
ethnic American

NICHOLAS TAWA

THE SCARECROW PRESS, INC.
Metuchen, N.J., & London 1982

Library of Congress Cataloging in Publication Data

Tawa, Nicholas E.
  A sound of strangers.

  Bibliography: p.
  Includes index.
  1. Folk music--United States--History and criticism.
2. Music, Popular (Songs, etc.)--United States--History
and criticism. I. Title.
ML3551.T29   781.7'2'00973   81-21235
ISBN 0-8108-1504-4   AACR2

TABLE OF CONTENTS

PREFACE

A Sound of Strangers is a study of musical acculturation in those American ethnic communities that were first formed toward the end of the nineteenth century and that continue to today. As far as I could determine, the present book is the first written on this important subject.

Taken up are the musical traditions brought to America by the millions of peasants and urban workers from southern Italy, the Mideast, and Eastern Europe, and by the Chinese, Japanese, and East European Jews. These were men and women whose ways of life had few points of contact with American practices. The resultant tensions were great, the reconciliations difficult.

Omitted from the discussion is the music arriving in America from the British Isles, Scandinavia, Germany, Spain, and France. For the most part it was brought here by earlier immigrant societies whose traditions had many associations with, or were the antecedents of, the dominant American culture that confronted the later arrivals. In addition, a great deal has been written about this music by sympathetic American historians.

I was impelled to enter upon this work after it became painfully obvious that music historians have ignored or misunderstood the new immigration's contributions to American musical culture, that most sociologists have paid scant attention to the arts dimension of immigrant life, and that the many ethnic Americans I knew felt, as Dr. Otto Kinkeldey, America's first professor of musicology, put it: "The skin and bones of the immigrant experience have been studied to death; the soul of that experience has been left out."

When Dr. Kinkeldey discovered, in 1949, that I was

of Syrian-Lebanese extraction and had grown up in Boston's
South End with Chinatown on one side of me, Jewtown on
another, and Greektown on still another, he asked me to explore and present a paper at his Harvard University Musicology Seminar on the survival of non-Anglo-Saxon traditional
music in the South End. A few months later Dr. Archibald
Davison, of the Harvard University music faculty, suggested
that I examine and write a study on the remains of troubadour-
like song forms among the emigrants from the Mediterranean
basin who had settled in Boston. Both men kindled an interest in ethnic musical cultures that has remained with me
to today.

The evidence upon which the book rests is drawn
from four sources. The first is my own intimate acquaintance with several of Boston's ethnic subcultures, particularly
those of the Syrian-Lebanese, Greeks, Armenians, Jews,
and Italians. The second is my experience in working with
all of Greater Boston's ethnocultural associations, in conjunction with the annual Whole World Celebration and the
International Ball sponsored by Boston's International Institute, on whose Board of Directors I once sat. The third
source is the wealth of interviews of first-, second-, and
third-generation ethnic Americans and autobiographical reports submitted by students enrolled in my course on American Music. The fourth is the literature of histories, sociological studies, biographies, autobiographies, and periodical
articles that seek to illuminate the ethnic experience. I
have tried to base most of the conclusions advanced in the
text on corroborating materials drawn from all four sources.

My introduction to ethnic cultures other than the
Syrian-Lebanese and Armenian ones (several relatives had
married Armenians before coming to America) began at six
years of age, when twice a week I was made to join a special speech class designed for children to whom English
was a second or unknown language. I entered it knowing
only Arabic, and only after kindergarten and first-grade
teachers had failed, after numerous spankings and rattanings,
to impress the desirability of learning the English language
upon my young body and mind.

The class was small, numbering about a dozen boys--
Syrians, Jews, Greeks, and Chinese. What is more, the
same students were kept together from one year to the next.
Willy-nilly, the boys became friends, and each took to invit-
ing some of the others to his home. By ten years of age

I had witnessed ethnic celebrations unknown to my parents, consumed a variety of exotic foods, learned songs heard neither at school nor at home, and helped my friends at their chores, whether in their father's Jewish bakery or Chinese grocery or Greek pastry shop. None of the boys could drop in on my father's place, for it was four miles away--an ice-cream-cone factory situated in the midst of a Polish district.

At thirteen years of age I began working at the factory, part-time during much of the year, full-time during summer school vacation. I came to know some of the Polish workers well. Visits to their homes and attendance at their picnics followed.

Music, which I had loved from my earliest years, had remained relatively unexplored, as my parents had destined me for law school and felt that study of a musical instrument would fritter away too much of my energy. Though I was a pre-law major at Harvard, the new friends I made there were musical or literary. Most important to this study, one classmate insisted I compose an autobiography and keep a daily journal as a means of understanding myself and the world around me. (We were very intense young men in those years!) Thus began my still-persistent habit of writing all sorts of notes on 3x5 cards, which were then squirreled away in shoe boxes. During my undergraduate years I took up the study of violin, piano, and musical composition, and became increasingly involved with music.

Still sharp in my memory is the way my parents stared at each other in consternation, first when I turned down Harvard Law School in 1945 and entered graduate school to study music, and second when I announced I was going to marry a woman of Italian descent. Her parents reacted with equal dismay, thinking Syrians were short, crinkle-haired people whose dark skins were mottled with spots in varying shades of green!

My wife, Chela, and I had to learn how to cope with the demands of two extended and close-knit families, one Syrian-Lebanese, the other Sicilian-Piedmontese. Our solution was first to move to another city, and later, when we moved back to the Boston area, to live, as much as possible, simultaneously with both. It should be added that Chela's family was musical. Her father had been a professional oboe and English-horn player before ulcers got the best of him. Her uncle had been a trombonist with the Boston Symphony Orchestra and later was supervisor of instrumental music in the Boston public schools. Her brother is now director of all music in the Boston public schools, band director at Boston College, and manager of the musical entertainments for the Boston Patriot games.

Although I won several awards in musical composition, I found that a surer way to pay bills was to teach. Therefore during the 1950s we lived in Springfield, Massachusetts, where I was an instrumental supervisor responsible for the musical instruction in six schools in Springfield's North End. The students came mainly from impoverished homes--Greek, Italian, French-Canadian, Jewish, Armenian, Syrian-Lebanese, Puerto Rican, and black. To build a viable music program, we formed a parents' committee. It sought inexpensive secondhand instruments for the children (the school system supplied only tubas, string basses, cellos, and percussion), found money for band and orchestra uniforms, and helped form a car pool to transport students to concert engagements in and outside the district.

My job required frequent visits to ethnic homes, to attend meetings and to resolve the many cultural, social, and economic problems that resulted when a child entered the instrumental-music program. At first hand I witnessed the parents' hunger for music, their anxiety over the weakening of ethnocultural ties that affiliation with public-school music groups might entail, and their reluctant accommodation to the several phases of musical acculturation evidenced in their children.

In the mid-sixties I joined the faculty of the University of Massachusetts at Boston, whose student body was drawn largely from the several ethnic communities of the area. At the same time I began working with Boston's International Institute to help strengthen its instructional programs in ethnic culture and to cooperate in launching its series of week-long Whole World Celebrations, which quickly became popular showcases for the several music and dance heritages of the local immigrant societies.

I learned a great deal more, in these years, about cultures with which I had had mostly a reading acquaintance. My surname, Tawa, is common among the Japanese. Consequently I was often invited to Japanese social functions; Japanese-Americans were convinced that somewhere in my background lurked a Japanese affiliation. My mother's maiden name, Ahto, occurs in Baltic families (curiously enough, the Ahto family is blond, blue-eyed, and fair-skinned). This was one reason why Lithuanians were willing to speak freely with me. At the same time I gained a firsthand intimacy with ethnic cultural organizations and the problems their leaders faced. Among these organizations were the Ukrainian-American Youth Association, the Italian-American Youth Singers, the Portuguese Encantos Folcloricos, the Armenian General Benevolent Union, the Hellenic Ensemble, the Krakowiak Polish Dancers, the Israeli Folklorists, the Lithuanian Youth Ensemble, the Yugoslav Folk Dancers, and other music and dance groups representing the peoples from every part of Europe and from some parts of the Middle and Far East--Turkey, Syria, Lebanon, Egypt, Indonesia, China, and Japan.

Each year associations affiliated with from forty to fifty ethnic subcultures participate in the Whole World Celebration. Since 1965 I have formally interviewed all of their directors owing to my role of master-of-ceremonies at the performances. It did not take long for me to discover that neither these interviews nor the taped meetings that adhered to a punctilious agenda were useful for the purposes of this study. Microphones seemed to inhibit free and open conversation. Men and women talked stiffly, waited for questions to be put to them, and as often as not misunderstood what was asked or hedged their answers. Vastly more revealing were the overheard asides and the informal conversations over coffee that took place at rehearsals and backstage on performance days. The talk was swiftly recorded on 3x5 cards and filed away for later use. Invitations to family gatherings and communal celebrations provided further insights, and these, too, found their way onto 3x5 cards.

Indispensable sources of information have been the autobiographical reports written by all students enrolled in my two-semester course on American musical culture. Since 1965 about 450 reports have been submitted, most of them by third-generation, far less by second-generation, descendants of the new immigrants. The main object of these accounts was the recording of the musicocultural history of the writer's family as far back as the pooled memory of parents, grandparents, and relatives could penetrate. Every report was followed up with at least one conference with the writer, in order to verify the authenticity of the information given, to clarify ambiguous statements, and to explore promising lines of inquiry. The agreement was that I could write up the information contained in the reports and interviews, so long as the authors remained anonymous. This understanding has been honored, though in one instance it was impossible to conceal the writer's identity owing to the nature of the quoted material.

The distribution of nationalities among the students taking the course provided some surprises. While most of them were of Italian and East European Jewish descent, and a respectable number came from Slavic (mainly Polish), Hungarian, Greek, Armenian, Albanian, Portuguese, Lithuanian, and Syrian-Lebanese backgrounds, few of the enrollees were Irish, black, or Chinese. The absence of blacks and Chinese can be explained. Blacks are offered courses in non-jazz black musical history and in jazz and blues that probably interest them more. The Chinese may have avoided a course that they thought would concern itself mostly with the establishment of Western musical cultures in America. The lack of Irish students is puzzling.

As I assembled my notes preparatory to writing this study, it became obvious that the preponderance of my evidence concerned urban men and women of East European Jewish and Mediterranean origin. This, of course, is reflected in the pages that follow. To keep the book to a manageable length, I decided early on in the writing to focus on secular music. The need still exists, however, for a reliable study of sacred music's functions in the ethnic subcultures.

How trustworthy is the story that follows? Recognize that what follows is in large measure groundbreaking. Guidelines were few; opportunities for error, constant. I dare not pretend that what I have written is the Truth. My sincere hope is only that it leads us closer to the truth about the total immigrant experience.

ACKNOWLEDGMENTS

Permission to reprint text or music is gratefully acknowledged, as follows:

Two songs, in Pennsylvania Songs and Legends, ed. George Korson (Baltimore: Johns Hopkins University Press, 1949), pp. 437-38, 439-40. Quoted by permission of the publishers.

Two songs, in Helen Ware, "The American-Hungarian Folk-Song," Musical Quarterly (1916), pp. 434-41; and three songs, in Maud Hare, "Portuguese Folk-Songs from Provincetown, Cape Cod, Mass.," Musical Quarterly (1928), pp. 35-53. Quoted by permission of the editor.

Two songs, in Echoes of Naples, ed. Mario Favilli (Boston: Ditson, 1909). Reproduced by permission of the publisher, letter dated 4-27-81.

Five songs, in The Story of an Immigrant Group in Franklin, New Jersey, by Janos Makar (Franklin: Author, 1969). Quoted by permission of Botond B. Makar.

Three songs, in The Ukrainian Winter Folksong Cycle in Canada, by Robert B. Klymasz (Ottawa: National Museums of Canada, 1970). Quoted by permission of The Klymasz Collection, Canadian Centre for Folk Culture Studies, National Museum of Man, National Museums of Canada.

The Japanese Anthem, "Kimi ga yo," in Farewell To Manzanar, by Jeanne Wakatsuki Houston and James D. Houston (Boston: Houghton Mifflin, 1973). Copyright © 1973 by James D. Houston. Reprinted by permission of Houghton Mifflin Company.

Four Czech songs, in Bruno Nettl and Ivo Moravcik, "Czech and Slovak Songs Collected in Detroit," Midwest Folklore (Spring 1955), pp. 37, 40-44. Quoted by permission of the editor.

Eli, Eli, in A Treasury of Jewish Folklore, by Nathan Ausubel (New York: Crown, 1948). Copyright © 1948, 1976

by Crown Publishers, Inc.   Quoted by permission of
Crown Publishers, Inc.

One song, in E. May, "Encounters with Japanese Music in
Los Angeles," Western Folklore (July 1958), pp. 192-93.
Quoted by permission of the editor.

Kol Nidre, in Concise Encyclopedia of Jewish Music, ed.
Macy Nulman (New York: McGraw-Hill, 1975).   Quoted
by permission of McGraw-Hill Publishers and Macy Nulman.

Christopher Columbus, in The Two Rosetos, by Carla Bianco
(Bloomington: Indiana University Press, 1974).   Quoted
by permission of Indiana University Press.

Hymn of the Japanese-American Citizen's League, in To
Serve the Devil, II, by Paul Jacobs and Saul Landau
(New York: Random House, 1971).   Quoted by permis-
sion of Random House Publishers, Inc.

A
SOUND
OF
STRANGERS

Chapter 1

BACKGROUNDS, AMERICAN AND FOREIGN

●————————————————————————————

America by 1880 had already become the home of migrants
from Spain, France, the British Isles, the Scandinavian
countries, and Germany. The musical story of these people has been told many times. Also receiving the attention
of writers have been the handful of opera stars, symphony
conductors, virtuosic instrumentalists, and educated men
and women of means and high culture. In contrast, the
musical culture of the millions of people who migrated here
in the forty or so years beginning with the 1880s remains
largely ignored. Their story is our concern. These new
Americans arrived from areas heretofore scantily represented
in America: southern Italians, East European Jews, Poles,
Yugoslavs, Greeks, Magyars, Lithuanians, Portuguese, Russians, Ukrainians, Rumanians, Bulgarians, Armenians, Syrians, and Albanians. From across the Pacific had come
Chinese and Japanese. [1]

At first came mostly bachelors or married men without their families. They intended to work intensively for a
limited period, then return home with their accumulated savings. For a vareity of reasons, however, large numbers
of them remained in America. Soon marriageable young
women commenced crossing over to marry their single countrymen. Married men sent for wives and children. An increasing emigration of entire families ensued. Some groups,
like the Jews and Armenians, had existed as aliens in their
places of origin. Because they wished to escape persecution,
they usually came as entire families and with the intention
of settling here permanently. Few of these people knew
what to expect after they arrived in the United States. All
hoped to achieve a fuller life for themselves and their children.

The description of these migrations--the hardships of home, the bewilderment after disembarkation, the struggle to win a place in the American economic, political, and social scene--has been set down. But still we ask, what were their artistic and aesthetic attitudes? How did these strangers value and use what they and their ancestors had nurtured in the arts? What were the sounds of ethnic music within the American context; how and why did it survive here and accommodate itself to the necessities of hostile surroundings?

In trying to answer these questions, my intention is not to discuss in detail the music and musical practices of each ethnic subculture. A vast undertaking in itself, such an endeavor is beyond the scope of this study. Rather, I shall seek out the most significant principles governing the performance of ethnic music in America, to explain the relationship of these principles to a common immigrant experience, and to illustrate them with the comments of ethnic Americans, and, where appropriate, with musical examples and descriptions of actual music making.

Strange People and Strange Music

From the beginning, native Americans recognized these immigrants as really foreign, unlike anything American, British, or the more approachable European from the north and west. Their skin was darker or yellower; height, shorter; shape of head, eyes, and nose, unfamilar. They dressed, behaved, ate, kept their homes, and raised their children in what seemed an outlandish fashion. Their speech consisted of a meaningless jabber accompanied by outsized gestures. Their religions excited Protestant uneasiness, for these strangers were also religious aliens--Roman Catholics, Orthodox Christians, Orthodox Jews, and Buddhists. Some were even atheists. The new arrivals failed to show pride and interest in American democratic procedures. Few desired citizenship or assimilation into American life.

The nativist asked why did these people gesticulate so freely, speak so vehemently, value keeping "face" and "respect"? To the insular American these people lived by outworn rituals and retained superstitions out of place in a modern America. Their clannishness, tight family ties to the exclusion of other relationships, and uninhibited styles of living (exemplified by noisy and chaotic picnics, weddings, christenings, and funerals) were puzzling. They practiced strange secular-religious rites like the bar-mitzvah, festa, and Easter celebration uniting the Resurrection to spring-time fertility symbols. They celebrated their own national holidays; American Independence Day meant little to them.

As one Bostonian writes:

> My great-grandfather came down here from Nova Scotia, and my father tells me that he [the great-grandfather] and my grandfather thought all Italians in the West End were crazy, boozing it up when-ever they could. They couldn't keep their hands off you.... When they weren't fighting with each other, they were singing, playing guitars, or turn-ing up their radios real loud. One guy who lived across the street from my grandfather used to push his Victrola to an open window and play Ital-ian songs and opera all day. And no one com-plained. Instead of wasting their time and money on wine and music, he said, they should have cleaned themselves and their houses better, and gone to school to get better jobs. When he knew a festa was coming up, he used to visit his sister in Bangor [Maine]. [2]

Old musical habits persisted, however incongruous with the American scene. A paradigm of this sort of incon-gruity was witnessed by Louis Adamic in 1922:

> One night about six years ago, staying in a hotel on St. Clair Avenue in Cleveland, which has a large Yugoslav colony, I was awakened by a party of Carniolans passing below, singing a familiar Slovene song. I went to the window. They stop-ped on the corner and sang stanza after stanza. They had, apparently, had a few drinks and felt sentimental. A street-car rattled by; a moment later two speeding automobiles almost collided. In the distance somewhere a locomotive clanged and whistled. They sang well, but I wished they would stop and go on. The song would have sounded beautiful back in some quiet village in Slovenia, but here in Cleveland, in America-- no.... A policeman came from across the street and told the melodists that unless they shut up at once and moved on he would run them in. They

were, it appeared, disturbing the peace. Where
the hell did they think they were anyhow? Back
in the old country?[3]

The music in many instances seemed as foreign as
the immigrants who treasured it. Bizarre were the persistent minor and modal scales of the Jews and Slavs; the
quarter- and three-quarter-tone intervals of the Greeks and
Syrians; the intense nasal quality and unfamiliar ornamenta-
tion in the singing of vocalists from the Middle East and
Balkans; the whining, raucous, and unpredictable melody
produced by the strange instruments and the tinkly penta-
tonic singsong of the Chinese. None of these sounds had
correspondences in the tidy, plain, major-scale tunes sung
with square rhythms and open voices that Americans enjoyed. Nor did Sicilians always sound like Verdi; Rumanians, like Enesco; Poles, like Chopin; Jews, like Bloch;
and Japanese, like the casts in the musicals The Mikado
and The Geisha.

Translations of the song lyrics sung in ethnic communities sometimes revealed a point of view unacceptable to
moralistic turn-of-the-century Americans. The inhabitants
of immigrant communities, for instance, did not hold sex a
taboo subject. When older Polish boys and girls from Boston's Hampden Street area sang certain songs full of sly
references to the pleasures of bedding down with a lissome
sexual partner, they certainly behaved unlike proper Bos-
tonians. Yet parents refused to object. Similar songs are
easily found in the song literature of the Portuguese, southern Italians, and others. The prevalence of such songs,
however, did not import promiscuity, as some Americans
thought. Indeed, the Hampden Street parents tried to watch
carefully over their daughters' activities. One member of
the Polish settlement explained that, on the contrary, such
songs were ways of encouraging the young and preparing
them for marriage. [4]

Similar considerations hold true for the rather scurrilous ditties about simple Orthodox priests and their car-
nally appetent wives, popular with Albanians, Greeks, and
Syrians. Their performance did not portend an imminent
apostasy from Orthodoxy. One amazed woman of Irish descent, recently married to a first-generation Albanian-
American, heard a song of this type sung lustily by several
men during an Albanian Orthodox Church picnic. Even more
amazing to her, the priest, sitting on a nearby bench,

listened and smiled. [5] "A priest isn't God. His wife isn't the Virgin Mary. They don't go around with their eyes looking down on their breasts. They know what the world's about," was the explanation that seemed to satisfy the Albanian husband and his circle of friends. [6]

Puzzling to an American were other sentiments in the songs of immigrants--their fatalism, worldweariness, cynicism, laughter at hallowed principles and institutions, and outrageously passionate declarations of love. Some expressions were intimately related to the past and present experiences of the singers and were bound to rub off on their descendants. In turn, their children might eventually hand them on to Americans in general.

A fascinating task of the musical historian is the tracing of a sentiment in little evidence in nineteenth-century American culture and watching it gradually be introduced into the American mainstream by talented descendants of immigrants. Isaac Goldberg writes of one person who effected such a transmission. Describing George Gershwin and the background to his music, Goldberg states:

> Laughter comes easily to him, but so does a certain half-puzzled solemnity that does not sit naturally upon his brow. In those blue moments ... he is prone to regard himself as a rather sad young man, adrift in a universe foredoomed to unhappiness. Not, you will understand, a "greenery, yallery, Grosvenor Gallery, foot-in-the-grave young man ...," but an atavistic exponent, perhaps, of the melancholia judaica, --that Weltschmerz which the Jew seems to acquire with circumcision. [7]

The description of Gershwin goes hand-in-hand with an earlier one given by Hutchins Hapgood of a Russian Jew he met in New York: "Being a Jew, he was serious. Being a Russian didn't add to his frivolity, for he early imbibed a love for Tolstoy, Dostoyefski, Turgeneff, Gogol, Chekow, and others; and this didn't induce in him exactly a hilarious view of existence." [8]

Puzzlement over the immigrant's outlandish ways of thinking and behaving often led Americans to a disvaluement of non-American habits. Why was the foreigner disliked and laughed at? Bothered by this question, Enrico Sartorio explained the southern Italian's peculiarities found ludicrous

by Americans as owing to the simple peasant-village life he
had known overseas. In an Italian village, Sartorio writes,
no one really noticed what a man wore, or cared if he
shaved. "Early in the morning he called out to his friend
across the street as he went to the field." Everyone was
up early anyway; few noticed the noise. "He sang as he
crossed the village going to work and coming back; the
'stornello' of his friend answered his song. He walked in
the middle of the street as everybody else did, and did not
spit on the sidewalk for the obvious reason that there was
none." Therefore, states Sartorio, only through ignorance
of his unfamiliar American surroundings does such an Italian "gesticulate, talk loudly, sing in the streets, spit on the
sidewalks, to the great amazement and horror of the
American-bred in the big city. Think of his village, of his
life there [to find out] why he does it."[9]

Unfortunately not enough Americans expended thought
and effort to study the cultural habits of the new arrival.
Too many failed to distinguish between immigrants' peasant
culture and their countries' high culture. One is reminded
of the time the English statesman Gladstone employed flaw-
less classical Greek in a speech delivered to a Greek audience. When he finished, he was startled to find his listeners, who had not understood a word he said, congratulating
him on how elegantly he spoke English![10]

As innocent as Gladstone were some of America's
first writers on immigrant musical culture. Indicative of
their limitations, they frequently thought to interview only a
country's highly cultivated composers, conductors, and performers of symphony and opera. The American writers
would then publish these sophisticated musicians' denigra-
tions of their countrymen's plebeian musical accomplish-
ments and tastes. Oftentimes the articles concluded with
the hope that this musical elite, aided by the funds of phil-
anthropists, might some day rescue their benighted countrymen from the sloughs of musical vulgarity. Statements of
this type, for example, appeared in Musical America in the
first decades of the century, several of them coming from
the pen of Ivan Narodny in 1913.

Peter Rose wondered why writers even in 1970 continued making the same errors about ethnic Americans.
Why did they interview mostly the prominent and well-
educated immigrants? Why did they neglect the more difficult task of seeking out the ethnic commoner's cultural

traditions, social structures, and daily activities?[11] Nathan Glazer suggests one reason for the continuing neglect of such exploration: the a priori decision of intellectuals that the ethnic cultures of whites are of a low order and unworthy of serious consideration. Glazer claims that the intellectual interprets the professions of ethnicity as masks concealing anti-black racism and other prejudices:

> One argument of those who insisted it was only racism went: after all, how much of Polish or Lithuanian or Italian culture actually existed in these areas? Who read Mickiewicz, or Dante, in such areas? If there was no real commitment to the heights of culture, how could one claim that a positive motivation in favor of maintaining a community and its culture dominated, as against a negative hatred of outsiders?
> It has always meant, on the one hand, the high culture. But it also means ... simply the way of life--the customs.... I think it reflects snobbery to take the position that some communities have a right to protect their culture because it is high and others do not because we refuse to accept it as valuable. [12]

In truth the music enjoyed by ethnic Americans has often received a low valuation. As one established American composer of electronic music and influential teacher at a major university told the author in 1974: "After all, how long are those Italians to be allowed to continue singing that sappy Neapolitan crud [sic]?"

A curious way Americans persisted in misconstruing immigrants was to see them as quaint foreigners whose supposed possession of their own delightful musical culture somehow made their real economic and social problems less crucial. To give an early instance, a let-them-eat-cake attitude motivated one New York socialite's criticism of Konrad Bercovici for telling her and her circle that suffering existed in New York's ethnic slums. She rebutted him with the following chatter: "Poor as they are the Poles have Chopin. The Russians have Tchaikowsky. The Hungarians have Liszt. Dear me, dear me, they are so colorful!"[13] Obtuseness of this sort occurs in many stories and novels depicting immigrant life, written by lip-deep American authors in the twenties.

On at least one occasion American social workers created the color in the slums.   In 1919 the administrators of New York's Greenwich House organized the neighborhood's Italian children in order to stage a mid-May festival called "A Merry Masque." Its subject was Robin Hood and his "merry men." Confused Italian mothers saw their boys and girls dressed as daffodils, gnomes, fairies, English foresters, and Scottish lassies.   The children danced Scottish flings and sang appropriate British ballads as they rounded a maypole.   The actual words of one of the sung compositions went as follows:

> Oh, we are jawly outlars,
>   Green Shoiwood is our ho-ome.
> Up oily in the moinen' we,
>   Ter trip ut o'er de green,
> Wid dance an' mirt' an' ruv-el-ree
> An' love ter grace de scene.
> Up oily in de moinen' we,
>   Ter trip ut, trup ut mur-ril-lee.

The extraordinary conclusion of Zona Gale, who describes this scene, was that "the reason for the Masque and its chief value lay in providing the children in Jones Street with a bit of their rightful heritage--Play."[14] Nowhere does her article reveal any awareness of the children's Italian heritage.

Most Americans at least conceded Italians were musical.   At the turn of the century they thought the Japanese and Chinese to be musically hopeless.   Margaret Alverson, a prominent California voice teacher of that time, asserts: "Five discordant tones compose their scale, unmusical and untrue chords, or, one might say, discords." Against her better judgment she once accepted a Chinese voice student.   Reluctantly she admits he had talent.   But she adds: "Of course he never had the clear ringing voice that is the gift of the white race."[15]

Given such mistaken interpretations of Orientals and their cultures by ostensibly reputable musicians, hardly surprising was the run-of-the-mill American's inability to understand the music at all.   One Issei remembers that he and several other Japanese men once were working on the railroad near Thermopolis, Wyoming.   One Sunday they found a cave containing hot springs.   After undressing, steaming themselves, and relaxing a while, the narrator says: "We

got to feeling good and we sang Japanese folk songs, which
to Americans sound like people moaning and groaning in
great pain. Some boys walking by heard us. They saw our
clothes and thought somebody was being killed, so they ran
to get the police. How embarrassing!"[16]

Anti-Foreign Songs

In the early decades of the new migration many Americans
were disposed to criticize and poke fun at the foreigner
through music. "The Jew was a joke! The college [musi-
cal] tribute to Solomon Levi perfectly visualizes the part he
played in the eventful eighties, " writes Daniel Chauncey
Brewer, [17] a nativist who believed Jews victimized Americans. He complains that the song "Solomon Levi" fails to
make Jews out to be the infamous creatures they really are:

> My name is Solomon Levi,
>   At my store on Salem Street
> That's where you'll buy your coats and vests,
>   And ev'rything that's neat;
> I've secondhanded Ulsterettes,
>   And ev'rything that's fine,
> For all the boys, they trade with me,
>   At a hundred forty-nine.
>
> (Chorus)
> O, Solomon Levi!
>   Levi! tra la la!
> Poor sheeny Levi,
>   Tra la la la la la. [18]

Closer to Brewer's viewpoint was a song published in
1896, words by Charles Gilbert, music by J. A. Parks, entitled "How It Happened (or The Jew of Lombard Street). "
It inveighs against Jewish international financiers "whose
treachery and bribery have blighted our fair land. " The
song begins:

> There was a Jew in Lombard Street,
>   And he was wondrous wise,
> He lov'd to see his millions grow
>   And pile up to the skies;
> Said he to all his brother Jews,
>   Who lov'd their ducats, too,
> "There's too much money in the world

> To profit me and you";
> Then all the sons of Israel cried,
> "Thou art a mighty Jew;
> In finance thou art weighty
> And we bow down to you.
> We'll seek the Gentile congress
> Far across the briny deep,
> And strike the silver dollar
> While the unsuspecting sleep. "

Other invidious songs fostered by anti-foreigners depicted immigrants as undesirables to be excluded from America, particularly if they were Chinese and Japanese. These exotic newcomers threatened the "American way of life. " "John Chinaman must stay home / To eat his rice with sticks" went the pro-Grover Cleveland song "Wave High the Red Bandana" in the presidential-election year 1888. [19] Eight years before, a Philadelphia publisher had issued "The Chinese Laundryman, " words and melody by Frank Dumont, and popularized by Charles Backus of the San Francisco Minstrels. The first stanza describes the Chinese man as addicted to rat pies; the second, as a dishonest gambler intent on becoming a citizen and policeman in order to advance his own sordid interests. The last stanza is more offensive than funny:

> Me soon gettee money very plenty
> And wantee gettee nice littee wife,
> Me lovee her better dan chou chou
> Me likee her better dan life,
> Me feedee her rice and opium
> Me buyee nice littee house,
> For dinee me fixee de rat-trap,
> To catchee nice littee mouse.

while the Chorus ridicules the Oriental's musical sensibility:

> Oh ching chong opium, taffy on a stick,
> No likee brass band, makee very sick,
> Melican man listen, sing you littee song,
> With a chinee fiddle and a shanghai gong. [20]

Asian women were portrayed as of the easy kind, their affections lightly bestowed and as lightly put aside. This is the thrust of the final quatrain in "The Jewel of Asia" (1896), words by Harry Greenbank, music by James Philip. The song was widely performed in America in the last four years of the nineteenth century. A white man announces to his Japanese ladylove that he now adores a white woman. Her reaction:

> And she laugh'd, "It is just as they say sir--
> You love for as long as you can!
> A month, or a week, or a day, sir,
> Will do for a girl of Japan."

When American workers found foreigners competing for their jobs, resentment welled up in their ranks. Beginning in the 1880s broadside ballads depicted immigrants as undercutting honest workers, taking away their jobs, and acting as willing tools of powerful bosses. A longshoreman's broadside ballad, now in the Harris Collection at Brown University, states:

> They bring over their 'talians, and Naygurs from the South,
> Thinking they can do the work, take beans from out our
> mouth,
> The poor man's children they must starve, but we will
> not agree
> To be put down like a worm in the ground and starve
> our families.

Another song, a railroad worker's broadside, denounces the immigrants for their strikebreaking activities:

> The Russian Jews soon spread the news
> About their jolly times,
> And all the bums from Baxter Street
> Rushed for the railroad lines,
> The Italians made themselves at home
> And soon began to call
> For William H., the railroad king,
> To pass the beer along.

Other songs portrayed Jews, Italians, and Slavs as addicted to various vices, delighting in revolting diets, and glorying in filth and vermin. Their dress, habits, and modes of recreation met with musical ridicule. Immigrants might hear these insults in almost any public place frequented by Americans, especially in establishments where alcohol was served. When questioned, first-generation ethnic Americans mention encountering scurrilous ditties in cafes, nightclubs, saloons, and vaudeville halls, as well as on the streets and while taking transportation back and forth to work.

According to one elderly Greek man, a particularly nasty song was sung by young "Americans," habitués of a saloon near the corner of Washington Street and Broadway, in Boston's South End. He claims that just after the turn of the century, whenever he walked down Washington Street on the way home from work, he was likely to hear:

> Greasers one, greasers all,
>   Greasers piss in the downstairs hall.
> Wet your wrists, dunk your heads,
>   Think you smell like flower beds.
> Make a noise like "Itchy koo,"
>   Stupid Greek and slimy Jew,
> Can't speak English worth a damn,
>   Leave this land to Uncle Sam.

These were "tough guys," he told the author. Therefore he went by them smiling, "as if it was a big joke." Sometimes "they'd throw some kids a few pennies and get them to chase after me with the song."[21] The memory of the experience still rankled in his mind when the author questioned him some forty years after.

At times the taunts in and out of song became unbearable, and the long-suffering foreigner turned on his victimizer with a violence incited by the sudden release of pent-up emotions. This was the case with Nicholas Bendetto, an Italian musician. A brief, unsigned item in the 1898 Musical America reads: "Robert Wemple was stabbed last week by Nicholas Bendetto, a member of the Banda Rossa [directed by Eugenio Sorrentino], at Stein's Harlem Casino, in this city [New York]. Wemple and two companions had been taunting Bendetto about his style of playing. The hotheaded Italian rushed into the kitchen, secured a keen-edged potato knife and stabbed Wemple in the right thigh. Bendetto was arrested."[22]

When they thought of Italians at all, far too many Americans imagined an organ-grinder with a monkey.[23] The image conjured up in the first stanza of the popular "Sidewalks of New York" is an exercise in nostalgia to Americans, an anathema to sensitive Italian-Americans:

> We would sing and waltz
> While the "Ginnie" played the organ
> On the sidewalks of New York.[24]

In another song, "The Girl That Keeps the Peanut Stand, "[25] Italians are ugly, filthy buffoons. The sheet-music's cover lithograph pictures an Italian organ-grinder in the background, his unappetizing daughter in the foreground. The song's second stanza ridicules her as follows:

> Her hair was frizzled o'er her brow,
> Her eyes were slightly cross'd,
> Her face was thickly freckled o'er
> Like mildew mix'd with frost,
> Her gown of richest calico
> Hung low upon her neck,
> And sundry graces round her shed,
> With spots of grease bedeck'd, Oh!

Prejudice in Educated Circles, American and Ethnic

Disparagements of immigrant culture came not only from the vast company of the ignorant and provincial Americans but also from the small group of ostensibly sympathetic, cosmopolitan, and highly educated viewers of the ethnic scene. Jacob Riis, a respected reporter on New York's slum life, felt bewildered and repelled by the singing of Syrian men in a tenement flat near Mulberry Street. He found no art in the reed pipe's wail and tambourine's jangle, nor in songs rendered with what he perceived as "agonizing expression" and "shockingly bad voice" by the "worst singer" he had ever heard. [26]

Echoing Riis, an American scholar studying Jewish immigrant life heard Jewish secular music and pronounced Yiddish songs to be filled with rank bathos and silliness. The singers, he wrote, were possessors of "ruined voices"; the instrumentalists were experts in vulgar caterwauling and musical horseplay. [27]

Equally obtuse was the statement of John Freund, editor of Musical America, after he had attended a concert of Italian music. His review denounced the audience for favoring only Italian operatic music. With annoyance he observes that Italians avoid hearing symphonic and chamber compositions. Then he delivers the following pontification: "The fact is true, indeed, and it is a very unmusical mind that can take real delectation in an entire program made up of Puccini, Leoncavallo, Mascagni, early Verdi, and Ponchielli. "[28]

Perhaps Freund was the person instrumental in encouraging Ivan Narodny to write the series of Musical America articles on ethnic music in New York, in which Greeks, Italians, and Hungarians are pronounced unmusical or indifferent to the arts and found worthy of praise only if they took up artistic music of the type performed by symphony orchestras. 29

Regrettably the mass of commoners could detect little fellow-feeling or appreciation of their popularly based culture in their better-situated countrymen. Similarly German Jews discouraged their East European coreligionists from retaining the amusements imported from the Slavic lands. The East European newcomers flocking into the slums embarrassed the wealthy, well-entrenched German Jews of New York. Their manners and music lacked refinement and revealed an insensitivity to the finer nuances of the cultivated experience. At about the same time the more affluent and educated Italians, most of whom had come from northern Italy, described the southern Italian peasants living in the American slums as incolti (uncultivated) and zoticoni (boors). The division into mutually exclusive classes, one small and snobbish, the other large and poor, was a characteristic of every ethnic society in America.

To their horror some musical members of the upper crust manqué found themselves identified with their less sophisticated countrymen. In self-defense they set about refining the musical crudities out of the ignorant and (they hoped) impressionable slum-dwellers. The East European Jews of the Lower East Side were urged to attend lectures on music appreciation and uplifting concerts sponsored by their moneyed fellow-religionists from uptown, who hoped thereby to obliterate the addiction to uncouth Yiddish songs and vulgar dances. Educated Italians tried to suppress the demeaning organ-grinder's trade; at the same time they formed themselves into cultural societies to demonstrate the high couthness of the membership to critical Americans. 30 So acute was the embarrassment of a few of the better educated that one or two spoke favorably of the Johnson Law of 1921 and the Immigrant Act of 1924, which shut off the immigrating hordes from the United States. "Who needs the guffoni?" asked an Italian alumnus of the Boston Symphony Orchestra.

Immigrant Reactions

The foreign-born learned to resist the efforts at "bettering" them culturally. They resented both the self-elected elite from their own ethnic group and the other proselytizers for high culture as intolerant busybodies. In addition, they felt irritation at the statements of narrow-minded Americans that, though the newcomers might attend church on Sunday, their enjoyment of the rest of that day with singing, dancing, and drinking was "Sodom and Gomorrah revived. "[31]

Especially those foreigners living in America's smaller villages and towns heard this kind of accusation. Thus Constantine Panunzio, a poor immigrant recently arrived from Italy, found incomprehensible the strictures of a Yankee family in Sherman, Maine, against dancing, singing secular songs, and attending concerts and theater performances. Again, Maurice Hindus, newly come from Russia, heard similar sentiments from Baptists in a town farther south. With thorough exasperation Hindus decries the American small-town intolerance of dancing and secular music, those "exhilarating diversions" he found so much a part of "the ritual, the glory, the justification of living. " Dancing, he writes, "gave color and rhythm, thunder and melody, to an otherwise monotonous and dismal life. " For similar reasons M. E. Ravage laments the idiocies concerning music voiced by educated Missourians. Around 1906 Ravage's "American" roommate at the University of Missouri, an excellent musician, expressed shame over his pronounced talent for the violin. He belittled his performance as "a frivolous diversion, " adding that it was "a bit effeminate for a man to care for music. " More amazing still, the professors themselves, particularly those in the arts, adopted "an apologetic tone for being interested in such unmanly things as poetry, music, or painting. "[32]

In reaction the majority of immigrants learned how to avoid their countrymen and women of superior rank, even while they continued to render them the respect that had become habitual after years of indoctrination. As for Americans, the foreign-born regarded them as intent on strangling every pleasure that made existence tolerable. Prejudice bred prejudice. The antagonism rendered the foreigner was countered with a distrust of most Americans. As a result the majority of first-generation ethnic Americans attempted to keep outsiders divorced from their private lives. A young professional Italian-American musician concludes that this attitude affected all the older first-generation men of his acquaintance:

> Old Italians usually celebrate wedding anniver-
> saries, birthdays, and holidays. They are ex-
> tremely prejudiced against non-Italians. They feel
> secure and happy only when they are among Italians.
> One night at [a well-known Italian restaurant where
> he entertained nightly on the accordion] I hired an
> American guitar player to work a special 50th an-
> niversary party with me. The people complained
> about him because he was American although his
> playing was excellent. The manager of [the res-
> taurant] called me aside and told me to hire Italian
> musicians only, if I wanted to keep my job. 33

No entente cordiale lightened the antipathy of many foreigners toward Americans. Typically, an old Greek gentleman, Dmitrios, had no use for anyone outside his ethnic society. In a voice trembling with indignation he once commented about some of his experiences: "The Americans laughed at our holy hymns when we made a street procession out of the church. Why did they find the "Khristos Aneste" something to joke about? Have they no feeling what we think? And then they drink too much and make insults at the girl singer in the Greek nightclub and restaurant, poke at her as if she was a belly dancer. Who needs them? I spit on the devils. "34

One must add, however, that not all nonethnics were ugly Americans; nor were all of the foreign-born as vehement in their denunciations as was Dmitrios. In actual fact the vast number of Americans had little contact with immigrants. At the same time, a number of the new arrivals lived out their transplanted lives only slightly aware of what some Americans thought of them.

Defining Musical Culture in Ethnic America

The next two considerations of this study concern what in general is meant by ethnic musical culture and what was the new immigrants' view of the American civilization surrounding them.

First, musical culture as understood in this study comprehends all the organized sounds considered important

by an ethnic society. The term also encompasses the habitual manner of performing musical works, the convictions and
feelings affecting the performance, and the special modes of
musical expression and interpretation valued by performer
and listener.

The characteristic music of the ethnic community,
while existing as entertainment, also acted to cement relationships between members. In this fashion it helped make
coherent an essentially voluntary and sometimes ill-defined
association of individuals. One Italian's first experience in
America, about the year 1910, provides a poignant example:

> When I came to New York, no one from my village
> was there. I found a place in the Italian section.
> But it was lonely. Only once did someone invite
> me [to their home]. I was afraid to go. One
> night at a festa the band played the "Marcia Reale,"
> and I began to cry and yell with the crowd. That's
> how I met my friend Johnny. He was yelling also.
> We hugged each other and got some wine and sang
> a lot of songs. He's a Calbrese, but he was okay.
> Our two families still get together on some Sun-
> days, to eat, talk, and make music. [35]

Without question the subject matter of song lyrics ex-
presses the commonly accepted values of a group. Additionally, a song's melodic curve, its rhythmic ordering, and its
performer's intonations--all three elements deriving directly
from the sound and pulse of a particular spoken language--
become attractive and easily assimilated vehicles for teaching and perpetuating these values, whether within the home,
school, church, or communal gathering. Thus music can
aid in prescribing normative behavior to individuals in a
society. [36]

Another and not inconsiderable function of music within an ethnic society is its anodynic effect. It soothes the
cares and calms the tensions brought on through everyday
coping with problems arising from family, job, and
community-related activities. Instead of feeling like a feck-
less greenhorn, alone, rootless, and unloved, immigrants
can share with their neighbors those emotions that take them
outside of themselves. As an elderly Greek man living in
Lowell, Massachusetts, states about a crisis in his life:

> The boss at the mill kept on calling us God-damn,

lazy greasers when we asked for more money.
All he'd give us was free chewing tobacco. [37] We
went on strike, and my wife complained about no
money, and the kids said I was a lousy American
and shamed them. So I took to staying at the café
and drinking coffee and oozu and playing cards and
listening to the bazookee player. It was wonderful
to hear our language without shame and nagging.
I'd maybe dance a little and sing the old songs.
You know, some of the songs are about fighters
in the mountains. [38] Me and the others at the
tables would enjoy ourselves and feel like men
again. [39]

People linked by a common heredity treasure their
native songs because these compositions embody memories
and traditions they find meaningful, can respond to, and take
strength from. It should be stressed, nevertheless, that
different ethnic groups have distinct musics, performed differently, sounding differently, and embodying different sets
of memories and traditions. For these reasons, "Dos Pin-
tele Yid" sung in the Yiddish theater, "Funiculì Funiculà"
sung in the Italian music hall, and "Ekh, Vdol' po Piterskoi"
sung in the Russian cabaret sound significantly unalike in
their scale structures, micro- and macro-rhythms, melodic
contours, and sense of climax. They conjure up dissimilar
images: the enduring Jew, the joyously singing contadino,
the brusque lover on Peterskoy Road. Only separate cultures could have shaped these songs. [40] The investigator
must therefore recognize the varying tastes, senses of the
past, and religious, moral, recreational, and social postures reflected in the musics of peoples from divergent
backgrounds.

Reactions to American Music and Customs

Not just a persistence of old habits but an inability to com-
prehend the musical practices of Americans caused a number of foreigners to stand apart from the New World's songs
and dances. American music making was a puzzle, particularly to Asians. Popular Western instruments like the
pianoforte had been unknown to most of them. The Syrian
immigrant Anthony Rihbany first saw and heard a piano in
the home of American missionaries, after he had permanently left his village and just before his departure from
Beirut for the United States. [41]

Another Asian, a Persian attending an American
school, states in a letter to a friend: "Are you used to
their music? My roommate likes his radio to go all the
time. He says it is 'popular' music. Well, it gives me a
big headache. He took me to hear what he says is a different kind--I think it is called 'classical,' and that gave me a
worse headache.... I miss our good Persian music. Do
you have a Persian record you could send me?"[42]

To many European immigrants, whose own music
more closely approximated that of Americans, the American
popular song seemed meretricious, lacking in real introspec-
tion, and only superficially emotional. As for jazz, it was
not music to them but a gimcrackery of jungle noises. One
comes upon statements like the following:

> My grandparents never did get used to the music
> here. They were bored with the symphony and
> found them too long and couldn't afford to go to
> opera. My father tells me they thought songs like
> "Yankee Doodle Dandy" [Boy?] and "The Band
> Played On" were silly and didn't make you think
> deeply or feel anything. Jazz they hated. My
> grandfather once smashed up my father's radio,
> when he was in high school, because he wouldn't
> turn off "that sound of animals, fine only for the
> crazy, uncivilized Americani." Give him "Torna
> A Surriento" and "Fenesta Che Lucive" any day.
> They had meaning!"[43]

Of course the newcomers understood the United States
through the limitations of their own experience. Much about
the new land confused them. One Jewish writer from Poland
describes her mother's response to the news that a neighbor's
son had become a professor in a western college: 'It seemed
absurd to me; during many years I carried a queer image of
him in my mind. For when I asked my mother what it
meant, she had said, equally uncertain, that a professor was
a man who played the violin at weddings, or a doctor who
required a large fee. "[44]

This same writer confesses that her parents never
understood America's Independence Day. The holiday struck
them as unintelligible and frightening, with its thunder of
guns and fireworks, ominous burnings of the American flag,
and minatory martial music: 'It was a day full of excitement and terror to our parents, who kept guard over us

children all day long. . . . No one whom I knew in the ghetto could really tell me why July 4th was singled out from all other days for special observance. . . . "[45] The pogroms they had endured remained vivid in their minds.

Lou D'Angelo is more amusing when he describes the effect of American holidays on Sicilians: "We paid almost no attention to American holidays like The Day of the Dead [Memorial Day], Lu Forte Gelato [The Fourth of July], or The Day of the Chicken [Thanksgiving Day]. "[46] Without familiar rituals, special foods, characteristic songs, and a tradition practiced by and learned from their fathers and grandfathers, such holidays had no meaning.

The twin threads of repulsion and amusement in reaction to the music and musical notions of Americans run through several accounts left by immigrants mentioning their musical experiences. One must keep in mind that almost invariably during this century's early years the term "American" was applied to any person outside the ethnic group who spoke English and had a white skin.

An Armenian woman experienced shock at her first sight of Americans. She arrived in America apparently on July 4th: "They were marching up and down the streets, soldiers with guns. Even women. And no one smiled. Like machines they ran you over if you crossed the street. And those musicians [sic] looked as if they were drinking. They played with no delicacy, so loud it made me cover my ears. Then a man, he looked angry, pushed me away. I was frightened and went back to my room and locked the door. That awful music, those drunks, and that beast with no manners! I never forgot. "[47] From that day, she claims, she avoided hearing American music.

A few penniless but worldly-wise and educated Russians, on the other hand, found Americans not frightening but innocent creatures whose bumptiousness could provide diversion, their lack of sophistication, a livelihood. Somewhat sardonically, Mikhail Jeleznov observes that after coming to America he could have made himself a professor of Russian literature in the Midwest, a housepainter, a paperhanger, a doorman, a waiter, a fake count or prince, or "a famous gypsy singer. " With mock-sadness he decided against becoming a singer: "I have no ear for music and cannot carry a tune. Famous gypsy singers, I understand, do not consider this a handicap [in America] if they possess a deep throaty voice. Unfortunately I lacked even that. The only time I sounded like a famous gypsy singer was when I had a cold. "[48]

The tendency of American and immigrant to midunderstand each other's musical culture applies mostly to the first few years of the settler's residence in America, and not to every American and immigrant. In actual fact some immigrants attempted to jettison their native culture immediately. On arrival they tried immersing themselves in the American cultural stream. But usually these were young people under twenty years of age or persons living completely within the American society and distant from the nearest ethnic enclave. On the other hand the preponderance of evidence underlies the confusion of the first half-decade or so an immigrant spent in the New World. Only after the acclimatization of a few years living and working in the United States and meeting constantly with Americans through force of circumstance did attitudes and cultural practices alter appreciably.

Some Immigrant Traits and Music

The men and women coming to America before discriminatory immigration laws stemmed the flow had to concentrate on settling in a strange land. As a consequence scarcely any of them had time or opportunity to write up their experiences. Unfamiliar with American ways and uncomfortable in the English language, they also were reluctant and often unable to reveal their minds and emotions to those first few Americans seeking to explore their thoughts rather than their manner of physical survival. Unhappy contacts with proselyting Protestants, Americanizing social workers, and intolerant high-culturists, who sallied forth daily from missions, settlement houses, and other institutions seen as threatening, reinforced the resistance to change and distrust of intruders. [49] As a result their feelings about their own vis-à-vis American music, in these early years when their commitment to their own cultural inheritance was at red heat, is recorded in only a handful of trustworthy accounts.

Nor is the experience of more recent immigrants altogether useful. The longstanding overseas ways of life of the late nineteenth century are ended. The smaller stream of recent arrivals originates from a more modern source. A greater sophistication about the world and more than superficial knowledge of American popular music comes with them; a more tolerant and less insular America greets them.

The immigrants of some seventy-five years ago were different sorts from these. Yet in one regard Italians then and now behaved similarly. Bruno Roselli describes the typical Italian man arriving around 1900 as ready to rush out and purchase a musical instrument when he had accumulated a few savings in order to give his children music lessons. Though certainly not true for all Italian immigrants, the compulsion for music, nevertheless, appears in their statements far more than in those given by members of other immigrant groups, save for the Jews. Rosselli's listing of additional traits, however, could well apply to a majority of Christian immigrants from the peasant class--the fear of the evil eye, the desire to be respected and envied for one's dutiful children, the belief in working with the hands, the apprehension that too much education for the children led to alienation from the family, the enjoyment of festivals and other celebrations, the drive to earn and hold on to money, and the reluctance to give to charity. [50] As will be seen, all of these traits had ramifications in their relationship to music.

Loyalty and cooperation scarcely seem to have extended beyond the confines of the family circle, especially among Mediterranean peoples. Peasant experience had taught the value of self-preservation and suspicion of outsiders. Attempts to strengthen communal ties in America would frequently founder on the rocks of selfishness, anarchic individuality, and a readiness to discover the worst in each other. For these reasons the institutions necessary to preserve their musical culture would remain weak. Their songs lived on only so long as they were passed on within the family. The musically talented among their young would find few outside of their family to assist them with money for their training. Nor would they easily discover concert organizations for their exposure or audiences for their encouragement. In short, many immigrants believed charity began at home and should remain there. The decay of their national culture was an inevitable result.

The father hoped to transplant the strong family structure that defined the role and behavior appropriate to each member. He tried exacting an observance of the strictest morality from his daughters. Though he might love music and dance, he detested the way American men

and women tightly clasped each other's bodies and engaged
in dancing activities that bordered on the lascivious to him.
Roselli mentions the American manner of dancing as abhorrent to southern Italians. Greeks revealed a similar dislike.
As one Greek father explained: "When we see a woman so
close to a man not her husband, we know she is no good."

The strong disapproval of mixed dancing in the American manner was also common to Asian people. Monica
Sone, a Nisei, once had the temerity to ask her Japanese
father about dancing lessons for herself. He became over-
wrought and refused his permission absolutely. Such gyra-
tions, he said, were suitable for women in American burlesque shows and geisha girls but not for his daughter. [51]
The Chinese father discouraged Western social dancing for
similar reasons. He felt mixed dancing of this nature "can
legitimately occur only between lovers or married couples
at home, or between prostitutes and their customers in a
brothel. "[52]

One recurring explanation for shunning American popular music comes from immigrants. During the first years
after their arrival they say they might otherwise have accepted its sound if they hadn't connected it in their minds
with morally questionable activities. Close social dancing
and the suggestive blandishments of the burlesque stage were
cited. (The reference here is to the activities countenanced
in the more permissive cities, not those of the straitlaced
towns and villages of America.) They interpreted this music's enjoyment by their impressionable children as a serious sign that America's debauching fashions had insinuated
themselves into innocent minds and displaced the rich legacy
left by one's own ancestors.

Bitter about his children's falling away from their
family's heritage, a Ukrainian gentleman once stated vehemently: "Our songs have a lot about love in them, yes,
and maybe about how nice to do certain things, too. They're
to enjoy and to laugh at. No one rubs against each other
when they sing them or hear them, like with the Americans.
Those American songs say it is alright to taste [sex] any-
time. I hated them and wanted my children to stay away.
They wouldn't. They danced and sang and became Americans. "[53]

Moral condemnation of American popular music and
dance arose from no profoundly held religious beliefs. The

evidence is convincing that the Christianity of many immigrants from Eastern Europe and the Mediterranean was in-
terwoven with a simple paganism and a faith in amulets,
magic, and ritual. These last were considered a means to
propitiate malign forces and gain support from potent divin-
ities. [54] A characteristic vehicle for giving expression to
these people's beliefs was the secular-sacred festival com-
memorating a religious event or a saint's day. For an ethnic American the festival provided an opportunity to renew
one's credit with a supernatural being, take surcease from
labor and worry, and recreate the happier moments of the
Old Country. Food, music, and dance infused the entire
celebration.

Especially the southern Italian's festa delineated this
type of activity to Americans. Because of their great numbers and stubborn clinging to old ways the Italians could not
help but receive notice. The more circumspect northern
Italians and the Irish-Catholic Church hierarchy at first had
tried to bar the contadini from Sicily, Apulia, Calabria, and
Abruzzi from holding these celebrations. They found such
activities embarrassing and lacking in decorum. The festa's
opponents, however, met with defiance. Without the festa,
"religion was cold, formal, and lacking in significance" to
southern Italians. "They fought hard for it, and eventually
in many cases they either organized their own church or had
their own way despite the Irish hierarchy's accusations of
paganism. "[55]

The communally initiated, communally sponsored, and
public ethnic festival has become comparatively rare amongst
most non-Italian groups in recent years, except for occasional revivals. These revivals are almost always nostalgic
reminiscences of a nearly defunct way of life. Yet a variety
of such festivals were held annually a few decades ago by
most ethnic groups. Today they are replaced to some extent
by international cultural fairs sponsored by institutions catering to ethnic communities, like the International Institutes, or
by municipal administrations of cities with significant ethnic
American populations.

Everything just said notwithstanding, the immigrant's
typical day in the Old Country had not usually unfolded with
feasting, dancing, and singing. For a significant number of
persons, these leisure activities were first savored in the
United States. The descriptions left by newcomers of their
daily lives in their homeland are often ones of working hard

all day and looking only for rest in the evening. [56] A constant diet of music and dance is incongruous in such a setting.

Adults came here expecting to work long hours. For some, work continued to be the only thing they knew and believed in; leisure and music to occupy that leisure signified little in their new lives. For too many man, after unremitting daily labor, leisure was a vacuum filled with the amusements of the saloon; whatever music they heard formed a subordinate counterpoint to drinking, gambling, and womanizing. [57] The vocation of some Italians was to travel American streets as organ-grinders. Normally they rented their instruments from an Italian boss, the padrone. Some young Italian musicians worked directly for the padrone, who might or might not prey on their ignorance, exact slave labor, and pay subsistence wages. Music for such persons could only be a joyless occupation. [58]

In contrast to the above, reports exist of men and women who worked hard in the day and enjoyed music in the evening, whether as a recreation transferred from their homeland or a taste recently acquired in America. Truly, the testimonies of a majority of the newcomers point to music as touching their lives in more than an incidental fashion. Among the reports are several describing the writers as workers supervised by tolerant foremen and allowed to sing on the job so long as they kept busy and proved efficient. The managers mostly of small, few of large, factories are reported to have permitted their employees to sing. A case in point is a small factory-bakery on Boston's Hampden Street, owned by the author's father. In the 1920s and 1930s it employed about twenty workers, first- and second-generation Syrians, Poles, Italians, West Indians, and Greeks. [59] The machines required constant supervision. Temperatures in the summer hovered around 110 degrees or higher. Men sometimes stripped to their shorts and stood in tubs of water in order to survive the workday. Nevertheless, for much of the day the men listened to each other's national songs or sang American popular works. To pass the time, to keep from going insane, to enjoy the songs they loved were some explanations given for the impromptu concertizing.

Evidence also exists of workers rebelling when prevented from singing or listening to music while on the job, among them Jewish cutters and stitchers in a New York clothing manufactory, Hungarian parts-assemblers in a Cleveland tool firm, and Armenian agricultural workers in fields near Fresno. One such incident involved a band of Italian railroad workers whose boss was working them hard. One Friday afternoon "a greasy shabby-looking Italian" appeared "with a hand-organ on his back." The laborers paused in their work and asked him to play. He began Verdi's "Anvil Chorus." "As the mighty notes rolled out from the breast of that dingy organ, the crowd listened with ... profound reverence [and] breathless silence." The grinder struck up "that liberty-inspiring hymn" "L'Inno di Garibaldi." The men forgot their weariness. "Unconsciously, spontaneously, the pent-up emotions, like a dam bursting at the surging onrush of a mighty torrent, broke out in song and wild acclamation." It was then the boss came along, became annoyed at the work stoppage, and ordered the organ-grinder to leave. The laborers protested. After the boss punched one of them, a general fistfight commenced between him and his henchmen on one side, the Italian workers on the other. The altercation ended when the entire group of Italians quit their jobs and abandoned the camp. [60]

The East European Jews, whose two and a half million settlers make up the second largest of the ethnic groups to arrive after 1880, are surpassed in number only by the five million southern Italians. In several important ways these Jews differed from the Italians and most other immigrants. For one thing, they were bound up with their religion and permitted it to permeate their thoughts and actions. They were disposed to respect their religious teachers, nourish music as an essential component of worship, and value learning as a means for understanding God's commandments. Consequently, after their arrival in America, the Jews continued to hear a variety of sacred musical works in their homes and synagogues. In addition, they urged their children to study and attend college. The higher learning these young people acquired would include literature, art, and cultivated music.

Jewish life in Eastern Europe had been for most an urban one, of shtetl (small-town) living and of working at small trades. The Jews could therefore adapt to urban living in America more easily than other groups. Furthermore, persecution had strengthened the feeling of community and brought about the development of mutual-aid organizations to assist fellow Jews in distress. All regarded Jewish charity in such a cause as an important blessing.

At the same time institutions had emerged to facilitate urban existence. Not surprisingly, after their arrival in
America a large percentage of these Jews, as compared
with other immigrants, were prepared to discover and aid
talented but needy music students; to establish music classes, artistic institutions, and performing groups; and to encourage their musicians by attendance at concerts and
musical-theater presentations. 61

     Because they already were accustomed to dwelling in
the midst of, treating with, and competing against outsiders,
Jews would quickly acclimate themselves to American conditions and achieve an enviable record of economic success.
Far more than any other ethnic group they and their descendants would swiftly penetrate the musical cultures of
others. Soon they were to be found participating in American popular music, Negro jazz, Italian opera, and the symphony orchestras and chamber-music organizations that for
many years had been the special preserve of the Germans. 62

The Transplanting of a Musical Culture: A Quick Overview

It was to be expected that foreigners would continue to con-
sole themselves with the music familiar to them from birth.
In 1949 the author asked a Lebanese man of about fifty-five
years of age why he had come to the United States. He replied: "Why did I come? In the Old Country my belly was
empty, my spirit hungry, my honor stepped upon. In America I heard it was easier and I left. Here I eat my piece
of cheese, sing with my lute, and keep my enemy far from
me. Praise God!"63 He had endured hunger and harass-
ment from the Turks during his boyhood in a village near
Beirut. He escaped with his uncle to the New World when
he was about twenty-one. The South End of Boston replaced
his ancient village; a presser's position in a sportswear factory, his painful stint as a farm laborer. On weekdays he
worked seemingly endless hours. On weekends he and his
friends met to enjoy homemade arrack, cheese and olives,
conversation, and music.

     In addition, the recently arrived foreigners made up
songs to encompass their first experiences in America. Such
a work is "Christopher Columbus," sung by Italians in America and Italy. First, it praises what the Italian saw as good
about America:

> And America is long and wide and beautiful,
> It is all made of roses and flowers,
> It is all covered with roses and flowers,
> Long live America and those who go there.

Then he warns of the bad:

> We came here from our villages,
> We didn't find any straw or hay,
> We had to sleep on the hard ground,
> Just like animals. This was our rest. [64]

Furthermore, immediately on arrival the immigrants would discover new musical sounds sometimes contending with, or as often occupying a place beside, the music of their homeland. A Croatian newcomer recounts his first glimpse of America from shipboard: "I stood gazing at the [American] flag intently for some time.... Then the band began to play various American national airs; and the sight before my eyes of the wonderful city of New York filled me with pride and ambition."[65] This was his first experience of music unlike his own, yet of music he might want to make his own. The process of Americanization had begun. It would never cease.

The newcomers little suspected that soon after setting up residence on these shores they and their children would create and enjoy a large number of songs that inevitably were a blend of overseas and American idioms. Some of these works and the vocalists singing them soon won their way into the affections of the American majority. Hasidic rhythm, warm Neapolitan melody, and exuberant Polish dance blended with American blues, popular ballad, rag, and jazz in musical compositions denominated as American.

Before long the children of a few immigrants-- Ruggiero Ricci and Yehudi Menuhin, to name two--would achieve fame as performing artists of serious music; others--like Aaron Copland, Paul Creston, and Alan Hovhaness--as composers of works of the highest cultivation.

Though some of the new arrivals may have enjoyed opera and symphony abroad, most lovers of cultivated music acquired the taste in the United States, where they first gained the leisure, means, and opportunity for attending performances. What the immigrants were most likely to

have brought over with them were the traditional and currently popular songs and dances learned in the village of
their birth. True, the simpler operatic arias of Bellini,
Verdi, and others fell into the popular category in Italy.
A great distance, however, separates the occasional rendition of these few unassuming arias from the complexities of
full opera performances. Moreover, in their native villages,
these immigrants had had neither radios, television, phonograph records, nor motion pictures with sound to bring them
a world larger than their own and musical works executed
by professionals more competent than the now-and-then amateur players and singers of their district. If later the
fruits seemed more fragrant, the daily living more care-
free, and the music sweeter in the Old Country than in the
United States, distance and the nostalgia induced by foot-
looseness in an unfamiliar world went a long way toward
making them so.

Visits to the old village after long residence in America often brought on a contrary opinion. The testimony of
several first-generation travelers who revisited their rural
birthplaces in southern Italy, Portugal, Yugoslavia, Greece,
and Syria gives weight to this conclusion. As a case in
point, after several decades' residence in America, one
elderly Greek woman returned for a summer's visit to her
former Aegean-island home. To her chagrin she learned
that her relatives there were hungrier for money than for
relaxed living. Her cousin Yiorgo, whom she had described
to her friends in America as "the big musician" in the family, was unable to play more than a faulty tune or two on
his guitar and had little inclination to sing. No sequence of
church suppers, community musicals, picnics, and parties
with feasting and music enlivened the monotony of existence,
at least not to the extent they did in America. [66]

Most immigrants had departed from rural towns and
villages that could provide few of the amenities of urban
living. Constantine Panunzio, an Italian immigrant from a
village in Apulia, describes his life abroad and the music
he heard there as necessarily simple. None of his neighbors
had money. Their main diversions were the religious festivals they took precious time out to celebrate--Carnival, Passion Week, Easter, Corpus Christi, Christmas, and the festa
for San Corrado, the town's patron saint. "Aside from these
feasts and celebrations, the townspeople have little of a social character. The town maintains a municipal theater
which is open for two or three months in the winter. In

the summer the band gives concerts in the Villa Garibaldi.
There are few, if any, community dances or functions, and
seldom do the people go out on picnics or social functions
of a similar character."[67]

Even better-off farmers could indulge in only a limited number of cultural activities. A second-generation
Portuguese-American has left an account of his great-
grandparents's way of life on the Cape Verde Islands in the
late nineteenth century, before misfortune forced a sale of
their "plantation." Though his family owned a sizable es-
tate for growing sugar cane, it could enjoy few of the pleasures associated with urban living and perforce had to assume
a "fairly simple life-style." He continues: "Fiestas, mastros, and Canta Reis [were] their only true sources of entertainment. Fiestas usually took place on such occasions
as weddings and christenings and New Year's Day. Mastros
took place on holy days. Whereas Canta Reis took place
only during the Christmas holidays. In all of these occasions everyone would participate [and] each occasion was
full of wine, song, and dance."

Fiestas were days for family reunions. Starting at
noon, there took place an enormous amount of eating, drinking, dancing, and singing, lasting late into the night. "Music was usually provided by a small group of amateurs
[playing] guitars, violas ["mandolin-like instruments"], tri-
angles, and tambourines." The sound was a "blend of
Portuguese and island tunes and rhythms, very similar to
Latin American tunes. Unfortunately none of my relatives
could recall any tune from this period."

Portuguese farmers and fishermen participated in the
mastros for St. Pedro and St. Paul, when the blessing of
the fishing fleet and the arable lands would take place. A
thirty-foot pole, to which were added "two or three mast-
like sails made from the limbs of fir trees," had vegetables,
fruit, and fishes tied to it. Prayers were said near the
mastro and at the shore line. At sunset the mastro was
pulled down and the feasting and music began in earnest.

The one other time for music making was the Canta
Reis of the Christmas holidays, a form of door-to-door
caroling. Otherwise the occasions for enjoyment and music
making were circumscribed, for the Cape Verde Islanders
had to struggle to eke out a living.[68]

The Immigrants from Urban Areas

That lesser number of immigrants who had come from the cities and larger towns, in contrast to their more numerous country cousins, proved to have had a more extensive acquaintance with musical works. Though city-dwellers might have worked hard in their homeland, at least their hours of labor had a daily limit. Evenings and weekends provided them with some spare time. Money wages made possible some discretionary spending. For a nominal charge, or none, they were able to attend concerts and musical-theater performances. Municipal bands played in the squares in cordial competition with itinerant street musicians. Cafés and music halls featured fine singers and instrumentalists performing a repertoire of popular songs and dances. Encouraged by their musical urbiculture, some residents had scrimped a few spare coins for a musical instrument and a spare hour or so to learn to play it. A fortunate one or two took lessons with competent musicians.

Among the many amateur musicians arriving in the United States, only a small handful had come from the ranks of farm laborers. Most had resided in urban areas. Typically a Polish-American writer describes his maternal grandfather and grandmother as growing up with music in a Warsaw suburb and in Krakow, respectively. The men in their families worked in minor trades--carpenters, stonemasons, and small storekeepers. Yet several of them had also learned to perform with skill on musical instruments.

Questioned about his Polish past, the grandfather replied:

> I came to America when I was sixteen years old [1914]. My father was a good violinist--played at weddings. My brother was a drummer and my younger brother played accordion.... We played "mazurek"--like a polka. The popular instruments were clarinet, string bass, violin, and trumpet. There was [frequent] singing and playing together. At the weddings we played "Mazurek" and "Krakowiak".... At funerals the rich had [us?] playing a drum, clarinet and cornet.

Both grandparents spoke of singing in choruses organized and conducted by the local parish priest, of partici-

pating in outdoor serenades to celebrate a relative's or
friend's birthday, and of enjoying "the Polish custom" of
dressing up each Saturday night and attending a neighborhood
hall to dance and sing the Polish popular songs of the day.[69]
Whatever city they may have come from, other urban-born
immigrants report similar experiences with music.

An extraordinary amount of music making seems also
to have taken place in the self-contained Jewish shtetls of
Eastern Europe. "From earliest infancy," Ruth Rubin
writes, "the Jewish child in the Pale heard singing and
chanting, humming and intoning. In the home, in the back
yard, in the narrow village street, in the chedar, in the
synagogue, at the Sabbath table, during holidays...."[70] As
an instance of how this musical activity was translated into
one person's life, Mary Antin speaks with affection of the
fiddling, singing, and dancing at weddings enjoyed by the
townspeople of Polotzk, even including "the most pious men."
She speaks, too, of the "lullabies on lofty themes" her mother constantly sang for her. Sabbath dinner was a delight,
she says, especially when "my father led us in singing our
favorite songs, sometimes Hebrew, sometimes Yiddish,
sometimes Russian, or some of the songs without words
for which the Hasidim were famous."

At times an entire afternoon was given over to music
and dance, while "somebody blew on a comb with a bit of
paper over the teeth." Polkas, waltzes, mazurkas, quad-
rilles, and lancers were dance tunes for which they "did
not hesitate to invent new steps and figures." She concludes
her description with: "Sometimes we sat in a ring and sang
all the songs we knew. None of us were trained--we had
never seen a sheet of music but some of us could sing any
tune that was ever heard in Polotzk, and the others followed
half a bar behind.... We had Hebrew songs and Jewish and
Russian, solemn songs, and jolly songs, and songs unfit for
children...."[71]

The several descriptions just given point to two conclusions. First, the immigrants who had the greatest and
most continuous contact with music came from urbanized
areas. Second, prior to the departure for America, these
people sought out and performed mostly the popular and traditional music of their homeland. Scant mention is made of
any constant diet of symphony and opera.

Significantly, a direct correlation exists between the

size of the urban area in Italy and the number of Italians who came to America familiar with opera. The larger the city, the more likely the staging of operas, the greater the availability of free or inexpensive musical performances, and the more frequent the gratuitous presentation of operatic excerpts by wind bands and by café and music-hall singers. As a large majority of Italians did not come here from cities, whatever knowledge and love for opera they had came mainly after they settled in America.[72] We must agree with Erik Amfitheatrof's statement: "Though the older [Italian] immigrants surrounded themselves nostalgically with Italian foods, Italian songs and photographs of Italian opera singers, actually they had barely participated in the rich culture of Italy."[73]

Music and the New Ethnic Communities

After they arrived in America most immigrants hastened to form their own ethnic colonies where the modes of living congenial to them could continue. Some articulate spokesmen explain this gathering together as owing to a need for emotional fulfillment brought on by the foreigner's feeling of estrangement in unfamiliar surroundings. A desire to bolster one's feeling of psychological well-being and personal worth, several writers claim, grew out of the hostility voiced by some Americans against all newcomers.

Within their own enclaves the immigrants felt respect for themselves and their heritage. Konrad Bercovici sums up the first reactions of immigrants to the impact of American culture, as follows:

> Only in the first year or so after immigration, in the bewilderment of the new surroundings, is the superiority of the nationality of this country [the United States] admitted. Soon afterward the imbued idea of superiority that is in every nation asserts itself. Bits of the old home become dear again. The national costume is put on during holidays. The old songs are revived, and old customs are reinstated with renewed vigor.... Hundreds of newspapers in as many languages, hundreds of churches, hundreds of national schools, hundreds of societies and groups are keeping all the old traditions alive.... They compare, weigh, and measure; and nine times out of ten they return to their

own life, accepting only reluctantly what they must. [74]

A third-generation Italian-American explains more simply: "My grandfather says we settled in 'Little Italy' to avoid the hostility of Americans and to retain the old customs and culture and pass them on to the next generation. He learned [in America] to be proud of his Italian heritage and came gradually to love opera here, although he complained he could hear only a few presentations of it. "[75]

Russians tried to establish Little Russias;[76] and Poles, Little Polands, where they might throw off "the traits of the New World, as of a magic garment, and [live] here the life of their native villages, " holding to their old customs and enjoying their native songs and dances. [77] To one American observer, when Greeks observed Good Friday by draping their stores in purple and black and holding a solemn midnight procession down American streets, with candles burning and ancient Orthodox hymns sounding through the night, he felt as if he had been set down in an Athens neighborhood. [78]

Yet despite the similarities to the homeland the immigrant community held to a subculture neither wholly foreign nor, of course, wholly American. The musical activities of its residents functioned to ease the transition between the old and new. Little by little the foreigners might, and their children would, enter more fully into the American mainstream. [79] Meanwhile social and cultural societies were established and music making fostered that had few counterparts in the Old Country. Rather, they "originated in the new world as a response to urban surroundings. "[80]

Though having the earmarks of an exotic importation, the music of the ethnic community constituted an essential component of the complex mechanism created to aid the newcomer's adjustment to the United States. It follows that, with the adjustment completed, the music could no longer function as it had. It would either disappear as superfluous to the lives of third- and fourth-generation descendants of the settlers, or gradually change to reflect the increasingly Americanized tastes of the young.

Though mostly from rural areas, the new arrivals did not rush to live on farms. American banks refused

loans to penniless foreigners. Urban jobs were more easily
found. The village social life preferred by settlers was impossible in rural isolation. Immigrants desired the company
of their countrymen. The ethnic enclaves of the cities provided this companionship. Some, however, did settle in
smaller towns and villages, but usually these were inhabited
mainly by people from one country and often from one neighborhood. [81]

    The new arrivals became conservators both of the
music they had known and of the national music in which they
could take pride and set forth their feelings and beliefs about
the world they inhabited. The parochial walls of the Old
Country were breached to some extent. Settlers of the same
nationality were soon sharing each other's musical works.
A small but growing number of former peasants began taking
an interest in their country's artistic music and its performers. Chopin and Paderewski for the Poles, Verdi and Caruso for the Italians, became symbolic tonics to strengthen the
feeling of self-worth in their countrymen. [82]

The Role of Isolation in Perpetuating Ethnic Culture

Some degree of isolation from American influences was essential if the music imported by the settlers was to survive.
As one young man relates of his family's living in the Italian
section of Lawrence, Massachusetts: "My grandfather
brought his songs from Naples and taught them to his children and they taught them to me. It cannot be concluded
that there was any clash with American music among my
grandparent's or parent's generation. In their situation,
there was simply no interaction between the two cultures."[83]

    The turn-of-the-century culture that immigrants
handed down to their children, though seemingly unchanged
here, often did experience considerable alteration over the
years in the foreigner's homeland. [84] American cultural
isolation perpetuated a narrowness of interests that sometimes disturbed the more recent arrivals from across the
seas. A young Italian who had landed in America after
World War II and gone to live within the large Italian colony in Boston's North End spoke with astonishment of how
ignorant of the world he found the North End's older inhabitants. Equally surprising to him was the continuing demand for old songs that no longer had much currency in
Italy: "At a typical North End feast, I was asked by an

old man if I knew the words of the "Marcia Reale" (Italian
Royal March), because he didn't remember them.   I was
shocked and surprised because I didn't even know that the
"Marcia Reale" was still played, and that it still is requested on American soil!"   The young man claims that he
and the friends he had left behind in Syracuse, Sicily, knew
more about American music than most men of his age who
had been born and brought up in the North End.   "Italy has
passed them by, " he said. 85

The most important center for the perpetuation of any
ethnic culture was the home.   Furthermore, the mother,
more than the father, was the cement binding together all
family members.   To be taken seriously, therefore, is the
mother's role as preserver of culture and conveyer of it to
her children.   In the ethnic community she usually had less
education and lived a more isolated life than her husband.
For these reasons she was more immune to American influences than her husband and children.

The children were in the mother's charge as her
husband sallied forth daily to gain a living in the larger
American world.   She cooked the meals, observed the customs, and sang the songs that transmitted an ethnic identity
to her young.   Whatever her nationality, the mother is identified in source after source as the person who gave the
writer his or her first taste of music, encouraged nascent
musical talent, and insisted on purchasing an instrument for
and giving music lessons to her child--at times battling her
husband to get her way.   Whether she had come from Poland, Italy, Syria, China, Greece, or Japan, she guided her
child's first musical steps and almost always along traditional pathways.

Her cultural importance looms large in Angelo Bertocci's recollections of his life in Boston in the year 1923.
Bertocci says he hardly ever saw his father, who worked
long hours for meager pay.   Though money was scarce, his
mother decided one day that no matter the cost she wanted
a player-piano in her home.   Towing the young Angelo along
to serve as translator, she proceeded to a piano store.   An
astonished proprietor surveyed this foreign customer in the
"obviously cheap serge dress and the Filene's basement
hat. "   His surprise increased when she insisted on purchasing not the low-priced but the $600 piano: "It cost six
hundred dollars, more than half a year's wages and obviously an extravagance.... And we bought with it several

dozen Italian popular rolls including 'O Sole Mio, ' 'Funicul î Funiculà, ' 'Santa Lucia, ' but also 'I Pagliacci, ' 'La Traviata, ' 'Aïda, ' and 'Rigoletto. '" After delivery to the house, the piano lived in a newly designated "parlor room, " where it served to entertain the family and give the Bertoccis standing among the neighbors. [86]

The young man quoted earlier, whose parents had come from the Cape Verde Islands, says that his mother taught him many old Portuguese songs. From his earliest recollection the entire family customarily spent entire evenings with music, often at his mother's instigation. Furthermore, in the family's Portuguese neighborhood (in the town of Wareham, on Cape Cod), the fiestas, the mastros, and the singing of Canta Reis continued to be observed meticulously, with much of the preparation for their celebration left to her and the other Portuguese mothers. [87]

For years music remained a primary vehicle for preserving the first-generation ethnic's identity in a strange land. "The melodies and songs of the homeland" provided a "common bond, " alleviated sadness and loneliness, and enhanced the sense of belonging to an identifiable group. [88] A lonely George Papashvily, newly arrived from Russian Georgia, admits he carried his songs around in his throat "as some have pocket pieces to touch. " Wherever he worked, whenever he walked the streets, he sang aloud "little bits that wouldn't stay out of my head. Chougouri sacartveloah, Oh del la del lo (Our Georgia is a ringing lute, we are the strings upon it). " People turned and laughed; he couldn't stop, for singing was his all-important comfort. [89]

Parents naturally would try to teach their young the way of life they admired most. The home, national church and school, participation in national youth organizations--all attempted to show a child "who he was and where he came from. " A third-generation Armenian-American sums up his and his parents' relationship to the culture of the immigrating generation:

When my parents were born, they represented the second generation of Armenian-Americans in my family. My grandparents raised them ... as Armenians first. Cultural traditions were stressed and ingrained in them from the time of birth. Before they became aware of themselves as Americans

... the importance of Armenian culture, including music, had permanently sunk in. But while my grandparents enjoyed this music for escape, or a reminder of home, or even for spirit-lifting entertainment, my parents picked up on it purely for its entertainment value. They and other Armenians of the same generation loved its sound and loved to dance to it. It is this music which was most often heard in my house as I was growing up. [90]

To the many undereducated immigrants[91] music and dance were the most comfortable forms of expression. Unaccustomed to thinking verbally, they found reading and educational lectures less attractive. A band concert, a favorite singer's performance, a possibility of hearing one's native music--for these they would turn out.[92] To listen to a talented amateur musician was a pleasure. To hear their own children perform was the dream of many. Jerre Mangione, in Mount Allegro, nicely captures the attitude of such immigrants when he describes an Italian mother's feelings:

It was mainly of music that she thought when she thought at all about culture. Music, and not of art. She had an ancient Sicilian prejudice against books and sincerely believed that if you read too many of them, you were bound to go mad. Painting, unless it resembled photography, was of little interest to her. But music was something else. Music was food for the spirit. Without music there could be no real happiness.... If she could only manage to have her four children--or even one--play arias from Verdi and Bellini or play dance music (how she could dance!). Or if they did not prove to be that gifted, if only they could play the accompaniment to the songs as those we heard during the long winter evenings from newly arrived Sicilians who sang to ease their homesickness. If only they could play anything, how happy and proud she would be![93]

Outside the home the ethnic community would provide a variety of mechanisms for keeping its language, traditions, and music alive, through its church, temple, or synagogue, cultural organizations (including its own schools), holiday observances, religious festivals, formal and informal social meetings, and commercial places for entertainment. From time to time new arrivals from, letter-exchanges with family remaining in, and visits to the Old Country would help reinvigorate ethnic memories. Not always, however, for as often as not the more recent émigrés had fair educations and chose to live among Americans, one's overseas relatives had moved to a city and altered their ancient village ways, and visits to the old village, instead of reinforcing ethnicity, underlined to what extent the visitor had taken on American colorings.

All things considered, millions of men and women in all sincerity did try to transplant what they and their ancestors had treasured into American soil. They would nurture their native arts, try to make them flourish, and attempt to convince their progeny of the value of continuing along ethnic ways. In 1952 a Lebanese father, who had been in America for two years, was celebrating his baby daughter's christening. Surrounded by a company of his countrymen, he sat beside the crib, took up his lute, and sang:

Oh daughter of Libnan,
   I shall not forget thee.
Nor shall my children forget
   The grace of thy form,
   The fragrance of thy skin,
   The magic of thy glance.
I shall treasure thee, daughter who gave me birth;
I shall celebrate thee in song
   With tears in my eyes
   And love in my soul.
We will always remember thee in thy beauty. [94]

The song "Ya Binth il Libnan" (Oh Daughter of Lebanon) had its counterparts in the musical compositions valued by every ethnic group. Such songs succeed in reflecting the general ethos of the immigrants who loved them. They capture the vital force that brought into being the concepts, usages, and habits characterizing each ethnic group. To forget their music, to cease celebrating their native land in song, would have meant that the immigrants had lost touch with who they were. For the sake of their own spiritual well-being they could not afford to forget.

Chapter 2

RESIDENTS, MUSICAL AND UNMUSICAL

●──

During much of the present century American writers have
tended to stereotype or, more often, dismiss the musical
ways of life pursued by the recent settlers. Only a few
researchers, like Joanne Purcell, Kenneth Peacock, and
Maude Hare, have attempted to ferret out some of the musical values in the new subcultures, values that dictated a
different perception of scale structure and tone production.

In their interviews first-generation ethnic Americans
from the Orient, Middle East, and Balkans have mentioned
their sadness at the amusement their singing afforded American listeners. They spoke, too, of their bitterness at
public-school educators' constant criticisms of their children's musical abilities. These criticisms came as letters
from music supervisors, low report-card marks in "Music,"
"Effort," and "Conduct," and afterschool detentions to punish
"poor" singing.

On the other hand Italians were manifestly musical
according to several authors writing in the first decades of
the century. With appalling superficiality they asserted that
the Italian newcomers were constantly singing, playing instruments, and happy in their poverty. Thus most Americans
at the turn of the century did subscribe to the concept of
musical nations and races. Italians were in; Chinese and
Syrians were out.

The truth was different. The melodists and tone-deaf
were distributed among all ethnic groups. The unmusical
were a ubiquitous lot among Italians, East European Jews,
Hungarians, and whatever other group one could name.

Humans Without Music
_____

Many new Americans evidenced throats unused to singing and feet unaccustomed to dancing. How many is difficult to determine. Without question they constituted a considerable minority.

One fitting this category, Abraham Rihbany, writes that he scarcely ever heard music or saw dancing in his native El-Shweir, a town fifteen miles from Beirut. Daytime was for work only, nighttime for sleep. [1]

The Rihbany story is repeated in the lives of other immigrants. What is more, a goodly number of them never did enjoy music after arrival in America. [2] This was true of Chicago's Russians, writes Jerome Davis. In 1922 he published a tabulation of Russian men's recreational interests. Only eleven percent of them admitted to any interest at all in music. In contrast, over half of them frequented the local saloon. [3] Confirming Davis's findings, Alex Simirenko discovered that about seventy-five percent of Minneapolis's first-generation Russians had no musical instruments in their homes. [4]

At times the reports appear contradictory. In 1938 Harry Shulman wrote he had uncovered negligible cultural activity in New York's ethnic communities. He then qualifies this statement by saying that, while pictures, books, magazines, and toys were rarely found, musical instruments "were relatively common, particularly among Italian families." [5] Based upon slender evidence like this, as well as on the prevailing stereotype, other writers have woven music into a tapestry of warm, affectionate human relations among Italians.

Contradicting Shulman's findings, Mario Puzo, who grew up in New York City, writes of his Neapolitan neighbors: "I never heard an Italian singing. None of the grown-ups I knew were charming or loving or understanding.... I wondered where the hell the moviemakers and storywriters got all their ideas from." Bearing Puzo out, Pietro Di Donato noticed scarcely anyone in his neighborhood with the time to play instruments. Certainly he himself didn't. Beginning at the age of seven (the year was 1917) he was put to work in a drugstore: "I received the catechism of my working hours--directly from school to the drugstore, off from six to seven for supper, quit at nine p.m.; all day Saturday; Sunday afternoons off." [6]

Two explanations for the contradictions can be offered. One, Italians did purchase pianos as status symbols, to cut a <u>bella figura</u> among their friends. As many of the instruments were player-pianos, no urgent necessity arose for studying them. Also, other instruments like the violin and guitar were often purchased with the vague hope that someone somehow might learn to extract a sound from them. Lessons and daily practice did not necessarily follow their acquisition.[7] Two, most reports on the proliferation of instruments among Italians begin in the late thirties and concern the second or third generation, not the first.

This last observation applies to other ethnic groups. The same Simirenko who found most Russian homes without instruments also says that this was true only for the first generation. In about sixty percent of second- and third-generation homes he discovered guitars, violins, and pianos.[8]

Especially during the first three decades of their American residence hardworking foreigners found the often-romanticized life of the ethnic community a ridiculous fiction. More typical for the ethnic poor, claims Mary Vorse, was a Sicilian mother's life in Brooklyn. Vorse met her in 1920. Her husband had been dead for thirteen years, years in which the widow singlehandedly had struggled to raise her children by working in sweatshops--that is, when work was available. Her body seemed worn down by "anxiety, sorrow, and starvation." One child stood "listless at her side." The woman "had never sung monotonous Sicilian songs," neither near Palermo where she was born nor in Brooklyn.[9]

Ghetto-dwellers like the Sicilian mother, if they heard music, heard it fortuitously--on the streets, at a wedding or two, in church, or during an occasional picnic. Their own homes remained mute.[10] If their behavior altered at all, dance usually proved more stimulating to them than the less active execution of songs. "Just thump out the rhythm and throw out the tune and they'd still dance as if nothing had changed. They wouldn't even miss my accordion playing," a third-generation musician of Polish descent said of his paternal grandparents, who had discovered dancing after they had reached forty years of age. A Greek-American writes that his maternal grandparents' musical experiences were limited mostly to the Sunday chanting at church. His mother grew up hearing little music at home. Eventually she discovered that she loved to dance. But she always remained incapable of listening "to music as music."[11]

No Music for the Musical

Among the immigrants without music were some with decided musical inclinations. Unfortunately their new American life precluded the enjoyment of a pastime they held dear. Belonging in this category were hundreds of Minnesota's Finns, who had to give up their musical traditions for years to labor on "primitive farms." Only after they had provided for the physical needs of their families could they begin to think of forming choruses, bands, and orchestras like the ones they had known in Finland. [12]

Now and again, letters back to relatives abroad contain the complaints of writers who were musicians and possessed instruments but had no time for playing after work. The daily routine had to be work, bed, and ready for work again. [13]

The saddest examples of humans denied music were the genuinely talented youngsters. Their parents denied them musical study and insisted that they work and contribute to the family income. [14] In one instance from the early thirties a Jewish boy living on Harrison Avenue, in Boston's South End, exhibited extraordinary aptitude for the violin and composing music. He was largely self-taught, though his Quincy School teacher encouraged him to continue. Despite his musical promise, his parents confiscated the instrument, made their son devote all his nonschool time to helping in the family bakery, and demanded the teacher cease "corrupting" him. He is today the proprietor of a small bakery and plays hardly any music at all. [15]

A tragic instance of talent denied is provided by Florence Kelly. She writes of the many Italian children she knew who were lost to the arts because they had to work. At one time a music teacher at a settlement house discovered a musically precocious Italian newsboy. "The lad's parents were bought off for a stipulated sum," with the understanding that the boy would no longer hawk papers. "For four years the child Angelo" studied voice. "But a presidential election came, cold and sleet threatened the troop of children who huddled in newspaper alley until one and two o'clock in the morning awaiting the latest night extras and the first editions of the morning papers. Angelo was among them--the greedy peasant family had not withstood the temptation to get both the music teacher's gift and the newsboy's earnings. Weariness, cold, and wet did their work; pneumonia followed the election night and Angelo never sang again. " He died. [16]

The Failure of Efforts at Self-Enrichment

Several accounts tell of men and women who purposely ceased to sing the old songs from home and attend functions where the music performed would link them to a group non grata in America. [17] Whether for this reason or because they wished to atone for what they perceived as their cultural deficiencies, a few immigrants tried to acclimatize themselves to the atmosphere of symphony and opera. The results were often ludicrous. During the late twenties one Syrian man with no consciousness of his own cultural traditions heard somewhere that Beethoven, Verdi, Rembrandt, and Shakespeare were worth cultivating. He was soon to be found nodding at Symphony Hall, staring at the fashion-mongers in the Boston Opera House, wandering in a desultory manner through the Museum of Fine Arts, and puzzling over the incomprehensible lines delivered by the Shakespearean actors at Boston's Emerson College. All his attempts proved futile. He had understood nothing. He gave up these activities and turned to stamp collecting. [18]

With humble Italians the avenue to cultural betterment was usually Italian opera. But music's absence in their pasts weighed them down. Pascal D'Angelo writes of the summer of 1919, when he worked as a pick-and-shovel laborer: "I began to hear much about 'Aida, ' but I did not know exactly what it was. Federico up on Hudson Heights had been to see it; but he was unable to tell me much about it except that there was a fine parade in it. " D'Angelo finally attended an open-air performance at the Sheepshead Bay racetrack. Taken by the spectacle, he wanted "to rush home to our box car and compose another Aida, even though I did not know one note from another, as I still don't know. And music, which I adore, is a language I have yet to learn. " He attempted to understand musical theory and history, to study voice, and to play the mandolin and guitar. He failed in every musical endeavor he took up. [19]

The author has met several people from impoverished backgrounds who first took up music during young adulthood. But it was too late. They lacked patience for studying music books. One relinquished violin study because the thumb and little finger of his left hand remained stiff and constantly

ached. Besides, he failed to master any kind of vibrato.
Another found playing the piano impossible because his hands
never worked together and he had difficulty reading the printed music. When such people played at all, they tended to
play by ear and not by note.

The Avoidance of Music

For every settler who attempted to become educated, however futilely, in music, another stood adamantly against
participation in any musical activity, calling it a waste of
time and money, [20] a recreation for the idle rich, [21] and a
corrupting pastime for the industrious members of the working class. Furthermore, it would be argued, most professional musicians led a hand-to-mouth existence. [22]

Investigation of this attitude amongst Boston's first-
generation men and women has established its greatest prevalence with people who customarily worked in laborious jobs.
Others were shopkeepers or craftsmen--plumbers, tailors,
cabinet-makers, bricklayers, or electricians. A few were
professionals--dentists, lawyers, doctors, and engineers.
Financial security was a major concern for the least affluent; wealth accumulation a preoccupation of the comfortably
situated.

One hesitates to exempt members of any ethnic society from this group. Though the author has no reliable sta-
tistics to cite on the distribution of people chary of music,
he has discovered them in every subculture. Greeks, Syrians, and Chinese were least hesitant about admitting their
hostility. Italians and Jews were more apt to applaud music
and musicians when speaking to the author. But their children and grandchildren would confide that they really neither
engaged in musical activities nor encouraged any of their
family to do so. [23]

Ignorance Through Default

Many ethnic enclaves were not geared to compensate for the
lack of cultural direction in the home. Organizations necessary to perpetuate national song and dance and to encourage
musically talented youth were nonexistent or few and weak,
especially among migrants from the Mediterranean basin.
Inevitably a large number of children grew up with trifling

knowledge of and vaporous affection for the music of their parents' native land. [24] A 1942 study of eleven- to fifteen-year-old boys and girls of Italian parentage showed almost thirty percent of them failing to name a single person of Italian origin famous in the United States; and almost sixty percent, anyone famous in Italy. [25]

Typical of ethnic groups where music played an insignificant part in community lives are Boston's Albanians. A second-generation young man writes that he had rarely seen a musical instrument in an Albanian home or an interest in performing or listening to music in an Albanian person. Nor did any "effective unifying cultural organizations" instruct youngsters in their musical heritage. As a result, "whatever musical culture there is is dying and American music is taking over." He concludes: "Taking myself as an example, I can honestly say that I've never felt any feelings of hostility or rejection of the older generation's [musical] culture.... My parents were too busy making a living ... and there aren't now any programs through which a person can learn very much about Albanian culture. "[26]

Surprising is the discovery that some ethnic groups like the Czechs and Poles, who had the reputation of possessing strong cultural organizations abroad and a determination to continue them in America (choruses, orchestras, band, and musical-theater companies) also included a goodly number uninterested in, and unwilling to support, the cultural organizations that a few dedicated men and women tried to foster. Numerous complaints appeared in Polish and Czech newspapers and other publications on the indifference of their countrymen. [27] Some writers worried over the lack of a sense of national character and of a dedication to furthering a national culture. [28]

His curiosity aroused, the author, from 1974 through 1977, questioned the leaders of over forty Greater Boston cultural organizations participating in Boston's annual Whole World Celebration--Italians, Ukrainians, Poles, Hungarians, Czechs, Lithuanians, Greeks, Turks, and Syrians. With few exceptions, they complained that a tiny handful did all the work to keep music and dance groups together. They themselves had to visit the homes of neighbors constantly to win new, or discover what had happened to old, members. Attendance at rehearsals was irregular; membership turnover high. Children might appear more or less regularly. But they dropped out with late adolescence.

Only one or two groups, among them the Polish
Krakowiak Dancers and the Ukrainian-American Youth Association, seemed to suffer less acutely from these problems. These more fortunate groups, however, had national
reputations for excellence. Demand for their appearance
was strong and transcended ethnic boundries. Success had
fostered a pride in membership.

Nevertheless, as was pointed out to the author, even
the successful groups worried about raising money for themselves and keeping up their membership. One leader observed: "No one ever handed us anything on a platter. You
have to go out and fight for what you believe and take a lot
of crap while you're doing it. For every one guy that offers to help there are ten who only want to criticize and a
hundred who don't care if you exist." This person and several other commentators had been active in music and dance
organizations for over thirty years. Some of them were
looking for younger people to take over their duties. Alas,
they had had no success in finding anyone.

The Fostering of Ethnic Music by Urban Educators

An unusual activity of a handful of American urban educators,
for which they deserve commendation, was the stepping in
where parents had proved deficient and communal organizations weak to teach children something about their national
music. True, songs from different countries mingled together during the public-school music lesson. Yet students
like the Italian youngsters of New York City's Greenwich
Village did get to know something of who they were musically:

> The teachers in the lower grades complained
> that the Italian children seemed to have nothing in
> their backgrounds upon which the school could draw.
> If the children read Pinocchio, learned to sing
> Santa Lucia, or danced the tarantella, it was be-
> cause these ... were part of the general school
> program, taught to school children of different
> backgrounds indiscriminately. Efforts to ascertain
> how much traditional folk knowledge the children
> of the locality possessed tended to confirm the ex-
> perience of the schools. When groups of children
> were asked to sing, the Italian songs which they
> knew were either currently popular Italian songs

which they had heard on the family's phonograph,
or those which they had learned in school and
which they mingled interchangeably with songs of
other origins. Out of a group of some thirty
children who were asked whether any could dance
the tarantella, the only two who could do so had
learned it in school. [29]

Around the year 1910 music and dance educators,
directed by the composer Arthur Farwell, then Supervisor
of Music in New York Parks and Piers, rehearsed and
staged an annual Children's Folk Dance Festival, in which
ghetto children, among them Jews, Italians, and Hungarians,
were taught to execute in costume the dances of diverse
peoples. [30] A similar idea later invested the many annual
cultural fairs sponsored by the International Institutes located in cities with large immigrant populations. Gaspar
Jako, Executive Director of Boston's International Institute
and expert in the history of these fairs, has stated they
were meant first to educate ethnic Americans unfamiliar
with their own culture and to give them a sense of pride in
their background, and second to help other Americans appreciate the contributions each ethnic group has made to
American culture as a whole. These fairs were also begun to help stem the erosion taking place in ethnic families
where Americanized children were becoming increasingly
hostile to their parents' way of life.

Ethnic members of an Institute were invited to participate in a yearly celebration of the food, music, dance,
crafts, and costumes that distinguished their subcultures.
When minds proved rusty, feet clumsy, and voices recal-
citrant, the festival's organizers stood ready to help ethnic
Americans locate the literature that described their authentic songs and dances and to rehearse dancers and singers
so that performances would appear finished and authorita-
tive. [31] First organized in the 1920s, these fairs continue
to the present.

Emotion and the Music-Lover

The many people desiring music's performance outweighed
those with little involvement in music. Though reluctant to
contribute money and effort to cultural organizations as such,
these immigrants did listen to music at home, encourage
their children to take lessons, and attend communal events
featuring song and dance. [32]

In what manner did these people enjoy music? The books written about one of the various ethnic minorities almost invariably claim that the people comprising the society are conspicuously emotional in their outlook and that music reflects this emotion. [33] At times the assertion is laconic, with hardly any explanation given, as in Joseph Remenyi's on the Hungarians. [34] At other times some explanation follows, as in August Vaz's comments on the emotionalism of California's Portuguese: "There is in the mystique of the Portuguese a great longing, a great yearning that they sum up in the word saudades--a seeking that is at once sentimental and realistic; at the same time ... there is a deep rooted feeling for home and family, for quietude, a feeling of will and at the same time a resignation to fate--so well shown in the traditional songs of the fado. "[35]

The fado was commonly sung with eyes almost shut, the face tilted upward and wearing an intense, abstracted look, and the torso moving sympathetically to the lilt of the melody. In his study of the fado Rodney Gallop writes that the Portuguese audience insisted on an unaffected delivery and criticized the professional, bel canto type of voice as untraditional. The singer tried to project the sentiments of the song, whether sad, wild, passionate, or erotic, by means of free rhythms, rubato, and syncopations. Oftentimes the verse was improvised. [36]

The agitation of feelings and the sensuous, if not sensual, appeal possible in song is made explicit in Harry Petrakis's description of a singer, Daphne Callistos, and her audience in a Greek-American taverna. She is asked if she knows the songs of Pontu, Epirus, and Crete. Yes, she replies, she knows them all, the lullabies, love songs, and laments. Petrakis continues:

> A lament is a morose and melancholy song, and Apollo [the guitarist] played them with feeling. But as she sang I had the strange sensation I was hearing a quality of despair I had never heard before. Her voice, haunting and mournful, led us down the path where the stream of woe pours into the river of lamentation. At the tables men stirred, and a wind of pleased muttering swept the room.
> When she finished the lament, Apollo changed the tempo to a lilting melody of a festive mountain dance. Daphne placed her hand on her hips and threw back her head and her voice, suddenly bawdy and vibrant, assaulted the room.... Her ardor

paid homage to the woodland spirit of fertility and
abandon.... When she finished a storm of applause rose from the room of men....
    When Daphne sang an unhappy ballad or a la-
ment, she had the old men weeping for the good
days of their lost youth. When she sang a dancing song from Macedonia and suggestively rendered
the lyrics of a shy man and his bold wife, the old
men went wild with delight. When the greybeards
finally rose to dance, they exhausted themselves to
demonstrate their unflagging virility, and leaped
off the floor like drunken and festive roosters.[37]

An informative paragraph, whose contents parallel
and augment what Petrakis wrote, is taken from a lengthier
explanation of the music enjoyed by Syrian-Lebanese men.
The commentary was written by a Syrian grocer, amateur
musician, and sometime poet who lived in Allston, a suburb
of Boston:

What did Anglo-Saxons know of the overwhelming
of feelings that drove a man out into the night to
bathe in the beauty of the stars and moon; the
placing of a palm on the cheek; the uplifted head,
and the unbidden singing of an improvised taqs-
seeme to all the quiet loveliness all around, "Ya
Leil! Ya Leillee, Ya Leil?" What did they know
of the group of haboab [cherished friends] who bid
goodbye to their wives for a day, and took their
oud, their arrac, their mazza and disappeared into
the countryside to that cold-running brook on Hum-
za's farm? All day they sang beside it, of love,
nature, life--and late at night returned home to
their wives and sang for them a popular thu-thoo'a
or two, with a swinging beat and dancing, and
guffaws that awoke the children. Sleepily they
wandered out, rubbed their eyes and began to
clap their hand to urge on the dancers.[38]

Change the names of the people and the songs, and
the Greek or Syrian scene, with few other alterations, could
become an Italian, Russian, or Serbian one.

The description of settings in which music elicits intense subjective reactions is found plentifully in the writings
of Jews, to whom the emotion-provoking violin and any music
that moved them sounded "Jewish."[39] Samuel Chotzinoff has

written a great deal on how the delight of many Jews in music, including art music, centered around the arousal of their feelings to a white-hot pitch. In one instance he tells of a Mr. Kooners's pleasure in hearing a Bach sonata that sounded "Jewish" to him, and whose composer "could just as well have been a cantor in a synagogue in Minsk as in a Lutheran church in Leipzig." Mr. Kooners's daughter Elena, a cellist, played Bach with a highly personal and sentimental tone and phrasing: "Her pent-up emotions were released by her fingers and bow; every note vibrated with nervous passion. Even the double stops and chords throbbed with emotion."[40]

A most extraordinary description of a Jewish piano teacher, Mrs. Zamoshkin, is given in Chotzinoff's A Lost Paradise (New York: Knopf, 1955):

> She quite discarded, for the most part, the printed notes, especially in intricate or rapid passages! In the slower, lyrical sections, she brought out what I presumed was the soul. On these she lingered, caressing some notes by raising and depressing her wrist, while her face assumed a pained expression and she shook her head ecstatically, as if the beauty of the moment was too much for her to bear. When she arrived at the last page she pressed the loud pedal down and kept her foot on it remorselessly and with flashing arms and fingers let loose a babel of sound such as I had never before heard. Though it had little relation to the notes on the page, it was a stirring finale in itself, and when it was over I saw that Mrs. Zamoshkin's face was triumphant, though covered with sweat. "You may have noticed," she gasped ... "that I left out some of the notes. But I didn't leave out the souls of the Poet and Peasant! No! That I didn't.

Music frequently acted as an emotional palliative to those who felt inadequate and alone as they coped with the problems of daily existence. Thus Eddie Cantor speaks of his father's recourse to violin playing because it "built around him" a life "of music and dreams to shield him from this strange city he didn't understand, from all the harsh tumult and clatter of iron and steel that were flying up around him."[41] Peter Roberts tells of isolated Italian laborers listening to Italian recordings and grateful that they had "something to think of besides work and sleep."[42]

Two of the most dejected people as a result of being
alone that the author has ever met were a young Italian
couple. Immediately on arriving in the United States in
1932 they went to work on a farm in Derry, New Hampshire.[43] Here they were cut off from amici and every
vestige of an Italian way of life. Though experienced as
farm laborers, the husband and wife hated working on the
land. Evenings before retiring they sat on the stoop, singing to guitar accompaniment and weeping. One of their
favorite songs was the serenade, "Mi par d'udir ancora,"
from Bizet's The Pearl Fishers, which the author, who was
eight at the time, still remembers in a ludicrously corrupt
version: "My pa, you dear, anchor the rascals in a mess
so far." The couple began to wander off during the day to
play the guitar and sing. Tasks remained unattended. When
the inevitable dismissal took place, they left swiftly for Boston, faces beaming, eyes tear-filled, singing a song in a
minor key and march tempo as they walked jauntily down the
dirt road.

The combination of weeping and singing, even of a
happy ditty, comes as no surprise to anyone at all conversant
with the tastes of ethnic Americans. For example, to many
Jews, "happy singing is sad,"[44] sad songs excel all others,[45]
and a way of showing deep appreciation for any music lay in
weeping.[46] Invariably Italian audiences called for songs of
parting, like the extremely popular "L'Addio A Napoli" and
"Torna A Surriento," which left the eyes of singer and audience brimming with nostalgia. Similarly several accounts
describe Poles snuffling into their beer at a picnic when a
favorite singer delivered one of those mournful love songs
they preferred above all music, like the lamenting "Alas, I
erred, for I knew not how to hide the love that ached within
me, that haunted my dreams at night."[47]

The propensity to feel sadness is delineated extrav-
agantly in one explanation of what constituted a successful
party for Russians in America. M. K. Argus writes that
his fellow Russians never understood the American slogan
"Keep Smiling" or the requirement that everyone have a good
time at American parties:

A Russian party is considered a success when it is
drenched in melancholy and weltschmerz.... If
there is a singer at the gathering, she will sing
about the misery of life, the frustrations of love,
the tragedy of death. If an actor is present he

will inevitably declaim Russia's favorite peom, one
that has been recited for generations in every part
of our vast country, "The Deep Grave Dug in the
Fresh Earth." The guests will sigh; the hostess
will beam with unhappiness, such a successful
party! [48]

Music as Pure Sound

The sensuous preoccupation with the voice and the sheer delight in vocalizing musical sounds were characteristics of
singers from the Mediterranean basin--Italians, Greeks,
Lebanese, Syrians--and of Jewish cantors from Eastern
Europe. A special, indescribable kind of feeling, "ecstasy
mixed with pain, " a Greek musician called it, might affect
singer and listener when conditions were right. Jo Pagano
writes of an Italian man strolling through a Colorado town
at night, singing "in a voice that was at once powerful, lilting, and raucous.... He sang ... abandoning his heart and
spirit enthusiastically to the intoxication of his own voice. "[49]

At a testimonial dinner given some years ago in honor
of a prominent Boston Italian, an amateur singer, half-
flushed with wine, sang Tosti's "Marechiare. " He gave a
loving stroke to every note, lingered with a singular projection of otherworldliness on the melisma in the tune's center,
and ended with an exuberance of spirits on "A marechiare,
a marechiare sorride un balcone. " It was less an interpretation of the song's subject, more an exaltation of personal
well-being communicated luxuriously through sound. The
singing roused the audience to noisy shouts of approval.
One excited old man dashed forward to embrace the singer,
kiss him on both cheeks, and force him to gulp down a full
glass of wine. [50]

Without doubt Enrico Caruso's strong regard for the
elemental excitement of naked sound goes a long way toward
explaining the extra dimension of beauty in his voice that
listeners found irresistible. Alfred Kazin tells of how he
and his Russian-Jewish parents reacted to Caruso's recorded
singing of selections from La Juive, played on a hand-cranked
Victrola. It was not so much the music nor the penetration
into the theme they found moving, as it was the sensuous
appeal of the voice:

Caruso, "that Italyéner, " seemed to me the

echo of some outrageously pagan voice at the roof
of the world. When I pushed at the hand-crank
and the wheezy sounds of the orchestra in the
background came to me as the whispered turnings,
sighs, and alarms of the crowd around the circus
pit, there on high, and rising higher with each
note, that voice, that golden voice, leaped its way
from one trapeze to another. We sat hunched in
our wonder, our adoration, our fear. Would he
make it? Could any human being find that last
impossible rung? Rachel! Quand de Seigneur la
grâce tutélaire.... "What a voice!" my father
would say over and over, deeply shaken. "What
a voice! It's not human!" ... Then, his face
white with pleasure, with amazement, with wonder, "Oh that Italyéner! Oh that Italyéner! What
a power he has, that Italyéner!"51

Music Education in the Ethnic Community

Music was an indispensable accomplishment in many households, not a mere luxury. 52 It was thought of as a grace
elevating the immigrant above the American. Thus a
Carpatho-Russian writes of his conviction that Americans
are "at the bottom of the list in the arts, especially music." Building a skyscraper is more important to them,
he claims, than creating a beautiful song. "To the Slav,
music is a necessity; to the Anglo-Saxon it is entertainment."53 Similar sentiments were voiced by writers from
almost every ethnic group.

A commitment to music was taken seriously by ethnic
Americans such as these. If a child demonstrated any talent, a teacher was engaged, practice supervised, and a
constant exhibit of the student's advancing prowess seen to
within the family circle and, when possible, the community. 54 "I was treated with respect and admiration by my
entire family: aunts, uncles, cousins, grandparents, and
parents," writes one young instrumentalist.

Regular practice was insisted upon by at least a few
parents. Some fathers tended to see their youngsters as
artists in the white, and daily musical exercise as the
burnisher bringing talent into a dazzling luster. Achille La
Guardia wanted to make a "second Sousa" out of his son
Fiorello. The boy became expert on the banjo and cornet

and almost a professional musician, until he turned to government service and politics. [55] Guy and Carmen Lombardo had to report daily after school to their father's tailor shop, where they first helped out, then commenced their practicing. "There was no fooling around during those practice sessions; music was a serious thing. Papa provided the best teachers available and didn't want to waste his money. "[56]

One favorite story Chotzinoff heard involved a Jewish student sent home with a note from the teacher: "Your boy needs a bath. " The reply came instantly: "Don't smell my boy, learn him. "[57] If the American ideal for a boy was to have him join the school football team, the ideal among many Jews was to have him learn to play a violin well and join the school orchestra. [58]

Entry into a profession open to poor immigrants was in the back of some parents' minds when they insisted on steady, painstaking practice. The penniless father of Ruggiero Ricci, the great violinist, made his son practice six hours daily. "Be a fiddler or a garbage man, " he warned.[59] Benny Goodman's Russian-Jewish parents could ill afford "advanced education" for their son, so decided "music might give [him] the approval, recognition, and security which was part of the golden promise of the United States. "[60] Harold Arlen states that his father, a cantor, started him on piano lessons "so I would be a teacher and not have to work on shabbas. "[61] And Harry Ruby, the songwriter, says that Lower East Side parents who could scarcely afford pianos bought them for their children: "These people, who had barely enough to eat and pay the rent--for some reason they wanted their children to learn something. Everybody got lessons in the hope that it would lead to something. "[62]

The passion for obtaining an instrument and giving children music lessons is vividly summed up in Jerre Mangione's Mount Allegro. He writes that in the twenties many Sicilian parents considered it a social disgrace not to have a player-piano, a set of Verdi-opera rolls, and a piano teacher appearing weekly to instruct the young: "Every child tall enough to reach the piano was regarded as a potential concert artist, " he claims. The piano gave parents "a medium for reviving their musical memories of Italy, and it was a perfect excuse for forcing a musical education on all their children, something that only the rich had been able to afford in Sicily. "[63]

Piano and Violin Study
_____

The piano and violin were by far the most popular instruments for study, the former mainly by girls and, in contrast to American preferences, the latter by boys. Writing
of his first piano students on the Lower East Side, Konrad
Bercovici states they were adolescent girls, "dark daughters
of Sicily, corn-colored ones from Poland, red-haired ones
from Russia, all ill-fed, ill-clothed, and very eager."[64]
On 10 January 1903 a New York Evening Post reporter
writes that Italians, even the extremely poor, gave their
daughters piano, their sons violin and mandolin, lessons.
An identical observation appears in the 10 September 1906
New York Tribune. [65] In Hamtramck, Michigan, four times
as many Polish-American girls as boys studied piano; twice
as many boys as girls, the violin; and these included the
children of laborers with scarcely any money. [66] It almost
goes without saying that the violin was the preferred instrument for Jewish boys, and the sons of Russian, Ukrainian,
Hungarian, and Rumanian immigrants. Moreover, among
Greeks, Armenians, Syrians, and Lebanese, if a boy took
up an instrument, it was normally the violin; a girl, piano.[67]

Some years ago the author was the conductor of a
school orchestra made up of eleven- to fifteen-year-old boys
and girls from polyglot backgrounds, all living in the econom-
ically depressed North End of Springfield, Massachusetts. In
the fifty-member string section, the majority were boys of
Jewish, Greek, Armenian, French-Canadian, Syrian-Lebanese,
and Italian extraction; the lesser number of girls playing
strings included one or two blacks, Puerto Ricans, and
Americans.

When first- and second-generation parents were asked
why they encouraged boys to take up the violin and girls the
piano, the replies irrespective of ethnic origin were unex-
pectedly similar. Parents said studying an instrument was
a more serious undertaking for boys than for girls. Boys
might decide on a musical career. The number of positions
available to a pianist was limited. Violinists were in greater demand by far. Another consideration was that the violin
seemed the most expressive of all instruments to them, and
the most loved. Like the voice, it could ravish the ear and
"speak to the heart. " On it players could most effectively
replicate the sound of their own national music, whereas the
piano had no counterparts in their past experience. Although
national songs and dances were available in piano arrange-

ments, the effect was considered less authentic than on the violin. Surprisingly, even the Poles concurred in this opinion, despite the piano compositions of Chopin.

As for the piano, during the twenties it was often purchased in the shape of a player-piano because music from piano rolls was better than no music at all. In addition, parents thought of the piano as the most socially acceptable instrument for young ladies. It allowed them to play sedately, without encouraging the wild and unrestrained outbreaks of feeling the violin was capable of inciting. Yes, they did adore highly charged music; but not played by their daughters.

Engaging an Instructor

In the first two decades of the century a private lesson could range from twenty-five cents to one dollar in cost. Oftentimes the ghetto-dweller could ill afford these prices. Potential musicians would have been lost by default if it had not been for the rise of the settlement music school. When money was scarce, the settlement music school offered lessons either free as a scholarship or at nominal cost.

A constant problem for parents was the locating of competent teachers. Music charlatans frequently gulled the unwary. This the composer Paul Creston (born Joseph Guttovegio) pointed out when he spoke of his own early musical training in New York City. His father, a poor housepainter, knew nothing about selecting a reliable teacher and sent him for six years to a mediocre musician "who taught all instruments but played none." For the innocent the settlement music school fortunately offered a solution. Its faculty usually consisted of trustworthy instructors with fine credentials.

The first settlement house in the United States, patterned after London's Toynbee Hall, was founded in 1886 in New York's Lower East Side. Its purpose was to assist the urban poor by offering a variety of services--educational, medical, recreational, and social. In 1894 Emilie Wagner started her Settlement Music School in the Lower East Side. She offered classes only on piano and violin at first. Her success was immediate. The number of students increased, as did the teachers and courses offered. By 1907 eighteen teachers were instructing twelve hundred youngsters--Jews,

Italians, Poles, Russians, Ukrainians, and Bohemians--on a
variety of instruments. Lessons could be had for as low as
fifteen cents. Violin outfits could be purchased for $4.50;
pianos used for practice at a five-cent-per-half-hour charge.
If neither lesson nor instrument could be paid for and the
youngster showed promise, the settlement house assumed the
expenses. A junior and senior orchestra gave ensemble experience to instrumentalists of all ages. Free or inexpensive admission to concerts by professional performers was
provided. [68] The idea of the settlement music school spread
to other cities. Philadelphia in 1909, Boston in 1911, and
several other cities soon after had their own. [69]

Parental Attitudes Toward Lessons
_____

A couple of unanticipated answers emerged from the respons-
es of ethnic parents to questions concerning the kind of teacher they wished for their children. They, of course, preferred
above all to engage a capable private teacher from their own
subculture. By so doing, the knowledge of one's own music
might increase at the same time as the performance capacity
of the student. Failing to discover such a teacher, which
often happened, the parents turned to a musician outside
their group or sent the child to a settlement music school
for instruction. They knew that the musical literature the
child would study might only exceptionally be that of the
ethnic group. Indeed, it might comprise mostly the "classical" compositions of German and Austrian composers.
Nevertheless, their hostility was directed not to this music
but to American popular music. Besides, the most highly
placed people of all nationalities regarded the possession of
knowledge about "classical" music as a cachet of respectability.

If a musical career was intended, then the course of
study prescribed by nonethnic teachers was probably more
efficacious than the nonchalant or disorganized methods of a
few teachers within the subculture--an opinion stated by several Italians and Greeks, in particular. While the youngsters took lessons, their parents and musically knowledgeable friends could provide them with their own native music
to study and perform in the family circle and elsewhere in
the community.

The author has examined the music that scores of
youngsters studied. Along with the expected exercises and

facile pieces carved out of the opera of major composers like Beethoven and Chopin, ethnic compositions purchased or written out for the student by some family member were plentiful. To cite two typical examples, a Syrian-American girl showed the author several works for piano given her by her mother and uncle. These she had dutifully studied and later played "for the family and for company." Among the works were songs and dances either published in Beirut or Cairo, or written down for her by a friend of her uncle. In all the songs the vocal melody and the pianist's treble part were identical. At about the same time an Italian-American violinist presented the author with several pieces of music that his grandfather had insisted he study. They included a collection entitled Le Belle Canzoni d'Italia and a manuscript book containing his grandfather's favorite Italian melodies.

By giving music lessons to the children, some parents hoped to keep their families united. Guy Lombardo's father, for example, "wanted desperately to keep his family together" in the New World. Music, in addition to all its other virtues, offered promise as a means of achieving this goal." In the town of London, Ontario (a hundred miles out of Detroit), where the Lombardos lived, Italian families customarily formed "musical trios, consisting of violin, flute, and harp. Into the hands of the first-born, Guy, Papa put a three-quarter-sized beginner's violin. Carmen found himself with the flute. "70

Parents also saw to music lessons for several other reasons. One Jewish mother from Poland told her daughter: "In America, to be a gentlewoman, I hear, you must know how to play the piano. So you go take lessons. "71 One or two far-sighted adults realized their children had to learn to live in an American world. They tried carefully to balance ethnic with American instruction. This was the reasoning behind the decision of Jade Snow Wong's Chinese father that she should receive "some training in Western music." He had already sent her older sister to a conservatory in San Francisco and was pleased that she now was able to play "Beethoven, Chopin, and Mozart to perfection at important Chinatown socials and taught piano lessons. "72

Examining the question of voice study reveals a paradox in ethnic thinking. Most music-lovers enjoyed song above all other forms of composition and idolized the human voice, but also felt instruction in voice not as essential as

on an instrument. The consensus was that a person could
start right off singing. Surrounded by song, a vocalist
learned by example. Whether right or wrong, this was the
opinion of the greatest number of ethnic Americans who responded to the author's questioning. "The natural voice can
be beautiful," said one Ukrainian, "but a raw violin sound
cuts you like a knife. "

Parents providing their children with voice lessons
normally had designs beyond the learning of traditional and
popular songs. The object of such training was opera--
national opera and operetta, to be sure; but whatever the
ethnic background, Italian opera also. Writers in the Polish-
and Hungarian-language newspapers of Cleveland point with
pride to young men and women who had mastered the difficulties of Italian-aria singing and were on the brink of professional operatic careers. On occasion the author has had
to listen to the singing of girls of Greek and Armenian extraction. The mothers were certain their daughters had
futures with the Metropolitan Opera. Instructive in this regard is the childhood of Maria Callas in New York City.
Her Greek mother learned to adore opera and purchased a
player-piano, a Victrola, and scores of piano rolls and recordings of opera. These the young Maria heard over and
over again. Later, although her father bitterly opposed a
musical career, her mother's will prevailed. Maria Callas
started on the road that led to engagements in every important opera house in the world. 73

The author cannot overemphasize the extent to which
Caruso had captured the fancy of thousands of ghetto-
dwellers. Alfred Kazin, in A Walker in the City, Samuel
Chotziniff, in A Lost Paradise, and Robert Merrill, in
Once More from the Beginning, have written of his impact
on East European Jews. Several of the author's students
of Greek, Lithuanian, and Armenian descent have spoken of
parents who had studied voice and grandparents who had admired Caruso. One or two said that old Caruso records
were still owned by the family. We can surmise that the
interest in Italian opera may have begun with the enjoyment
of Caruso's singing.

Musical Education in the Home
_____

Young men and women knowledgeable about their cultural
pasts who were interviewed by the author often give the

credit to what they heard at home. A third-generation
youth, whose grandparents had come from Naples and settled in Lawrence, Massachusetts, writes that his grandparents and parents had repeatedly sung their favorite songs in
his presence. Without his thinking about it, he memorized
and now frequently sang "O Sole Mio," "Carmè," "La Spag-
nola," "Caro Mio Ben," "Ciribiribin," "Comm' E Bella A
Stagione," "Canzone De Rosa," and "Siete Fatta Per Baciare"
for his own amusement. His family also guided him to an
Italian "maestro," who taught him to appreciate the music of
Italy in general, and the songs and dances of Naples in particular, while giving him instrumental lessons. [74]

A young woman of Italian descent gives a similar list
of secular songs she had learned as a child. She adds that
on holidays, her family had customarily gathered together
and performed pieces her grandmother said were traditional
in their home circle as far back as she could remember.
Some of these compositions the young woman knew well and
now sang for her own children on holidays: "Il Bambino
Gesù" on Christmas Eve, "Buon' Capodanno" on New Year's
Eve, "La Canzone del Venerdî Santo" and "Il Cuor della
Notte" on Good Friday, and the "Marcia Reale" on Italian
national holidays. She ends by stating that today she
"thumps the tunes out" on the piano as she sings, whereas
"in the old days" a little orchestra of violin, mandolin, and
accordion played by her brother, father, and a first cousin,
respectively, provided an accompaniment for the voices. [75]

Education Outside the Home

Many a private teacher working within the ethnic community
felt it a responsibility to teach students to value the subculture's outstanding musical compositions, whether traditional,
popular, or artistic. To accomplish this end the teacher
alone, or in collaboration with other teachers in the community, formed musical clubs, societies, or associations. Through
these organizations they and their students performed in private musicales open to parents and friends, in recitals and
concerts for a general audience, and in appearances at neighborhood functions those works most dear to the public's
heart. [76] Cleveland's La Voce del Popolo Italiano, 11 November 1937, prints a report on the recent activities of the
nine-year-old Trinarcia Musical Association, directed by
Maestro Spoleti-Bonanno. Among these activities is mentioned a recital before an Italian audience, in which two of

the finest performances were given by the "sensational ... nine-year-old Celia Balbo ... in the difficult composition of Arditi's Il Bacio (The Kiss)" and by "the newsboy Caruso," Nick Candora, who gave a "fine rendition of Pagliacci." The reporter concludes with: "It is through activities of this sort that the culture of Italy is brought to America and her people."[77]

Likewise, Kazuo Ito writes that the West Coast Japanese provided for teachers, schools, and associations to transmit their music and dances and to teach Japanese instruments about which the West had little knowledge. He mentions in particular instruction in the bon dance, and in playing the koto (harp), shakuhachi (flute), and biwa (lute).[78] Like other Asian immigrants, the Japanese recognized that no music teacher outside the ethnic group could help instruct their young. Upon them alone depended the perpetuation of their national culture.

Where the effort to ensure such instruction was weak, as it was with the Syrians and Lebanese, then, when the first generation died, the special musical knowledge died with it. Today, few second-generation and almost no third-generation Lebanese are able to play the oud (lute), kabunja (violin), and kanoon (lap-harp).

Ethnic communities usually tried to establish some sort of institution or national school whose function it was to teach the language and also the traditions and arts that distinguished the subculture. Typical was the Free Cossacks Society of Rochester, New York, and its Ukrainian School, begun around 1922, which instructed the Ukrainian children in their language and culture, with heavy emphasis placed on singing. Periodically the children's choir and selected soloists trained at the school gave concerts of native songs in the Free Cossacks Society Hall.[79]

Opportunities for an informal education in one's national music were constantly available. Attached to every ethnic enclave were professional musicians singing and playing instruments in taverns, cafés, and music halls, at picnics, and for special occasions in private homes.[80] Their repertoire consisted mainly of the national songs currently popular in the subculture. Composed music mingled inextricably with traditional works in their presentations. Favorite musicians recorded their most-called-for selections and sold the recordings to their countrymen. Walking down

a street of an ethnic neighborhood during the warm summer
months, one would be likely to hear live or recorded music
floating out from the open windows of tenement flats and the
screen-doors of coffeehouses and taverns. In addition,
itinerant street musicians played guitars, accordions, violins, and barrel organs and serenaded the patrons of restaurants and the passersby at street corners.

With the advent of radio and the weekly ethnic-music
hour the decibel level in the community rose perceptibly
when the ethnic group's national anthem announced another
installment of this especially loved program. At times during the summer one could meander down the entire length of
an urban community and not miss a note of the music being
broadcast. The sounds caromed off brick, concrete, and
asphalt, converting the buildings and streets into one immense sound stage. More than a few men and women said
that whatever they were doing stopped and wherever they
were--a neighbor's house, the butcher shop, the coffeehouse
--they made certain the radio was turned on, in order to
hear the latest offering of song, news, and advertised spe-
cials of local merchants.

The Ethnic Community's Instrumentalists and Vocalists

Every subculture contained professional and semiprofessional
singers, instrumentalists, and composers who had come to
the United States with their countrymen. After a few years
had passed, young men and women trained in America to the
musical usages of their ethnic group augmented the older
generation of musicians.

Few of these people gained a national reputation.
Normally they remained in one area, often refusing to travel
because of the strong love for, and the feeling of obligation
to, their families. They taught, arranged, and composed
music tailored to a locality's requirements. They appeared
as performers wherever their services were requested.
Some musicians helped organize the music ensembles and
dance companies that amateurs in the larger ethnic enclaves
began increasingly to join in the twenties and thirties--Polish
Choral Society singers, Yugoslavian kolo dancers, Lebanese
dubke performers, and so forth. [81]

The preponderance of ethnic musicians, professional
and amateur, were singers. They were, first, the soloists

in the synagogues and churches; second, the members of
juvenile and adult choirs specializing in sacred music and
community choruses in secular music; third, the amateur
vocalists of musico-dramatic clubs and the professional
singers giving formal recitals in concert halls and the numerous popular singers performing in the easygoing ambience
of vaudeville halls, coffeehouses, and night spots.

Prominent singers were the cantor of the Jewish
synagogue and priest and precentor of the Eastern Orthodox
Church. The Jewish cantor was all-important in the con-
ducting of the synagogue service. Ideally he possessed a
beautiful voice over which he had virtuosic control. This
combination enabled him to sing in such a moving and dazzling manner that "he represented ... the true Shelich
Tzibbur, a person worthy of representing his congagation
before their Father in Heaven. "[82] Typical is the description of Cantor Feinstein's singing on Rosh Hashanah and
Yom Kippur, at the Madison Street synagogue in New York
City. Trembling with emotion, his voice "soared away into
the topmost reaches of the vocal scale in a hazardous display of trills, runs, and scales, like an acrobat doing impossible feats on a high trapeze. "[83] All things considered,
the singing of synagogue vocalist and of operatic tenor were
not so distant that many a Jewish cantor could not easily
cross over from one to another. Several, like Jan Peerce
and Richard Tucker, were extremely successful in both
capacities. [84]

A similar love for the voice guided Greeks, Syrians,
and Lebanese in selecting the priests for their parishes and
hiring precentors to intone the traditional Orthodox Church
hymns and lead the congregational singing. When a priest
renowned for the beauty of his singing visited a local Orthodox church, both the devout Christians and the ardent enthusiasts for fine singing rushed to attend Sunday service.
They would fill the church's interior and stand on the outside stairway before the open doors in order to listen to the
visitor "blessed by God." That evening a relative or friend
usually held a reception for the priest. The host's intimates
and nodding acquaintances openly solicited invitations in order
to be present when the inevitable invitation to sing caused
the bearded visitor to perform hymns and one or two traditional secular songs. [85]

Choruses in the Ethnic Community

After synagogues and national churches were established in America the Jews and the Christian Slavs and Hungarians, in particular, moved to organize choirs as adjuncts to the religious service. Cantors, priests, and precentors were among the first choir directors. Soon musicians from the community began to assist in the training of amateur voices, and the choral repertoire expanded to include secular works.[86]

As the second generation grew up, an added inducement to the formation of choruses was the need to teach children the language and culture of their forebears.[87] That this teaching was at times difficult a comment by Emil Lengyel makes clear:

> In a Hungarian West Virginia [miner's] colony I saw a Hungarian pastor sweat blood over the attempt to make immigrant miners' American-born children learn the Hungarian text to the then popular song: "Gloomy Sunday." You might have thought that the minister's own salvation depended upon his pupils' memorizing the depressing words of that dismal song, and it probably did.[88]

Preferring play, children went reluctantly to what they regarded as tedious practice sessions. They were made to go nevertheless, especially when their parents suspected they had voices worth developing. As Robert Merrill explains, he once attempted to avoid choir practice. His refusal to go was swept aside by his adamant mother:

> When I still refused to sing with the synagogue choir, she was stunned. "You don't understand, Moishe. You can't fight me. God gave you a voice and you gotta use it."
> "I wanna play ball."
> "You walk on your feet, you sit on your tuchis, and you'll sing with that voice. I hear you in the bathroom in the morning. You're going to sing."
> "I'll talk with my voice, Momma, like I walk with my feet. I walk. I don't dance."
> "You're still a pisher."
> "I'll pish, but I won't sing."
> "And I'll crack you in a minute. Don't be fresh with me."[89]

When Robert Merrill's father later objected to his taking singing up as a profession, his mother put down her husband with: "Caruso died on relief?"

Alongside juvenile choruses grew adult choral societies. Their purpose was the edification of the choristers and the recreation of the ethnic audience. They sang mainly traditional songs arranged for chorus and the easier and shorter compositions written by composers in the Old Country. These associations came in the form of choral clubs attached to the Czech sokols (gymnastic organizations), Armenian choral unions associated with a church or cultural center, and Hungarian workers' singing societies. 90 The Yugoslavs alone had at one time a minimum of 125 singing societies belonging in two federations, Serbian and Slovenian. 91 One of the most extensive of the nationwide singing federations was the Alliance of Polish Singers, to which about 250 choruses applied for membership between 1889 and 1939. 92 Characteristic of the functions of most federations, the Alliance sponsored singing conferences, held contests, and recommended musical compositions for performance. To the choral-singing competitions came organizations with names like Chor Halka, Chor Harmonia-Chopin, Chor Jutrzenka, Chor Moniuszko, Polsko Narodwy Chor, and Chor Halina--the names of six Polish choruses in Cleveland. 93

When asked about the importance of the choral movement, the general secretary of the Polish Alliance in 1913, Edward Budzynski, replied:

> Music has been a great ennobling factor in the life of our Polish colonies in America. More than literature or any of the arts it has remained one of the greatest ideals of our lives and enabled us to get away from the mania of the Dollar.... We have a semi-monthly magazine, Harmonia.... There are 3,653 Polish singers in the United States belonging to the Polish Musical Alliance, but there may be twice as many singers in independent groups. 94

Musical-Stage Companies

The singing societies did not always confine themselves to giving concerts. Several were also busily engaged in staging national musical dramas, operetta mostly, sometimes in cooperation with a musico-dramatic club.[95] Some clubs, like the St. Stanislaus Parish Dramatic Club of the Poles in Chicago, were self-sufficient and mounted productions of such quality their reputations spread throughout the country. Poles nationally knew about the St. Stanislaus Club's great singer-actress Agnes Nering. Chicago also boasted an admirable Polish playwright, Szczesny Zahajkiewicz, whose dramas, staged in the twelve-hundred-seat auditorium of the Polish community, were enthusiastically received. He wrote around sixty plays. "As ninety-five percent of Polish immigrants came from peasant stock, he based his plays on peasant life in Poland, and wrote them for local American consumption, mostly for amateur parish needs. Singing and music were interspersed."[96]

To American ears the most exotic-sounding of the ethnic musical theaters was the Chinese opera. According to William Henry Bishop, who wrote with little comprehension of and less sympathy with the Chinese opera in San Francisco: "The performers are continually marching, fighting, spinning about, pretending to be dead, and jumping up again or singing in a high cracked voice, like the whine of a bagpipe. A warrior of six feet high, though he may be Genghis Khan ... will sing in this same voice, and no other."[97]

A more readily understandable entertainment to Americans was the opera staged by local or traveling companies for European ethnic groups. This was the case with a performance of Tchaikovsky's Mazeppa by an itinerant Ukrainian opera company. Quite a contrast to Bishop's obtuse mention of the Chinese opera is the music critic's review in the Buffalo Evening News, 11 February 1933: "The director, ... conductor, singers, and stage designers covered [themselves] with glory. Not only was the music a constant delight, but the enthusiasm of the whole cast was soon caught by the audience of 3,000, nearly all of whom were Ukrainians, whose dream of freedom is kept fresh by this story of a hero born 300 years ago."[98]

Unlike the Slavs, the Italians in America had no great desire to organize themselves into choruses. What many of them did crave was the opera of Italy. This was true both for those who had already developed a taste for it prior to their arrival in America and for that larger number who only in the United States had found the leisure and

money to attend an entertainment appealing to their fondness
for melody, emotional drama, and colorful spectacle.

Even when no resident company existed, as was the
case in Boston's North End, amateur presentations were
staged to which whole families would come. The atmosphere
on such occasions was relaxed. Mothers chattered and bab-
ies cried. Experts exchanged information on cooking, child
raising, and the best sources for pasta, olive oil, and wine
(especially during Prohibition). When the show began, members of the cast found themselves vociferously praised, criticized, teased, given advice on how to sing, and urged on to
attempt greater musical exploits. [99] Intermittently in Boston,
Cleveland, and other cities a traveling Italian-opera troupe
would appear and offer presumably more sophisticated and
musically satisfying productions than most local performers
could muster. One of the best known of these companies in
the thirties was the Cafarelli Opera Company. [100]

Fortunate were those large communities that could
enjoy the performances of a resident company. Perhaps the
best-known resident Italian-opera company was that of the
Leottis, a Sicilian couple living in New York City's East
Side. They produced Italian operas during the twenties on
the stage of the Thalia Theater in the Bowery. As with
Boston's Italians, the Thalia's Italian "throngs packed the
doorways and [met] on a plane of equality unknown to Metropolitan audiences." Again as in Boston, entire families
and uninhibited conversation characterized the assembly of
spectators. In her description of the Loetti operatic performances Henrietta Straus relates a story that underlines
how completely committed some members of the Italian
audience were to this form of entertainment:

> It was not uncommon, when a scheduled singer
> failed at the last minute to appear, for some one
> in the audience to volunteer the role. There was
> one performance of "Pagliacci" when, shortly be-
> fore the curtain was to rise, the manager came
> out and asked if anyone could sing Silvio. A man
> in the audience called out that he was willing, al-
> though he had not done the part for several years.
> "All right, " replied the manager, "come along. "
> And Silvio, who in more prosaic moments was a
> barber, became for the nonce a most impassioned
> and convincing lover. [101]

Turning from the Italians to the East European Jews, unquestionably one of the most vigorous of the ethnic musical-stage offerings was that of their Yiddish theater. Its American beginnings came around 1883, when Abraham Goldfaden fled Russia and opened in a rented Lower East Side hall with his first productions of Yiddish drama liberally larded with songs and dances.[102] By 1900 several companies performing regularly before New York's Jews gave employment to about three hundred performers.[103] Other companies established themselves in every city with a large Jewish population. In addition, these companies willingly traveled to other cities for performances. For example, the Cleveland Yidishe Welt noted in 1938 that the Detroit Yiddish Troop, led by Julius Nathanson, gave three local performances in March, "including Bei Mir Bist Du Schoen, the great hit," written by Louis Freeman, music by Sholom Secunda, and lyrics by Jacob Jacobson. In October and November the Jewish Actor's Union of New York performed A Mame's Liebe (A Mother's Love) and Freiliche Mishpoche (Happy Family)--the latter reputed to contain "twenty beautiful songs and good comedy."[104]

The Yiddish theater produced its own stars, like the comedian Mogolesco and the famous Mr. and Mrs. Thomashefsky. Actor-singers made popular the Yiddish songs written for their voices and personalities. The inevitable offerings of recordings and sheet-music copies of their hits followed any successful stage appearance.[105] In account after account of the Yiddish theater are found descriptions of outrageous comedy and boisterous horseplay mingling with tragedy and bathos of the most sentimental kind. The uninhibited audience laughed, groaned, and wept with the actors.[106]

Concerning Yiddish musicals, Samuel Chotzinoff writes: "They ... were founded on the universal theme of the Yiddish stage, the Russian Jewish immigrant and his difficulties in America. And while there was plenty of music and dancing and a humor unblushingly extravagant, pathos was always in the offing, and a person might have as good a cry at a comedy with music as at an out-and-out tragedy." These musicals, Chotzinoff continues, frequently opened with a Russian scene in which a religious festival is celebrated. "In due course, the hosts of the party, an aged rabbi and his wife ... dance a pas de deux ... with a hearty agility." Then they danced amorously, the rabbi trying to embrace his wife, who simultaneously provokes and eludes him. The typical second act, invariably laid in New York City, was replete with nostalgic song and dance recalling life in the old <u>shtetl.</u> It also featured the laughable attempts of immigrants to cope with the English language, and usually introduced a bold Americanized young woman in pursuit of a shy Talmud student. 107

Like most of the ethnic musical-stage companies, those of the Yiddish theater found their audiences dwindling in the late thirties. Their activities ended with the onset of World War II. 108

Artistic and Popular Singers
_____

The recitals of vocalists were inexpensive to put on, therefore frequently encountered. First, we note that cantors did not confine their singing to the synagogue. They felt free to appear in concert and perform Jewish folksongs, 109 popular love songs, 110 operatic arias, 111 and hits from the Yiddish theater. 112

Operatic and traditional selections were the staples in the repertoire of most ethnic singers with any kind of artistic training. The former type of composition showed off their command of technique and mastery of fervent melody; the latter, their ability to project the sweet and homely sentiments. 113 Scarcely ever did any of them perform a selection from international, and mainly German, art-song literature.

Typical of most such concerts was a recent appearance of a young Armenian-American vocalist. She had recently graduated from the Boston Conservatory and was giving a recital sponsored by a Greater Boston Armenian cultural club. The first half of the program comprised several Italian arias from Verdi's and Puccini's operas principally, and songs of Alan Hovhaness, among them "Akh, Hoor E, " (My Heart Burns) and "Sirds E Numan Mer Lerrneroon" (My Heart and the Armenian Mountains Are One)--all sung to piano accompaniment. After intermission, <u>dumbeg</u> (drum), <u>oud</u> (lute), <u>duduk</u> (flute), and <u>kemanche</u> (violin) players came on stage to accompany her singing of traditional Armenian sentimental and dance songs.

In addition to the professionally trained vocalists every community boasted a natural singer or two (like the already-mentioned "Silvio," who was ordinarily a barber) who, without the benefit of voice lessons dared negotiate the same difficult hurdles as the highly trained soloists. Especially in Italian communities were such amateur singers to be found.[114]

Not least among singers were the specialists in popular song--like the fadistas in the Portuguese café, the demotic balladeers in the Greek taverna, and the ghuneeye in the Syrian-Lebanese night spots. Accompanied when possible by native instruments, they held forth daily, performing older favorite and currently popular works. It was to this sort of vocalist that ethnic Americans customarily turned for an evening's relaxation. It should be added that normally only the Greek, Syrian-Lebanese, Chinese, and Japanese men went to night places. This state of affairs altered gradually with the second- and particularly the third-generation of pleasure-seekers. At the turn of the century Chinese[115] and Japanese[116] men sought out popular entertainment of this sort. Respectable women stayed home.

Instrumentalists

Soloists mostly on guitar, violin, or accordion, members of conventional bands and orchestras, and performers in specialized ensembles consisting of ethnic instruments made up the instrumentalists of most communities.

Since few settlers had been acquainted with it abroad, the piano came into use as an instrument newly discovered in America. Until the 1920s it received little notice from most ethnic groups. Thereafter its mention in the foreign-language press is normally in connection with a youngster trained in a more or less cultivated repertoire, or with a visiting virtuoso of one's own nationality playing international artistic music. As with the touring Polish pianist Josef Hoffmann, the newspaper editors felt that a bald announcement of the artist's local appearance did not presage a sold-out house. In 1937 when Hoffmann was scheduled to appear in Cleveland under the auspices of the Women's City Club, the editors of the Polish Wiadomosci Codzienne thought it necessary to insist: "All Poles should attend the concert." Later they tried to convince their readership: "When the American press praises the artist, it praises us all."[117] The ethnic turnout for artistic concerts, as these editors well knew, was not always what the cultural leaders wished.

The pianist gradually did find a place in ethnic communities as accompanist to a vocalist or another instrumentalist and as a provider of music for dancing. In time the pianist could even supplant native instrumentalists, at least temporarily. Significantly, in such instances some measure of acculturation is also evident. This is true for an evening's entertainment at an Azorean-Portuguese festival held in the mid-forties. A. H. Cayton writes:

> In cassock and with cigarette dangling from lips, the padre played [on the piano] various popular compositions such as the Portuguese song "Cantiga da Rua," his own foxtrot with the jocular title "The Slow Fox," "Maria Elena," and so on, to the crowd's intense delight. Much of the evening was given over to Portuguese folk songs, sung by men and women who unaffectedly went to the microphones.... The priest-pianist accompanied them "by ear" successfully; neither guitars nor violas were in evidence at this time.[118]

Though, like the cantor of Jewish society, the priest-musician is a familiar figure in ethnic Christian societies, his playing the piano and composing American dance music would have been decidedly irregular in the years prior to World War II.

Far more familiar musicians to most European immigrants were the guitarist and violinist. A typical description of a guitarist in action comes from Harry Petrakis. He depicts a Greek taverna musician in a Midwestern city performing by himself, although later in the Petrakis narration he is joined by a singer. He played "bright Greek mountain dances," "bucolic love songs of Zakynthos and Thessaly, and old-country island melodies."[119]

The guitar was a superior instrument for the execution of dance rhythms; the violin was preeminent for the performance of expressive melody.[120] Certainly this was so for Eastern Jews, Russians, Hungarians, and Rumanians.

We must add the accordion to the guitar and violin as a component of many of the modest instrumental ensembles peopled by semiprofessionals. A self-taught Polish contrabass player organized one such ensemble in Boston, in 1905. He located four other Polish men proficient on violin, cornet, trombone, and accordion, rehearsed them in krakowiaks,

mazurkas, polkas, waltzes, and foxtrots, and found them
engagements at Polish affairs.[121] A counterpart to this
small group was the quartet of violin, clarinet, accordion,
and trumpet organized by Wojteczek Zegleniak around 1913
in Titusville, Pennsylvania, to play in Polish saloons.

The largest ensembles usually numbered about a
dozen members. But whatever their size, the orchestras
carried out comparable functions. An Italian barber and
self-taught mandolin player put together a Boston "orchestra," whose instrumentation included two guitars, two mandolins, two trumpets, two trombones, one clarinet, one accordion, one contrabass, and percussion. Over the years
some inevitable changes in personnel ensued. But from the
1920s well into the 1950s the twelve players gathered every
Wednesday night at the barber's house to rehearse Italian
dances and songs, novelties, mazurkas, rhumbas, polkas,
and waltzes. The barber-musician's grandson writes:

> Whenever arose a social occasion at which a band
> was required for dancing, the band of the required
> size would be selected from this group of twelve
> musicians. They played at every conceivable type
> of function--weddings, christenings, banquets, and
> just plain parties out in the country which some-
> times lasted more than one day. I was fortunate
> to have attended a number of the functions at which
> this band played, and I shall never forget the vital-
> ity of the music, and the musicians, and the force-
> ful vigor it elicited from all those who danced. It
> was definitely music for fun.[123]

Most large ensembles, however, were on-again off-
again organizations. As illustration, Remus Kozina supplied
a ten-piece band to the Hungarians in Franklin, New Jersey,
which stayed together only from 1905 to 1910. The twenty-
one-piece Franklin Hungarian Band, established in 1918 by
Stephen Bendes, also lasted a few years. Bendes tried again
in 1925; the new band soon ceased its existence. Bendes obtained more steady employment in 1936, when he started a
Hungarian Boy's Band.[124]

The very large ensembles that managed to survive
longer than a few years had to travel incessantly and had
conductors with a flair for showmanship. The widely known
Creatore Band was one of these. Samuel Chotzinoff attended
a Creatore concert and describes the director as commanding

every musical phrase like a general, turning swiftly from
one side to another, pleading for expression from the trom-
bonists, stimulating the cornetists to achieve intense levels
of sentiment.   When Creatore conducted the "Miserere"
from Verdi's Il Trovatore, he knew "he was dealing with
emotion, with the human heart." He looked dejected; his
head hung down; his shoulders hunched up.   Hands "were
outspread, frozen in a gesture of resignation."   At the cornet soloist's rendering of Manrico's "Ah, I have sighed to
rest me," Creatore "crawled" to the soloist!   Then "he
straightened up and beat time in great sweeping motions,
almost in the cornetist's face.   The cornetist, raising his
instrument and his head toward the gallery, blew soft, sad,
tawny notes ... while Creatore begged and implored him to
give of himself and his art without stint.   The effect on the
cornetist was hypnotic, for he played with an extravagance
of emotion which went to the heart."[125]

In most instances the performer on an ethnic instrument played alone or in the company of one to four musicians.   The author himself has witnessed a rustic Italian
pifferaio (fifer) and cornamusaio (bagpiper) wandering the
streets during a festa, a Greek lyra and santouri player in
a restaurant, a Slovak cimbalom entertainer at an evening
social, and Russian performers on balalaika and a rather
primitive accordion in a small café.

Players like these would also make up the membership of ensembles like the Russian balalaika orchestras (such
as the one giving a concert in New York City in 1910),[126]
the several Yugoslavian tambouritsa orchestras,[127] the Ukrainian bandurist bands,[128] Greek orchestras like the Royal
Athenian Strings,[129] and the numerous Hungarian and Rumanian gypsy bands.[130]   All of them specialized in national
music.   Their peak of activity came before World War II,
for their most devoted following consisted of first-generation
ethnic Americans.

Finally, this enumeration of ethnic musicians would
be incomplete without mention of the men and women writing
new song lyrics and music for their countrymen.   Some were
humble laborers unaccustomed to writing verse or with hardly any musical training.   One of these, Axel Simonen, was a
Finnish steelworker.   About 1930 he made up the words to
the "Song of Steel."   Shortly thereafter a fellow steelworker,
Edward Pylkas, added the melody.[131]   Another occasional
inventor of songs and also a steelworker, Andrew Kovaly,

states: "We who came from Slovakia sang much in those days [the 1900s], in saloons, and in church and Sokol halls. We would make up songs of our own about our life in Mc-Keesport and sing them to old Slovak folksong tunes we had known in the old country. "[132]

Usually the melody employed was an already-extant one adapted to fit a fresh text. At times, as in the case of the Simonen song, the melody was new-composed. A few years ago a first-generation Greek restaurant-owner and musician explained his motivation for writing songs. The music was original, he said, but patterned after traditional Greek tunes: "Many years ago the papers had many bad things to say about Greek people and we felt awful. So I made a song asking why all of this bad feeling. Why wasn't there love? My friends all learned it and once even I got to sing it on the Greek program. Everyone says it made them feel better. I was glad and I tried many times to do it again, to show how my people feel. "[133]

Ethnic Americans with greater musical knowledge tried their hand at more ambitious works. Mikas Petrauskas, a Lithuanian choral director, wrote operettas and choral compositions; Ferenc Laluc, a Hungarian orchestra leader, composed songs and colorful orchestral pieces; Abraham Goldfaden and other Jewish dramatists, assisted by Jewish musicians, created remarkable musical-stage works for the Yiddish theater. [134] As far as could be determined, however, these men had their greatest successes with ethnic audiences when they confined their efforts to strongly melodic and easily singable strophic songs and to rhythmic dances set forth in brief, repeated four- and eight-measure phrases.

Complex through-composed songs, string quartets, and symphonies, these composers scarcely ever wrote or performed. For many years only negligible demand existed for such compositions. Composers who desired recognition for their artistic productions had to look outside their ethnic society to find it.

Chapter 3

THE SOUNDS OF MUSIC IN THE ETHNIC COMMUNITY

●————————————————————————————————

Music-lovers from various Massachusetts ethnic groups have
responded in a gratifying manner when asked to describe
their favorite works. They revealed a preference for brief
compositions lacking in complication and giving the impression of natural spontaneity. They told the author that the
best music unfolded like a sequence of personal events involving freely changing feelings, ideas, and images--one
succeeding the other in unpremeditated fashion.

A majority of the respondents desired one feeling to
predominate in a work, to help integrate the succession of
impressions elicited by text and sound. Because music was
almost limitless in its imaginative appeal, a fine musical
work could make a commentary on life significantly beyond
that of literature and the other arts (at least this was their
contention). They also spoke of music's value when they
met socially with others. Since few close relationships existed outside the family, they preferred to keep their meetings with neighbors at the coffeehouse, tavern, club, or
café impersonal. By singing to and for each other they
could express emotions they felt deeply and had in common,
without an embarrassing admission being made to each other.
Yet all could thoroughly enjoy an hour or two together and
return home refreshed.

The Music
_____

The most desired compositions were strophic songs, that is
to say songs whose verses are all sung to the same melody.
Hundreds of such songs arrived here with the immigrants.

Among the songs of the Hungarians in Franklin, New

Jersey, were several "flower" compositions in praise of a beloved (Example 1) and marching songs recalling the men's youthful experiences as army recruits (Example 2).[1] Pieces like these took on new connotations in the United States. For one thing, the images they conjured up could no longer be experienced firsthand. Outside the door existed no Hungarian meadows and flowers. A wistful yearning to return to remembered scenes encroached upon the feelings called forth by the real countryside described in the songs. A vision of things past invoked emotions originally never envisaged in the songs. The beloved lost to a rival stood as a surrogate for everything the singer had loved and lost. Again, his former living apart from mother and brothers to serve a limited time in the army was now a permanent separation. A contemporary poignancy infused the words "Who will guard me, O Lord of Heaven above?" In short, immigrants sang songs like these both because they were in a familiar idiom and because in America they became infused with new meanings stemming from the immigrant's existence in a strange world.

Owing to its preponderantly rural origin, every immigrant group had its songs invoking the flora of its homeland. For example, the Polish residents of Buffalo and Detroit, like Franklin's Hungarians, possessed traditional songs whose subjects recalled the fields, flowers, and forests of their homeland--like "Sliczne Cwozdziki" (Lovely Carnations) and "Zielona Ruta Jalowiez" (Green Grow the Rue and Juniper).[2]

As in the Old Country, the Greeks in Boston, Lawrence, and Lowell enjoyed works that traversed the gamut from harrowing laments with a decided Turkish flavoring in the melody to fast-moving humorous, and satirical dance-songs.[3] Sung for years in Greece, such works now satisfied the Greek settlers' robust appetite for the drama in lover's passion and the comedy in lusty frolicsomeness. All first-generation Americans from the eastern rim of the Mediterranean, from Albania to Palestine, enjoyed similar compositions. The imperturbable tunes and soft-edged lyrics of the American songs they heard were less satisfying. In contrast, the agonized lament seemed the expression of truth to the Middle Easterners. They took keen satisfaction in its tension-producing melody that moved in half- and three-quarter-step chromatic progressions, and in its extravagant images of emotional and physical ruin brought on by love's disordering of the senses.

In the Boston area alone they knew of neighbors,
ordinary people, who for love had acted in tragically bizarre fashion--of the young grocer slashing his penis in re-
morse over his wife's death in childbirth, of the disconso-
late restauranteur blowing off his head before the church
doors as his beloved married another, and of the bereft
cloth-cutter immolating himself in blazing gasoline soon after a tenement fire incinerated his betrothed. [4]

Although lunatic acts were rare in Middle Eastern
communities, these immigrants were certain that anything
might happen where passion was involved, and pictured it
thusly in song. They also knew that it might cause an
otherwise upright woman to err and an oblivious husband
to wear horns. If they chose to depict such a happening
humorously, it satisfied their taste for comic incongruity.
Indeed, men and women freely sang comic compositions of
this sort, interspersing jokes on similar subjects among
their renditions.

The Italians from the Mezzogiorno now living in
Boston and New York City persisted in singing their Neapolitan serenades. These compositions exalted the beautiful women, gentle climate, and lovely countryside around
the Bay of Naples (Examples 3 and 4). [5] Experiencing the
harsh weather of America's Northeast and the flinty regard
of their censorious hosts, these newcomers warmed their
sensibilities and renewed their own vision of beauty through
the languorous lilt of the triple-metered ode to balmy night
and delicate femininity. The sonorous and supple melody
curls up and down between major and minor keys a third
apart, between quiet adoration and impassioned pleading.

Songs on the Immigrant Experience

Songs on the subject of immigration, describing the moment
of departure, the voyage to America, and the loneliness
away from loved ones, soon appeared alongside the traditional compositions. In a Greek song sung by Menas
Vardoulis, of Pittsburgh, a young man bids a sorrowful
farewell to his mother and leaves for America, where he
fears he will wither away from pining for his home (Example 5). [6] An immigration song sung by Boston's Syrians
stresses the uncertainty of any reunion with one's family
(Example 6). [7] And a Yiddish lullaby tells of the wife left
behind and awaiting the passage money that will enable her
to rejoin her husband. [8]

The departing ones saw their way of life coming apart. Not for them the stiff upper lip and resolute going-it-alone of the Anglo-Saxon. Without inhibition they complained in letters and yammered in songs of their desolateness.

Another group of songs, complaints on the harsh life in America, followed as a logical consequence to the immigration songs. The Portuguese fishermen of Cape Cod sang fados maritimos, which told of the hard work, poor food, and low pay of the seaman (Example 7). [9] The Jewish sweatshop workers sang of the endless hours spent away from the wife and children they loved and who had become strangers to them ("Mayn Yingele"). [10] The Slovaks pictured in song the backbreaking labor and the danger of accidental death of the miner and steel-mill worker (Example 8). [11] These immigrants had quickly discovered that America had no streets paved with gold.

Cape Cod's Portuguese fishermen faced the same dangers and earned as uncertain an income as before, hence the continued "sad life ... of a sailor" they sang about. All too many Jewish fathers worked at least six, sometimes seven, days a week in New York's dingy factories. Though they felt the bond between them and their families, they rarely shared the home life that was the very reason for their existence. The "golden land of opportunity" seemed "merely a myth" in the face of "the stark reality of the sweatshops." The anguish in "Mayn Yingele" was real, not a sentimental fiction. [12]

Andrew Kovaly, the supplier of the song "I Lie in the American Land, " quoted in Example 8, explains that Slovakians often made up songs about their lives in America and sang them to old Slovak folktunes. Kovaly put together the words to his song after a good friend was killed under an ingot buggy in a McKeesport mill. At the moment of death his friend's wife and children were traveling to America in order to join him. Kovaly states: "The song made me feel better and also my friend's wife. But she cried very hard. I have never forgotten. "13

The Popular Love Song

On balance, the majority of musical compositions heard in the ethnic subcultures were neither traditional songs nor broadsides adapted to fit extant tunes. Rather, they were popular works of known and recent authorship, fashioned to

please an indiscriminate audience belonging to one cultural
society. Most such songs were imports brought to the attention of ethnic Americans through recordings, sheet music,
performances by local and visiting musicians, and motion
pictures with sound. In the writings about, and interviews
with, ethnic Americans, one is made aware of the importance, also, of musical dramas for introducing ethnic popular songs to their public.

For example, one stage work, Natalka Poltavka, by
Nicholas Vitalievich Lysenko (1842-1912), had a wide following among America's Ukrainians during the early part of
this century. A great deal of its popularity was owing to
the several strophic songs contained in the drama. Indeed,
the songs are not elaborate and display characteristics de-
sirable in popular music. The subjects are commonplace--
one song, "Petrus," is on steadfast love; another, "The
Winds Blow," on the unhappiness of lovers' separation. 14
The facile and attractive melodies to these songs have short,
clearly delineated phrases, and pauses coinciding with the
punctuations of the text.

Overlooked by many investigators is the existence of
ethnic popular songs that never appeared in print and oftentimes not in recordings either. Usually they were dissem-
inated by the singer-composer and possibly a few friends
who also were singers. Example 9 reproduces a dance-song
composed by a first-generation Lebanese-American entertainer, who sang it during the forties before audiences in
various Syrian-Lebanese enclaves. Again, its subject is a
favored one in ethnic compositions, the lover protesting his
love and pleading his cause. 15 The composer states that he
never published the music, although at one time he did make
a private recording, which he sold at the end of concerts
and through the mail.

A final popular-song example, a Chinese composition
on a young woman's yearning for her lover, has a history
common to several other pieces the author notated from the
singing of Boston's ethnic Americans. The Chinese vocalist
remembers the work as current some thirty or so years before (around 1920). 16 For some unknown reason the song
had remained in his memory. Typical of most singers'
comments on such pieces, he stated that at the time the
song was popular neither he nor his friends knew or cared
about its composer. Neither was it ever published or recorded, as far as he was aware. The informant believed a

friend of his father composed "The Maid in Love" (Example 10), but of this he was not certain. Further questioning established the more likely possibility of the song having migrated here from China. In America it was perhaps altered by a singer or two, his father's friend among them, for local presentation and sung a few months before disappearing from view. The probability also exists that the vagaries of memory caused some modification of the tune and text over the years.

Music at Public and Religious Events

A woman prominent in Armenian-American circles once told the author: "I think it's mostly through our own music that we can fully develop as mature humans and protect ourselves from the grossness we find all around. We can respond to such music more readily.... Anyway, some of us have tried to do something about it."17

She and others like her tried to encourage their countrymen to participate with them in an active communal social life. Soon social activity effloresced into multifarious communal celebrations: Christian religious holidays (especially Christmas, Easter, and important saints' days); traditional commemorations marking the change of seasons; Jewish, Chinese, and Japanese religious holidays; diverse national holidays; events significant to a local community; and communal picnics.

For a variety of reasons, priests, businessmen, public officials, and other persons with standing in the subculture promoted these celebrations, whether they were genuinely interested in music or not. Assuredly the hope of binding the people to the old ways (including religion), the possibility of improving one's own business position within the community, and the desire to enhance one's social stature also played a part.

The West Coast's Japanese community leaders recognized the importance of communal celebrations. Placing an emphasis on their common origin and shared recreational needs, these leaders and the associations they headed sponsored picnics, bazaars, banquets, and artistic performances. Music was rarely absent from any event. These Japanese hoped the gatherings would provide an efficacious means for passing their culture on to the young. Adults found adoles-

cents prone to resist social control and attendance at the
Japanese schools; they were ever ready to adopt American
usages, to the consternation of their parents.[18] Catechiza-
tion led to failure. Community events, they were certain,
would help alleviate the situation. Here was a problem familiar to, and a solution attempted by, every ethnic society.

Celebrations sanctioned by centuries-old customs
were reinstated in the New World. In her book on ethnic
festivals Dorothy Gladys Spicer writes that, although the
festive theme was interpreted differently in different ethnic
subcultures, everywhere "its same essential aspect [was]
retained. The solstices, the equinoxes, planting of seed,
and ingathering of crops [became] festive occasions observed
through ritualistic dance, procession, and song."[19] These
occasions normally had religious significance (though also
observed with an admixture of unbuttoned secular song and
dance).

The Celebration of Christmas and Easter

A typical instance of how the New World inception of an old
festive custom came about is afforded by the Portuguese of
Oakland, California. A few years after arriving in Oakland
four or five immigrants from Madeira met for a social
evening in the 1911 Christmas season. During the evening
they began to recall and yearn for their traditional Christmas festival. Thought led to action. Soliciting the aid of
several musicians, they erected a public Nativity altar,
decorated it, and added the traditional offertory tray. The
musicians stood about and played popular Portuguese works.
Swiftly the neighborhood residents gathered around. All
thoroughly enjoyed the music. The Christmas festival succeeded, for everyone felt lonely and longed for the old practices.[20]

Most festive celebrations began as modestly as the
one just described. The Polish Christmas festival in Hamtramck also had a tentative start. But it, too, quickly won
wide support. As in Poland, happy groups soon began "going around from house to house with 'Christ's Crib' and caroling."[21] Likewise, "as in the Old Country villages," Rumanian carol-singers commenced the practice of strolling
"from house to house singing the 'Good morning, old Christmas Eve,' 'The Eastern Star Is Rising High Above,' or the
'Three Wise Men from the East.'" Cleveland's and Youngs-

town's caroling <u>colindatorii</u> were adults; other Rumanian communities left the caroling to the young. [22]

Some carolers had bands accompany them on Christmas Eve. Among the activities of St. Josaphat's Parish Band, of the Rochester Ukrainians, was the custom of "Christmas caroling from door to door."[23] The Hungarian Brass Band of Franklin, New Jersey, also went from door to door playing old Hungarian carols like the traditional Catholic hymn "The Shepherds Are Rejoicing" (Example 11). [24]

A Portuguese-American youth has written an unusually detailed and informative account of caroling practices in the Portuguese colony of Fall River, Massachusetts. He writes:

> During the Holiday season, music always was heard in and out of our home. The most cherished Portuguese tradition, and one which I enjoy the most, is the singing from door to door of one relative's house to another. It could be compared to Christmas caroling except guitars, mandolins, harmonicas, accordions, and various other instruments are used to accompany the voices. The lyrics to the carols are impromptu, thought up as one sings. First, an individual sings, then the others as a chorus. An example of an impromptu lyric sung about my brother is:
>
> > My brother you're quietly sleeping,
> > Your family brings greetings with singing.
> > Let us in,
> > Before we decide to leave you.
> > You know that it's cold at your doorstep,
> > And yet you are slow to open,
> > A shot of whiskey or brandy
> > Would make us warmer to greet you.
>
> These lyrics sound poor, but in Portuguese they rhyme rather well. I recall a few years back, when I was ten years old, singing from 11 o'clock on Christmas Eve to noon of Christmas Day. This same singing tradition occurred also during the New Year holiday. The custom is that when the door is opened, the carolers enter for food and drink and ask you to join them as they go to the next rela-

tive's house. Usually a dance begins at the last
house visited for the night, and everything ends up
with a party of some sort. 25

In contrast to other Christian groups, the Eastern
Orthodox Albanians, Greeks, Syrians, and Lebanese had not
customarily celebrated Christmas with great festivities. Only after living in America for some years and being impor-
tuned by their children did they start giving presents and
planning some kind of home party. Interestingly, though the
Orthodox Christmas came on a different date from that of
the Western holiday and continued to be observed mainly as
a religious event, the exchange of gifts and the home celebration often took place on the "American Christmas, " December 25. At this time the carols sung in many Eastern
Orthodox homes in Boston were ones the children had
learned in public school or from the omnipresent Christmas-
carol books given away by the John Hancock Insurance Company. Also, the main course for the "American Christmas"
meal was likely to be roast turkey, the mothers perhaps
taking their cue from the American Thanksgiving. 26

Those Italian-Americans who "had a devout respect
for holidays and formal occasions of any description" normally celebrated Christmas privately, not on the streets.
Jo Pagano has written about an Italian family, the Maccaluccis, observing Christmas Eve. The narration begins with
visitors approaching the house through a wintry drizzle.
They noticed "the sounds of the gathering, the windows ...
all ablaze with light, and [they heard] singing and laughter,
the lilting strains of an accordion, the strum of guitars. "
They entered. Inside, the table displayed quantities of food
and wine. After dining, "all joined in the singing [of] the
familiar melodies of the land from which we had stemmed, --
O Sole Mio, Ciribiribin, Santa Lucia--folksongs, too, the
songs of the field and the plough, deep in the memories of
the oldest present. " Further pointing up the secular nature
of the celebration, Pagano writes that at 10 p. m. the men
began playing cards, leaving the cleaning-up to the women.
The adolescents danced, as younger children played boisterous games. As had been the custom in their homeland,
everyone made merry all night and "in a troop" attended
early-morning mass. Later they had Christmas dinner together. 28

The Maccaluccis undeniably sang secular works distant from the subject of Christ's birth. For instance, the

serenade "Ciribiribin" (words by Carlo Tiochet, music by A. Pestalozza), first published in 1899, describes a maid pining for her lover's kisses (Example 12).[29]

Alongside these advocates for Christmas merriment could be found immigrants with more somber views of the holiday. An excellent illustration is provided by several Sicilian-American families known to the author. On Christmas Eve they ate their pasta asciutto, a thirst-provoking macaroni dish flavored with salty anchovy sauce and garnished with small cubes of dry bread that had been fried in olive oil. They followed the course with baccalà, dried codfish that was soaked to soften it, then cooked. After their meal they went quietly to midnight mass. Scarcely a song was heard all evening and certainly no dancing.

In this context we recall Rocco Fumento's description of an Italian mother making holiday cookies on Christmas Eve. Her son alone kept her company. While she worked in the kitchen she sang a single Italian folksong whose words began: "You descend from the stars, sweet Jesus, the salvation of the world. Born in a lonely stable." Fumento speaks of the feeling of utter poignancy that overcame him as he listened.[30] This mother's sad solitariness should be set against every tale of gay and melodious fellowship as also typical of the Christmas Eve ambience in the homes of quite a few first-generation Americans.

The same contrast is found in the celebration of Easter. Some went to church and passed the remainder of the day with scarcely a stir. Others worshiped, feasted, sang, and danced until late into the night.[31]

Unlike Christmas, Easter was a religious holiday traditionally celebrated with many festivities by Eastern Orthodox Christians. Most families customarily kept open houses on Easter Day for all visitors and especially the neighborhood children. They decorated their homes and piled tables high with refreshments. Boys and girls trooped from house to house, greeting adults with "Christ has risen, Uncle [or Auntie]" and the singing of an Easter song or two. The children, in turn, received the kiss of peace, the reply "Truly, He has risen," and presents of money, decorated eggs, and packets of sweetmeats.[32]

The Syrian grocer, whose "What Music Means to Us" was quoted from earlier,[33] has left a description of the

Syrian-Orthodox Easter scene. He mentions men, women,
and children "walking in solemn procession with their priest,
cantors, and altar boys, and the faithful behind--demonstrat-
ing to a hostile world, once Turkish, now American--that
this was their proud faith of centuries. The swordsmen up
front, whirling, clashing scimitar on shield, ceremoniously
fighting with each other in mock battle, were the Christian
defenders of the faith. " He tells also of the Saturday night
Hujme:

> I wonder if the Americans knew of the meaning of
> the knock on the church door at midnight, to let in
> the Risen Christ, and, immediately, the sound of
> a thousand voices ringing out the ancient hymn "Il
> Messeeh am" (Christ has risen) and the greeting
> of friends with "Wallah am" (Truly He has risen).
> Then the sudden blaze of light as the church doors
> opened slowly, the surge of the crowd inside, and
> the Byzantine mass with its highly ornamented
> cantillation, which still has meaning to those whom
> America has not yet conquered. 34

The last paragraph describes the custom where the
entire congregation left the dark, black-draped church just
before midnight. On the stroke of 12 the priest's staff
rapped on the door, while the silent crowd looked on from
the street. The doors swung open to reveal an interior
brilliant with light and flowers. Noisy jubilation replaced
the quiet solemnity.

Other Christian Celebrations

Several other Christian festivals were celebrated variously by
the several ethnic groups. They included days commemorat-
ing the most significant events and memorable persons from
the New Testament, and others for a patron saint valued as
an interceder with God on behalf of the helpless and fearful.
The Portuguese from the Azores living in New Bedford and
on Cape Cod traditionally began their year with the Janeiras,
the feast centered on the visit of the Three Wise Men to
Bethlehem. Groups of singers carrying banjos and guitars
went from house to house thrumming and singing the customary "Santos Reis. " Examples 13a-b give two versions of
the traditional tune as notated by Maud Hare, the first from
a man born on the island of St. Jorge and the second from
his daughter. Hare conjectures that the melodies may derive
from the "Noite de Natal" of Portugal proper. 36

The most famous Portuguese festival brought here
from the islands was the Procession of Santo Christo, held
the fifth Sunday after Easter. Families attracted from
great distances came to watch the sacred statue carried to
the church, to worship, and to join in the merrymaking.
Concerning the procession, a Portuguese-American resident
of Fall River writes:

> As for religious music ... there was the famous
> song to Santo Christo which my father told me was
> written some time in the early 19th century--I can
> only remember this song being used in the proces-
> sional marches while the image was being carried
> through the streets during the local church feast.
> There were always bands in these processions,
> sometimes playing a drum roll to march by and
> other times playing this Santo Christo song, over
> and over. 37

A traditional processional hymn associated with the
holy person being honored, like the Santo Christo melody,
was usually repeated over and over again. Its monotonous
returning on itself sounded like a never-ending ritualistic
formula employed as a conduit to the divinity.

In the evening, more than one cantoriá ao desafio
was commenced. Guitar and viola players seated on a
platform accompanied the women singers usually in fados;
the men, in fados and the improvised quadras. 38 It is
instructive to note that the Portuguese women sang the popular sentimental love songs; the men alone the extemporized
songs. This distinct division of song types sung by the two
sexes was practiced by men and women from other lands
bordering the Mediterranean.

Portuguese festivals also aired several traditional
dance-songs. To give one instance, commonly heard at the
summer Feast of St. John (San Joäo Baptista) was Dançae
Moças (Example 14), one of several dance compositions associated with this "popular country festival. "39

Today the southern-Italian festa continues as the
most consistently observed ethnic festival in America, owing to the many Italian-Americans and their persistent loyalty to this tradition. As early as 1892 Jacob Riis noticed:
"The townsmen of some Italian village, when there is a sufficient number of them within reach, club together to celebrate its patron saint, and hire a band and set up a gorgeous

altar in a convenient back yard. The fire-escapes overlooking it are draped with flags and transformed into reserved-seat galleries. "[40]

The festa grew from simple beginnings into an elaborate celebration,[41] lasting over several days and involving several streets in the Italian enclave.[42] While the planning committee might comprise men from one village, the celebrants of every festa soon included all Italian-Americans.[43] An unidentified witness from The New Yorker magazine describes the setting of the 1957 six-day Feast of San Gennaro, held in the Mulberry Street area of New York City as follows:

> It was a scene of colossal, assured, offhand pandemonium, hinting at the existence of an imminent, inscrutable pattern--the effect sought, but never so surely realized, in the finales of operettas. The principal pastimes appeared to be the random infiltration of wholly occupied positions, the yelling of news to friends just out of earshot, and the patronage of canopied booths bulging with tortoni, torrone, zeppolo, hot pepperoni, pizza, Pepsi-Cola, sausage-and-eggplant sandwiches, lemon ice, cat-faced balloons, Confederate campaign hats.... Overhead, above the mantling archways of spiderwebby light fixtures, resident enthusiasts in undershirts and slips peered down contentedly from five tiers of tenement windows and fire escapes.[44]

The excitement of the festa made a strong impression on the young. One third-generation youth admits that he and his friends looked forward to all the feasts held in Boston's North End, which they enjoyed without reserve: "If one gets caught in the social swirl of a feast on a summer's night, America seems like a far off land and Italy is immediately present."[45]

Every account states that most of the music performed at a festa had little connection with the patron saint in whose name all the activities were launched.[46] In Three Circles of Light Pietro Di Donato tells of the Feast of San Rocco held shortly after World War I in West Hoboken, New Jersey. His description corresponds with the author's memory of similar Hoboken events in 1931 and 1932.[47] Di Donato tells of the paesanos gathering around the bandstand in the afternoon. Next the conductor arrived with his musicians, "no two of them wearing the same hat or uniform." After the speeches "the begowned and mammoth Madame Callastra, star of the Hoboken Open Air Opera Company," sang the "Star-Spangled Banner." This was followed by "the Italian national anthem, the 'Marcia Reale.'" Then professional and amateur vocalists sang operatic excerpts and Italian popular songs between instrumental selections. Now and again bagpipes, mandolins, and even a piano and harp joined in the music making. [48]

After what has just been described it should come as no surprise to learn that when Christian immigrants spoke to the author of the music important to them, they scarcely mentioned religious music. Moreover, save for one or two traditional hymns, religious music seemed not to be central to their festivals. On some occasions a few Italian women might walk barefooted behind a relic, cross, or statue and reiterate brief musical incantations (a practice that had almost disappeared in the years since World War II). Otherwise the music most appealing to them was secular. For this reason, during a festa held in Boston's North End at the end of the summer of 1976, the saint's statue was set down from time to time in the first day's street procession in order to bless a store or home. At these moments the band following the statue played what was considered appropriate. Three of the works performed were "The Isle of Capri," "Celeste Aïda," and "M'Appari Tutt' Amor," all of them love songs.

The author has kept a list of the compositions most frequently performed, year after year, at the festas he attended. The list includes operatic pieces like Verdi's "Ai Nostri Monti," "Sempre Libera," and "Questa O Quella";[49] songs of known authorship like Tosti's "Vorrei," De Curtis's "Torna A Surriento," Di Capua's "O Sole Mio," and Arditi's "Parla!"; and traditional ones like "Santa Lucia," "La Mamma de Rosa," "Carmè," and "Fenesta Che Lucive." To experience a full-throated tenor soloist sing the last of these songs (Example 15), its sorrowful message and ingratiating melody floating out on the soft night air, its auditors' chests heaving with sympathetic emotion, and its performance accompanied sotto voce by the murmur of conversationalists and the muffled shouts of vendors at the crowd's fringes is a unique moment unapproximated in the concert hall.

Harvest Festivals
_____

The harvest festival gave thanks for plentiful crops.   Unlike
the Italian festa, however, it was never widely observed in
America.   Now it is almost nonexistent, supplanted by the
American Thanksgiving.

     Several reasons can be offered to explain the harvest
festival's failure to survive.   The move into the cities had
taken immigrants away from their constant contact with the
land.   Urban jobs made a harvest celebration superfluous.
If held, the celebration seemed an anomaly, neither reflec-
tive of their present lives nor in keeping with their own and
American notions of appropriateness.   Even when immigrants
did become farmers, their scattered settlements and lack of
an integrated village life precluded concerted festivities of
any consequence.   Soon only a vague remembrance remained
of the festival that the transoceanic rural village had observed annually. [53]

     One of the few mentions of a harvest festival in the
first quarter of this century occurs in Konrad Bercovici's
On New Shores.   He writes of seeing one conducted by Italians living near Ventura, California.   Down a road decorated with banners and flags moved "a number of naively
decorated floats, upon which rode beautiful children dressed
as cherubs, flocking about papier-mâché saints."   After
them came several bands and "other floats, upon which the
Italians exhibited all that had that year grown in plenty in
their region."   Home celebrations that evening began with
the singing of arias and the listening to Caruso recordings.
Bercovici found the occasion to be "a real old-world festival which carried with it all the paganistic neo-Christian
spirit of Southern Italy."[54]

     The problems, real and imagined, involved in mount-
ing a harvest festival in America are illustrated in a 1953
account of Slovakian natives from the village of Vrobce, who
desired to stage one in Hightstown, New Jersey.   Svatva
Perkova-Jakobson writes that two trucks were rented.   In
one truck rode several people dressed in peasant costume;
in the other, Slovakians dressed as American farmers--so
as not to hurt American sensitivities.   The plan was to
traverse the town, making believe it was their old village.
Then they were to stop for a collation at the home of fellow Slovaks, the Portubskys ("They will be the landowners;
they are the oldest among us and they are here thirty years

already"). Some were fearful that Americans would throw tomatoes at them; others, that the Ukrainians and Poles might think the procession a form of political activity and take umbrage. A few refused to participate because the celebration struck them as insincere and a weak imitation of the real festival at home. At the end some eighty persons piled onto the trucks, along with an assortment of scythes, rakes, forks, sheaves, wreaths, ribbons, and accordions. A further problem arose: "The 'peasants and farmers' paused to thrash out what songs to sing when they went through the center of town. Should it be the American 'Old MacDonald had a farm, quack, quack, quack?... Then there should be ducks and pigs on the truck also, but the ducks are not harvested.'" Finally, all reluctantly proceeded through the town singing Slovakian songs and feeling great embarrassment as they did so. When they arrived at the Porubskys, they abandoned their timid behavior. They sang an old ritual song, had refreshments, then danced and sang until morning. 55

Another type of fall festival, one usually confined to the home and involving no public procession, was the annual "Pig Party," centered around the slaughtering of pigs for the winter's supply of meat. Accounts from Portuguese and Hungarian participants describe how in former years in America a pork supper with plenty of feasting and music regularly followed the butchering. 56

In most ethnic communities, however, if harvest festivals were held at all, they generally bore little resemblance to the practices of the Old Country. On most such occasions a large hall was decorated with autumnal motifs. People came dressed in native costume. While dinner was consumed, community choruses, bands, and soloists provided entertainment. Next came a couples parade around the hall, then dancing (usually American). The harvest festival thus reconstituted established a flimsy connection with the custom of the old village. 57

Some Japanese and Chinese Observations

Ethnic Americans of Japanese and Chinese descent had seasonal observances unfamiliar to most Americans. Possibly the best known of the Japanese celebrations was the Obon Festival, once held annually around the end of August. For several weeks before the holiday the Issei who were Bud-

dhists would teach the young Nisei of every faith the traditional bon dance. When the day arrived, a platform was
erected near the Buddhist temple. On the stand sat an assortment of samisen players, drummers, and vocalists.
Songs like "Tokyo Onde" and "Chochai Bushi" (Example
16)58 were performed. About 7 p.m. hundreds of dancers
in native costume began to execute graceful dance steps as
they circled the platform. A master of ceremonies urged
them on. After an hour or so of this activity the participants danced their way down a street lit up by Japanese
lanterns and lined with throngs of onlookers. In later years
an American-style dance band was hired to provide amusement for the young people after the completion of the bon
dance. 59

An important Chinese holiday, now rarely celebrated
outdoors, was the Tsing Ming, or Pure and Resplendent
Festival. Years ago it was observed on April 4 with feasting, parades, and music. Idwal Jones, after a description
of the festival, adds ruefully that Chinese celebrations have
moved indoors and become private affairs: "Now [1926] the
old grandeur has diminished though a quite eye-filling bout
with the dragon is still staged every New Year's. Parades
have been done away with. On the Pure and Resplendent
Festival the jollification is not visible to the passer-by.
The moon-kwang and the samisen are strummed only within
the family circle. "60

Fortunately Pardee Lowe has provided some idea of
what the music making was like in his father's household on
feast days. He writes that around 1910 he attended one of
his family's customary gatherings of relatives, known as
Hoy Teng, or Opening a Reception, which once took place
with each change of season:

> A group of seven Chinese musicians, five of whom
> were women, sat in one corner, flanked by two
> luxurious bamboo couches reserved for those who
> were overcome by too much food or drink.... To
> the accompaniment of the Law, a brass gong; the
> Yuet Kum, the moon guitar; the Tartar fiddle;
> wooden and skin drums, and clashing cymbals,
> they sang in shrill falsetto endless [Chinese] op-
> eratic ballads, mostly celebrating the past glor-
> ies of the Three Kingdoms. 61

Jewish Holidays

More than any other ethnic group, the East European Jews are fortunate in writers who have taken the trouble to relate with thoroughness their religious customs and sacred-music practices in the New World. Impressive are the many Jews interviewed by, or submitting reports to, the author who refer back to the first three decades of the century as a period when the love for cantorial singing was intense[62] and when the performing of religious music was a habitual exercise in the home.

If any Jewish congregation had sufficient wealth to support a cantor, one was immediately hired on an annual basis. The wealthier the synagogue, the more famous the cantor.[63] If the congregation had little money, a fine cantor might be hired at least to help celebrate Yom Kippur, The Day of Atonement, and Rosh Hashanah, Jewish New Year.[64] An admission charge for a seat in the synagogue was usual when a special and expensive musical effort was made to observe the two High Holidays. The charge underwrote the musical costs and aided with the other expenses of the synagogue.

Moses Rischin writes:

> Liturgical music, often launching its young practitioners onto the music hall stage, was stimulated by the ambitions of rival synagogues eager to redeem debt-ridden properties by attracting capacity congregations on the annual Pentitential days, for which seats traditionally were sold. Odessa's Pinhas Minkowsky and choir, hired at $5000 by the Eldridge Street Congregation, and other lesser priced cantors intoxicated worshippers with awe-inspiring hymns punctuated with sustained trills, bravuras, and free vocal fantasia.[65]

One of the most deeply felt of the cantorial chants, the "Kol Nidre" (All Vows) was regularly sung on Yom Kippur. Example 17 reproduces the East European Ashkenazic melody[66] and some of its variations. The text to this rhapsodic, rhythmically free cantillation was meant to void all vows. The words took on a special importance beginning with the Spanish Inquisition, when Christianity was forced on Spanish Jews. The music is of more recent, though unknown, origin. An ecstatic, intensely inflected melody synthesized and resolved some of the conflicting feelings within each listener.

In addition to the synagogal chants certain Yiddish sacred songs became prominent owing in part to their performance by favorite cantors. "Eli, Eli," for instance, its tune composed in 1896 by Jacob Koppel Sandler, won a tremendous following among American Jews after the popular Yossele Rosenblatt sang it repeatedly in concert during the early part of the century. Example 18 presents the work as it appears in Ausebel's A Treasury of Jewish Folklore. 67 The music's scale structure (the Ahavah Rabbah mode of E# F# G# A B C D E) is certainly not Western; nor are the intervallic patterns of the melody, which makes prominent the half-step to three-quarter-step progression of a'-g#'-f'-e'; nor is the close on high e". The performance of the song entails a projection of constantly increasing tension. The singer begins on a neutral g#'; the voice rises to b' and sinks down to d'; rises higher to c" and descends a second time; rises even higher to d" and falls back to the low d' again. Then finally comes the broad, inexorable sweep upward to the high e" and the end-climax on a long-held f" moving down a half-step to an equivocal resting place on e". The listener is left with no sense of repose. No lengthy fall of the melody has ensued to balance the intensity of the climax. With dramatic force the music pictures the personal outcry: "Oh God, my God, why have you forsaken me?" Like the "Kol Nidre," this composition had special significance to the Jewish immigrant adrift in a strange land.

Yiddish sacred songs of simple construction were heard in the home, particularly for the observance of religious holidays. A Jewish lawyer, interviewed in 1971, still remembered a few fragments of words and tunes to songs once sung by his father, sometimes on the ordinary Sabbath and always on the High Holidays. Example 19a reproduces the beginning of a melody he says his father liked to scratch out on the violin "for religious occasions." Thinking back to his childhood, the lawyer recalled that once or twice his father played and hummed the tune while executing "short hopping steps around the parlor."68 In every way the melody corresponds to the style of a Hasidic dance (see Example 19b). 69 The melodic and rhythmic resemblances of the two tunes are certainly close, starting with the third measure in each of the examples.

The Hasidic movement, which began in the eighteenth century among East European Jews, stressed the primacy of music and dance for achieving a personal religious experience beyond reason and infused with ecstatic joy. The dance tunes and songs originating with the Hasidim exerted an enormous influence upon all Jewish music. [70] As a case in point, the lawyer remembered that one of his father's songs began with the words "Shabes licht. " He had forgotten completely the melody and the rest of the lyric. Fortunately, in A Treasury of Jewish Folksongs, Ruth Rubin has included a Sabbath song, "Shabes Licht Un Shabes Lompn, " which opens on the words just quoted. [71] The melody is by Joel Engel (1868-1927), a noted Jewish composer and a collector of traditional Jewish music. When compared with the music quoted in Examples 19a-b Engel's tune shows unmistakable similarities in melodic movement and rhythmic patterns.

The three tunes do have several significant features in common. In this regard one notes the correspondences in the last two measures in all three tunes: the curve upward, from d' to a', then back to d'. In addition, the "Chorus" of the Engel songs employs nonsense syllables of the sort favored in the song-refrains of the Hasidim.

An unanswerable question arises--was the man really recalling his father's violin tune, or a dance confused in his memory with Engel's melody, or only the Engel melody altered almost beyond recognition owing to forgetfulness and the intrusion of other similar tunes? The correct answer may embrace all three areas.

The Sabbath is an important weekly observance among Orthodox Jews. Hutchins Hapgood writes that in a strict house the Sabbath of seventy-five years ago commenced on Friday evening with the lighting of the candles, followed by the grandparents' blessing of the parents and grandchildren. "The father then chants the hymn of praise and salutation; a cup of wine or cider is passed from one to the other; every one washes his hands; all arrange themselves at table in order of age, the youngest sitting at the father's right hand. After the meal they sing a song dedicated to the Sabbath, and say grace. "[72]

Jews were not always this solemn. Alter Landesman witnessed a more informal and gayer Sabbath, with Jews wearing their best clothes on Friday evening and Saturday afternoon, taking strolls, making social visits, and conclud-

ing the two days with a "Saturday night dance."[73] Undoubtedly the practices of most Orthodox Jews fell somewhere
between those described by Hapgood and Landesman.

National Holidays and National Anthems

Another category of public event, the celebrating of the national holiday of one's homeland, has received mention in
several writings on immigrants, which mention also the customary singing of the homeland's national anthem. Yet,
when the author interviewed scores of Boston's first- and
second-generation ethnic Americans, he was surprised at
how many had little or no awareness of the date of their
native land's holiday. Nor had they a great familiarity with
any national anthem save for the "Star Spangled Banner."
(The possibility exists that over the years the "Star Spangled
Banner" supplanted gradually whatever they knew of any other
anthem.) Some stated that they had paid indifferent attention
to their anthem when it was played in their village, finding
it less interesting than other types of music.   Others
claimed they had heard hardly any patriotic music at all, as
their holidays were usually religious ones and the music
mostly secular and popular.

Nevertheless, a large number of ethnic groups,
whether they had done so in the Old Country or not, did
observe their national holiday after their arrival in America,
if only as a means for achieving a collective identity.   Interestingly, in almost every mention of an early national celebration, the writer notes the performance of the American
national anthem.   In truth, it was an obligatory act for every
ethnic group to demonstrate its loyalty to the United States
in this fashion, before turning attention to another land.
Thus, when Thomas Burgess describes the Greeks of Bidde-
ford and Saco, Maine, observing Greek Independence Day on
April 15, he writes that three hundred men marched behind
a band to a soldier's monument.   After arrival, they listened
bareheaded to the "Star Spangled Banner, " then the Greek
National Anthem.[74]

We have at times the impression that the politically
conscious editors of the foreign-language newspapers and the
directors of foreign-language radio broadcasts, some of them
possibly encouraged with subsidies from abroad, were the
principal instigators of national commemorations--organizing
their observance, reporting with enthusiasm on the transac-

tions of the day, and praising the large turnout (often a fiction, part lie, part wish-fulfillment) of their countrymen. Without question some national celebrations had wide community support, and the editors and announcers were dedicated individuals. Regrettably, this was not always the case. For example, in the thirties several such celebrations in the Italian enclaves were said to have received subsidies from Mussolini's Italy.[75] Orators delivered speeches with some praise of Fascism. Hired vocalists led the audience in the Fascist anthem, "Giovinezza," and various popular songs sponsored by the Italian fascisti, like "Faccetta Nera" and "Addio, Virginia, Vado in Abissinia."[76] Whether many Italians attended is another matter.

In general, the observance of an Old Country's national holiday began with a daytime parade, the participants marching in national costume behind a band. At the parade's conclusion they sang the American and the homeland's anthem, then listened to a speech or two. In mild weather a communal picnic might ensue. In the evening some attended a community dinner followed by dancing; others went to a less formal celebration, where the serving of native foods, the performance of native songs and dances by community groups, and the pursuit of every kind of merriment was the rule. Still others might attend a special performance of an opera or operetta by one of their country's leading composers.[77]

In at least one instance the singing of a national anthem seemed less a nostalgic-patriotic gesture and more an outlet for frustrations linked to an elemental religio-patriotic antagonism against past and present enemies. About 1908 Edward Steiner heard recently arrived Albanians, in Jamestown, New Jersey, singing what he reports was their national hymn, and citing the words Ce me gre te Kollozhegt, Ch'u fillua Shocerija as the ones he heard in a room of the local Congregation church. He writes:

> The music is savagely martial, although the words are commonplace; for the Albanian, like the rest of us, is thanking God he is not as other people, especially the detested Greeks and Bulgarians. After the singing, the men danced. Shades of the Puritan ancestors! Dancing in a prayer-meeting room! But inasmuch as these were semi-civilized [sic] people, the dance was decent and full of religious symbolism. The men swayed

their agile bodies to the wild notes, bent the knee,
then two by two joined hands, forming a cross;
thus making their dance an act of worship. 78

What Steiner fails to point out is that the singing and dancing was done by people for whom the fight for self-
preservation had become a way of life.

A stark contrast to these Albanians, the Japanese
often sang "Kimi Ga Yo," their national anthem, "with feelings of sadness, of longing for a country they loved but
could not return to." The singing quietly reaffirmed their
determination to bear up under any tribulation however se-
vere. They therefore performed it "slowly and low as if
... reluctant to part with each note."79 Most of the Japanese who sang it did not consider it "a martial song or a
victory song, the way many national anthems are. It is
really a poem, whose words go back to the ninth century
...:

> May the peaceful reign last long,
> May it last for thousands of years,
> Until this tiny stone will grow
> Into a massive rock, and the moss
> Will cover it deep and thick.

It is a patriotic song that can be read as a proverb, as a
personal credo for endurance."80

This anthem was not necessarily sung by all Japanese. But for the Issei who valued it the words offered consolation in the context of the harsh discriminatory acts of
white Americans. 81 A moving description of the anthem's
value in a time of stress has been left by Jeanne Wakatsuki
Houston. During World War II her family, like all of the
West Coast Japanese, was forced into an internment camp.
One day her father had to compromise his honor by taking
a pro-American action he hated. His mental discomfort
was intense. That night his daughter heard him and a
woman friend singing Japanese laments. In her book Farewell to Manzanar (page 77) she describes the scene as follows:

> About the time I went to bed she [the visitor]
> and Papa began to sing songs in Japanese....
> After a while Papa sang the first line of the
> Japanese national anthem, Kimi ga yo. Woody,

Chizu, and Mama knew the tune, so they hummed
along while Papa and the other woman sang the
words. It can be a hearty or plaintive tune, de-
pending on your mood. From Papa, that night,
it was a deep-throated lament. Almost invisible
in the stove's small glow, tears began running
down his face. I had seen him cry a few times before. It
only happened when he was singing or when someone else sang a song that moved him.... Then
we would just stare quietly--as I did that night--
from some hidden corner of the room. This was
always mysterious and incomprehensible.

The melodies of anthems normally proceed at a slow
and dignified pace. While most are easy to sing, few are
memorable as music. In actual fact the music to several
national hymns are workaday tunes sharing hardly any characteristics with native music. Some are adaptations of imported tunes; others are arrangements or creations of nonnative residents in the country. In National Anthems (1967)
Paul Nettl discusses many anthems that fall into these cate-
gories.

On the other hand inspired melodies do exist, several
of them possessed by Slavs and Hungarians. The latter are
fortunate in having the fiery "Rákoczy March," whose tune
was used by many composers, among them Hector Berlioz
and Franz Liszt. Over the years this melody has been frequently performed by American bands and orchestras. Not
as widely known, but a fine melody that manages to be both
solemn and stirring at the same time, is the Magyar national anthem, the "Himnusz," composed in 1842 by Franc Erkel
(1810-1893) to a poem of Ferenc Koelcsey. Example 20
gives the simple yet effective melody along with one stanza
of the verse as stated by Janos Makar, in The Story of an
Immigrant Group in Franklin, New Jersey.

The Community Picnic
_____

Some events where music was heard had only local significance, like the installation of a rabbi in a Brownsville synagogue, [82] the day's mourning for the victims of the Kishnev
Massacre held by New York's Russian Jews, [83] the opening
of the enlarged Hebrew Cultural Garden in Cleveland, [84] the
dedication of a new Italian church in West Hoboken, [85] and
the unveiling of a statue to a Slovenian hero. [86]

One type of local observance enthusiastically taken up by the members of every ethnic enclave was the community picnic held on one or more summer weekends at a farm, rented picnic grove, or any other available area in the country. On picnic days every street of the ethnic district emptied of its inhabitants. Entire families rode on street-cars, trains, trucks, and rented buses, or pooled the available neighborhood automobiles in order to arrive at the meeting spot.[87] There, national dancing and musical entertainment was provided. Poor Italian granite workers might enliven their picnic with an accordion and two violins,[88] urban Italians with a large band;[89] Croatians with a tambouritsa orchestra;[90] and Jews with a mandolin ensemble.[91] Gypsy players came with the Hungarians; polka bands with the Czechs.[92] Singers were omnipresent--the professionals and the semiprofessionals on the platform, the amateurs singing from the tables.

Thus isolated in their country setting, ethnic Americans enjoyed themselves without the dampening effect of amused American onlookers and the hostility of embarrassed children. In the 1920s the Japanese looked forward to picnics as a means of celebrating their summer holidays in peace. They hoped white people would remain entirely absent and the Nisei children less censorious of their parents' "exotic" music: "Many Japanese went on picnics ... but when they saw the shadow of a white man they quietly hid their native foods and their chopsticks.... Since we were usually stoned and despised as 'Japs,' whenever we saw a sign of the whites we were instinctively on guard. I know an Issei who was called 'You goddam Jap!' by his own child."[93]

True, Americans subjected the Japanese to greater amounts of discrimination than they did most other immigrant groups. Nevertheless, members of other ethnic subcultures also spoke of the desire to relax outdoors by themselves and without the intrusion of American faces, which was an impossibility in the city. Also, when the stares of outsiders did not make them self-conscious about their "un-American behavior," the children more willingly participated in the activities enjoyed by their elders. Moreover, boys and girls would sometimes learn and perform the songs and dances of their ethnic society if surrounded only by family and friends.[94]

The traditional songs that children brought up in

America might find least appealing would at least have to be
listened to at a picnic--the Italian's "Lamento Funebre, " the
Portuguese's "Cantigas dos Campas, " the Bulgarian's "Dulgi
Glassove, " the Armenian's "Orovel, " and the Lebanese's
"Muwal Athaba Lebnaniye. " These songs were slow as a
rule, lacking a foursquare meter, more chant-like than
melodic, and characterized by pauses and long-drawn-out
notes. In most instances the singer sang with eyes shut,
head thrown back, and thoughts abstracted from the audience, seemingly in a trance. Usually a high-pitched "head
voice" rendered the music as a mournful cry, strikingly
out of the ordinary experience of Americans. In the United
States the performance of such songs occurred when the
vocalist was sure that no Americans were about. As for
the boys and girls, they were expected to listen respectful-
ly, however much they wished themselves elsewhere.

Monica Sone mentions the circumstances that encouraged one Japanese man to sing an ancient traditional
song at a picnic. At the same time she, a Nisei, betrays
her own impatience at having to listen:

> As everyone began to feel mellow and congenial,
> singing started here and there. Mr. Oshima was
> easily persuaded to sing, especially after a few
> bottles of sake. He crossed his legs and placed
> his hands dramatically on his knees. Then clos-
> ing his ... eyelids and tossing his head back to
> get a fuller range, he started groaning a naniya
> bushi.... Our parents loved naniya bushi. It
> was old Japan to them, a type of ballad singing
> in which the singer recounted favorite Japanese
> classic tales. It had a characteristic all its own
> so that once it was heard, no one could ever con-
> fuse it with any other type of singing. The sing-
> ers hung on to a note for what seemed to be an
> eternity. [95]

Although Sone found the song a "torture" to sit
through, she admits that Mr. Oshima had his eyes filled
with tears, so overcome was he with longing for his homeland.

At picnics the usual formal demarcations of what was
and wasn't socially acceptable became less rigid. Those attending came to put aside some of the restraints imposed by
duty, custom, and respectability that accompanied their

everyday activities, such as those inhibiting the free association of young unmarried men and women. Many an enamored youth could press his now-approachable sweetheart into assenting to marriage. Often, before the day was over, the overture to a wedding progressed with the suitor's parents broaching the subject to the young woman's father.

Here and there at the rim of the picnic grounds young couples strolled, conversed quietly, and occasionally stopped to exchange a pleasantry with other couples. The more musically inclined young men unlimbered guitars, mandolins, accordions, or other instruments, and commenced serenading their beloveds with assorted love songs. A Portuguese-American writes that, when a child, he watched his uncle court and win his Aunt Mary by singing Portuguese love songs to her at a picnic.[96] An Armenian-American mentions his oldest brother as gaining a bride with a "begging love-song of which there are many with Armenians." He says further that, when all the parents involved announced the engagement to their acquaintances at the other tables, a close friend of the young woman's mother paid the two singers on the platform to sing a traditional Armenian "pre-wedding song like the kind heard at picnics," in honor of the young couple. Two weeks later the formal betrothal, solemnized with the attendance of a priest, would take place. G. Schirmer has published an Armenian "begging love song" and a dialogue "pre-wedding song" which the narrator himself selected as being similar in sound and subject to what was sung on that picnic day.[97]

Other Armenian-Americans speak also of the "wedding music" heard at picnics. One young woman writes: "An Armenian picnic was not complete without a 'mock' wedding. These people loved the excitement and happiness of a wedding and so they would act out a wedding at these picnics. The people would gather around in a circle and watch the 'mock' wedding, and they would also participate in the singing of various Armenian wedding songs."[98]

Ethnic parents recognized that many of the mechanisms of their society militated against the older boys and girls freely meeting each other. They feared the loss of their young men to marriage-hungry female predators from outside the subculture. The singers on the platform were therefore encouraged to sing in praise of young beauty and love, while parents nudged their sons and urged them to converse with potential daughters-in-law.

The couples-dance, traditional in every East European and Mediterranean society, permitted a man and woman to face each other and execute stylized gestures of enticement, longing, and rapture. Picnics often featured this kind of dancing. A circle of onlookers would watch the older people commence the couples-dance. Shortly adults would begin pushing their hesitant young into the ring. At first the youths and girls danced with seeming reluctance. Then warming to the task and shunting inhibitions aside, girls were soon gliding gracefully around boldly capering partners, to the encouraging handclaps and exhortations of smiling matrons and their husbands. After the music ended in a final spasm of excited frenzy the exhausted young people would collapse under a convenient tree and presumably get to know each other better, now that the ice holding them aloof had been thawed a bit.

Coy dialogue songs, riddle songs with hidden agendas, and action songs enacting the play of love were also regular accoutrements of picnics and schemes for encouraging marriage. With scarcely a dissent ethnic Americans have said that, although in the Old Country a youth inevitably would meet and wed someone "of his own kind," this was not so in the United States. Thus an important function of the ethnic picnic, recognized by all, was the encouragement of young men and women to become "better acquainted."

Music at Important Family Events
_____

Birthdays, namedays, christenings, religious confirmations, engagements, weddings, wedding anniversaries, homecomings, and other significant family happenings--like a son's college graduation or passing the bar examination--were occasions for festivities and a "principal source of recreation" for family members and friends. 99 All these events required music, whether provided by a player-piano, phonograph, amateur musicians, or professional performers.

Instructive in this regard is Clement Valletta's story of an East Pennsylvanian village inhabited almost entirely by Italians who had migrated en masse from the same locality and brought their village band with them. The band provided music not only for all public occasions, but also:

for the paesani at weddings, funerals, confirma-

tions, soldiers' returning from the war, and in-
corporation [of the village]. The band played under the window of the bride to be married on Saturday, and it played at the reception, if the pae-
sano could afford it. When the Philadelphia bishop
would come to confirm children of the area, he
would be met by the band at the Whipscor train
station. A first-generation woman tells how she
had "four dollars' worth of candles, and automobile expenses, for the wake from Thursday to
Sunday when there was a funeral and the band."
At the Marconi Club, the band played Neapolitan
selections for boys returning from the service....
The band had a wide repertoire, from Neapolitan
street songs to selections by Verdi, Rossini, and
Leoncavallo. 100

The excitement produced in the father by the birth of
a first son is captured in several accounts coming from diverse ethnic groups. Oftentimes overwhelmed by his emotions at viewing his infant, the father turned to music and
dance to express himself. One young Bostonian writes that
the new Albanian father might experience an unpredictable
rapture at the party honoring the infant:

It is usually the new father who does all the singing and causes the commotion. My father told me
of a party [to celebrate the birth of a male cousin]
at which my uncle got so drunk and carried away
by the music that he lifted a man into his arms,
jumped onto a table and danced wildly with the man
in his arms, until the table broke, dropping them
both to the floor. There are many stories concerning new fathers who in the frenzy of the dance
and music have picked up dishes or glasses and
crashed them against the wall. 101

Music and dance gave spontaneous expression to the
father's deepest feelings when his child was christened. For
Greeks the evening celebration of the event frequently turned
into "a wild and festive night." Harry Petrakis portrays one
Greek father as dancing madly to the point of collapse, heed-
less of the warnings that he was going crazy and might drop
dead. "Full of wine and lamb and gratitude Leontis just
smiled. He danced and sang for love of his son, and he
did not care what others thought."102

The celebrations of Japanese at the birth of a first son seem to have been better controlled. Some Japanese customarily gave an elaborate party on the thirty-first day after the birth. W. C. Smith witnessed such a party in 1906: "The guests squatted on the floor and ate anything they wanted of food placed on a low table before them. The guests, most of whom were men (there were few women in those days) drank [sake] until one o'clock the next morning, singing and dancing to the music which the happy mother played on the samisen (the Japanese three-stringed guitar)."103

Wedding festivities, as with Americans, began with prenuptial parties, one for women only, another for men. The bride-to-be displayed her trousseau, heard practical advice on the management of a household, and listened to traditional songs whose subject was the loss of maidenhood, the ephemerality of beauty, and the uncertainty of a husband's affection. Thus reminded of her mortality, the bride was then made musically aware of the pleasures of the marriage bed and a home where she had a say.

In the late nineteenth and early twentieth century the custom among Orthodox Jews was to hire a badchen, a wedding bard, to attend the bride before the ceremony, in order to admonish her to seek virtue and recognize the seriousness of the married condition. Around 1895 Jacob Riis witnessed the activities of a badchen at the wedding of a clothes-presser to a shop girl, at Liberty Hall in the Lower East Side. Awaiting the start of the ceremony, the presser sat at one end of the hall. At the other end:

> From somewhere unexpectedly appears a big
> man in an ill-fitting coat and skull cap, flanked
> on either side by a fiddler, who scrapes away and
> away, accompanying the improvisator in a plain-
> tive minor key as he halts before the bride and in-
> tones his lay. With many a shrug of stooping
> shoulders and queer excited gesture, he drones,
> in the harsh, guttural Yiddish of Hester street,
> his story of life's joys and sorrows, its struggles
> and victories in the land of promise. The women
> listen, nodding and swaying their bodies sympa-
> thetically. He works himself into a frenzy, in
> which the fiddlers vainly try to keep up with him.
> He turns and digs the laggard angrily in the side
> without losing the meter. The climax comes.

The bride bursts into hysterical sobs, while the
women wipe their eyes. 104

The most famous badchen was Eliakum Zunser, noted
both for his composed and improvised music and verse,
mostly of the sad variety. He sang songs "directed towards
the specific bridal pair" and others showing "a deep affection
for his suffering people." He also "sang of his times,
pointed up the evils, satirized the guilty, stressed the
good."105

The bridegroom's prenuptial party had few serious
overtones. The time was spent eating, drinking, singing
merry songs, and teasing the groom. Typical of get-
togethers of this type, on one occasion an Albanian husband-
to-be was serenaded

with songs telling of all the hard times he was
going to have with his stubborn bad-natured
mother-in-law.... Or [they would] sing a song
or two which would warn the man to watch out
for his wife or she will be unfaithful to him.
One such song is loosely translated as "The Grist
Mill." In this song a wife goes to a mill to have
her wheat ground into flour. The man at the mill
tells her he will grind the wheat for free, if she
will spend the night at the mill with him. She
does this and goes home the next day, happy that
she saved some money. 106

A similar party was described by a Greek-American,
who also remembered one of the compositions the men sang
on the occasion. The music (Example 21) is in the form of
a kalamatianos, a Greek traditional dance-song. 107

Every subculture had musical compositions that were
regular components of the wedding ceremony. In the early
days of the century a proper Syrian wedding featured an outdoor procession of the bride and groom to the church. They
were preceded by the traditional sword-players and followed
by a chanting precentor. Women would hang out of the tenement windows along the way, singing the ancient zulagheet,
praise-songs for the bride, performed only by women, while
the precentor intoned an equally ancient hymn, and the
swordsmen danced in mock-battle. 108 Amongst Rumanians
the end of the religious ceremony saw the bride's godmother
place a marama, a married woman's headdress, on the

bride's head, "while the guests sang the doleful 'song of the passing maidenhood.' This is always a sad ceremony and many cry." Later "the fete would end with a wedding hora (the Hora Mare), a national circle dance."[109] Amongst Poles a customary practice was to say "farewells to the bride with songs on the threshold."[110] Amongst Hungarians existed the practice of placing a kerchief or a wreath on the bride's head as a "symbol of new womanhood," as the traditional songs marking this ceremony were sung. Example 22 reproduces one of these compositions.[111] Like so many songs meant for the bride, this one hardly encourages jollification.

Some of the sadness in the songs for the bride may have been owing to the high death rate among young mothers, deriving from the remembered primitiveness of the Old Country's medical practices and the unaffordability of American doctors' services. Some of the sadness, too, reflects the knowledge that a wife relied on her husband for her happiness, that a woman was helpless before the law and tradition.

There were, of course, the usual songs and dances that accompanied any festivity--the Neapolitan love song and tarantella,[112] the Czech pisni and polka,[113] the Jewish yidishe lider and kazatski,[114] and the Greek demotic ballad and kalamatianos.

It was not unusual for the partying to continue until the next day, or for uninvited guests to attend. On 6 May 1978 appeared a report in the Boston Globe on the Polish community of Webster, Massachusetts (a town the author knows fairly well, as his brother-in-law operates a large clothing store there and lives nearby). A wedding reception held at the Polish-American City Club is described that commenced on a Saturday afternoon: "You know how Polish weddings are, so there still were a few celebrating Sunday afternoon, but the thing that surprised the bride's family on First Street was that nobody seemed to know the three young men singing happy Polish songs on the front lawn."

Funerals also required music. No matter how poor, a person tried to provide for a dignified exit from this life, and for that reason paid money in to a burial society. If enough had been accumulated, a brass band was hired to play solemn music for the procession to the cemetery.

Examples 23a and b reproduce funeral marches once heard
in New York's Italian community and San Francisco's Chinese
community, respectively. Note, in the first example, the
first strain in seven, rather than the expected eight, measures; in the second example, the surprising division of the
melody into two strains of seven and ten measures. 115

The family's sense of fitness, the community's expec-
tation that proper respect would be paid the deceased, and
the general conviction that the dead needed musical propitia-
tion encouraged the hiring of a band. When a young teacher
in New York City, Mary Mellish heard a band playing a funeral march outside her classroom and supposed a wealthy
Italian was being buried. She asked the Italian boys in her
class for information:

> "No, " said Rocco, "he ain't rich, he's a poor
> guy. He works by the bake shop. "
> "How can he pay for a band of music?"
> "I don't know, everybody has to have a band on
> a funeral. If you no get a band, people talk about
> you. "
> "What do they say?"
> "They said that you are poor and no love the
> deads, you get bad luck, too, if you not kind to
> the deads. "116

When the funeral procession arrived at the gravesite,
lamentations were sung. The mourners then returned to the
deceased's home for a funeral feast and the singing of other
appropriate songs. 117 Example 24 gives a Greek enkomion,
which a young man says his granduncle, a former deacon,
used to sing at Greek-Orthodox funerals during the 1920s.118

Some ethnic families persist in singing the traditional
funeral songs. The Boston Globe article on Webster states
that many of the Polish inhabitants continue to sing "Witaj
Krolowo" (Hail, Queen). "The family and friends gather [at
the graveside] and sing the old hymn as has been done for
so many years in Poland. 'It can be a very emotional
scene,' Msgr. Kubik said, 'so we leave it up to the family
to decide if they want it sung. ' Most do. "

The Community's Musical Structures

Every ethnic settlement contained commercial enterprises

involved directly or indirectly with satisfying the society's musical needs. Importers shipped in published music and phonograph recordings for local resale; a few shops might manufacture ethnic instruments like the tambouritsa and balalaika;[119] some printers issued sheet music for ethnic use.[120] In addition, local retail establishments sold instruments, music, and recordings directly to members of an ethnic community. For example, the late twenties saw about thirty music stores, employing around fifty people and valued at $250,000, serving Chicago's large Polish settlement.[121] The best known of the stores catering to Jews was Katz's Music Store in New York City. The store retailed music and also served as a meeting place for Jewish literati and musicians.[122]

Where ethnic music stores were scarce or nonexistent the offices of the local foreign-language newspaper normally carried a stock of music for sale to customers. During the author's search for ethnic music he discovered a productive source in the newspaper office. Other suppliers failing them, ethnic Americans could try this outlet for the works they desired. Indicative of the value of such an arrangement is the experience of a Lithuanian laborer who worked in Chicago's stockyards at the turn of the century. One day he found himself out of work and almost out of his savings. He says: "Our money was going and we could find nothing to do. At night we got homesick for our fine green mountains." In the office of the Lithuanian newspaper, the Katalikias, he bought a song written by a Mr. Brandukas of Brooklyn, which was currently popular in Chicago. Translated into English, it reads:

Oh, Lithuania, so dear to me,
Good-by to you, my Fatherland.
Sorrowful in my heart I leave you
I know not who will stay to guard you.

Is it enough for me to live and enjoy between my
    neighbors
In the woods with the flowers and birds?
Is it enough for me to live peaceful between my
    friends?
No. I must go away from my old father and mother.

The sun shines bright,
The flowers smell sweet,
The birds are singing,

They make the country glad;
But I cannot sing because I must leave you. [123]

Other providers of musical items were peddlers sell-
ing penny sheets of the song texts alone, and bookshops and
general stores whose merchandise included some music and
recordings. [124]

In the same way that every ethnic enclave had one or
more musical associations that met on a regular basis, [125]
it had at least one public hall (maintained by a church, synagogue, temple, prominent community organization, or the
pooled efforts of several groups) that was available for concerts, musical-drama performances, and meetings enlivened
by music. Among Cleveland's Hungarians the East Side
Hungarian Worker's Home provided a roof for such activities;
among Brooklyn's Russians, the Russian People's House;
among Slovenes and Croatians, the National Homes; and
among New York City's Jews, several buildings devoted to
public use, like Pythagoras Hall and Sanger's Hall. [126]

In the cities inhabited by large numbers of immigrants were located theater buildings abandoned by the original owners, whose audiences had moved elsewhere. These
edifices were quickly utilized by one or more musical entre-
preneurs intent on attracting the patronage of immigrants
eager for diversion. Preeminent among New York's entre-
preneurs were managers of the Yiddish-theater troupes.
Alter Landesman, writing of the Yiddish theater, sets forth
an insight concerning the role of the stage in most subcultures: "Next in importance to the press was the Yiddish
stage in helping the development of a Jewish mass-culture
in America. " Immigrants "flocked on weekends to the Yiddish theatres" in order to "enjoy a few hours of pleasure. "
Landesman concludes: "The folk-religiosity of Yiddish
drama provided especially for those who had abandoned
Jewish ritual and no longer attended the synagogue, the religious pageantry of Jewish life. "[127]

Landesman's statement is relevant to the Chinese-
opera theater and its audience, many of them fallen-away
Buddhists and Confucians. [128] In a broader sense it is an
appropriate description of Italian musical theater's effect
on settlers in America. In 1927 Giuseppe Cautela wrote
about the Neapolitan sceneggiata performed in a New York
City theater, and reached conclusions similar to Landesman's. [129] (The sceneggiata was a musical dramatization

of a sentimental story, tragic or comic, often involving seduction, punishment, and forgiveness. The dramatization featured one popular song appropriate to the story, which was sung several times as punctuation to the action.)

Also popular were the variety shows aired in public halls and on theater stages. Typical was the grande spettacolo de varietà, an Italian vaudeville show consisting of dramatic skits, singing, dancing, clowning, and acrobatics. The performance either stood alone as the evening's entire entertainment or was divided into several sections inserted between acts of an opera or spoken drama. The Great Variety Spectacle of New York City presented well-liked Neapolitan singers like Clara Stella and Ria Rosee, "singing their big radio hits," and Carlo Buti, "everybody's favorite Italian popular singer."[130]

The Restaurant and Resort Hotel

Ethnic Americans expected to hear music at restaurants. The modest eating places entertained diners with recorded songs and dances; medium-sized ones, with a singer and a couple of instrumentalists; and large ones, with two or more singers and a half-dozen or more instrumentalists. Clients listened, danced, or sang along.

On occasion a strolling player-singer might wander between tables, playing for tips. One Italian accordionist once appeared for six months in this fashion at an East Boston restaurant. He states that singing would break out at the tables, particularly toward the evening's end: "Many times I was hired to play an hour overtime or to play at a house party after hours so the singing could continue."[131]

Some strolling musicians worked eating-and-drinking establishments in various parts of the country, picking up what money they could and moving on when earnings dropped. Adam Pista, a former Hungarian fisherman turned roaming fiddler-singer, was such a musician. He made up and sang works on common themes--sad partings from the old village, problems of living in America, and longings to return to one's homeland. Examples 25a and b reproduce two of his songs.[132] It is of more than passing interest that Western influence enters the music. Both tunes are in a major mode and sport an unambiguous harmonic scheme.

Japanese restaurants in California employed waitresses to play on <u>samisens</u> and sing when not serving customers. Some Chinese restaurants, especially for holidays and special celebrations, featured musicians in native costume, who sang and played on the brass gong, moon guitar, Tartar fiddle, drums, and cymbals. [133]

Sizable restaurants featured popular vocalists hired only to sing. To the accompaniment of Hungarian gypsy bands, Russian <u>balalaika</u> orchestras, Rumanian <u>cimbaloms,</u> Greek mandolins, Syrian lutes, or more conventional ensembles, these entertainers satisfied the customers' craving for song even as they enjoyed their food and drink. [134]

The resort hotel catering to an ethnic group's more affluent members offered a prolongation of these sensuous pleasures. Resort hotels multiplied during the twenties, as more and more immigrants became financially secure. Those lacking the means for a hotel room rented inexpensive satellite housekeeping cottages and rooms. Except for sleeping and daytime dining, this last group passed the day with friends at the hotel and participated in the hotel's evening functions. Whether the vacationing crowd was Jewish, Greek, Italian, or Syrian, it would nap, promenade, converse, and play cards in preparation for the delights of the evening. A few young people might exercise on tennis court, swimming pool, or baseball diamond, but rarely the parents. Save for some happy-go-lucky rock clambering, denominated as "mountain climbing," their chief exercise came with the singing and dancing after dinner. [135] A clarinetist who spent a summer playing at an Italian hotel observes:

> Boy, could they put it away, then dance it off until late at night. All day the place was quiet. At night it was a madhouse. The tips were good, but there was no rest for the musicians. One guy makes a request and pushes money at you so he can sing a song; another grabs your instrument to blow it; or a fat motherly type pinches your cheek while you're playing because you remind her of her <u>figlio.</u> We earned our keep. [136]

The Café

For everyday recreation, immigrants had their day-and-night

spots: Middle East coffeehouses, Italian caffés-cantants, Jewish "tearooms," Chinese hideaways, Slavic saloons, and Hungarian and Rumanian cabarets. William Saroyan captures
the atmosphere of such establishments when he writes of
an Armenian coffeehouse in California:

> This Coffee House was a place of great fame
> and importance in its day.... For the most part
> the place was frequented by Armenians, but others
> came, too. All who remembered the old country.
> All who loved it. All who had played tavoli [back-
> gammon] and the card game scambile in the old
> country. All who enjoyed the food of the old coun-
> try, the wine, the rakhi, and the small cups of
> coffee in the afternoons. All who liked to be in a
> place with a familiar smell, thousands of miles
> from home. 137

The tiniest coffeehouses were storefront or cellar
community centers. "A store was rented; a few marble-
top tables and wire-twisted chairs, several pounds of coffee, a few narghiles [water pipes], and a dozen or so decks
of playing cards were collected; and the coffeehouse became
a reality," writes Theodore Saloutos of the Greeks. Music
was an alternative to conversation and cards. Astute proprietors kept an instrument or two handy for customer's use.
A violin, santouri (zither), or guitar might appear. Songs
were sung. Tables pushed aside, dances were performed
to the shouted encouragements of the spectators. A successful dance rendition was rewarded with applause, drinks
for the performers, and the inevitable call Eis hygeia sas
(To your health). Saloutos adds that the larger Greek coffeehouses in Lowell, Massachusetts, employed a couple of
instrumentalists; the largest, four instrumentalists and a
singer. 138

The Italian equivalent of the coffeehouse cum music
was the caffé-cantant. Villa Vittorio Emanuele, the first
with a permanent stage for performers, opened around 1892
on New York's Mulberry Street. Italian popular singers of
the time regularly performed in places of this sort because
only there did they find an audience. Patrons entered free
but had to order drinks. Refused a salary, the singer followed each number with a promenade around the tables to
solicit money. Shortly a small admission fee was collected
to pay performers. Singers, however, still refused to give
encores until enough money was thrown on the stage to make

renewed singing worthwhile. Around 1898 Edward Migleaccio
(known as Farfarello) first appeared in a new kind of café
entertainment, the macchietta coloniale. Capitalizing on the
different modes of expression and changed manners of Italians in America, he created novel character sketches in prose
and verse set to music, ranging from comical satire to sentimental tragedy.139

A famous New York gathering place for Jews and Rumanians was Moscowitz's Wine Cellar, on Rivington Street.
A long, narrow basement; gas lamps, artificial-grape clus-
ters, and leaves pendant from the ceiling; painted murals,
photographs, and flags on the walls; and Moscowitz himself
enthroned on a tiny stage, cimbalom before him, red pep-
pers strung up behind--such was the scene. "Striking the
tense wires [of the cimbalom] with two little wooden sticks
he draws out from them the weirdest sounds, the saddest
chords, dissolving into the wildest dances."140 His was a
traditional and popular repertoire. He played, sang, and
paused between numbers to pour himself a drink. Moscowitz's ability to rouse the room was legendary.141

Hungarians enjoyed cabarets complete with gypsy
orchestra and throaty singer.142 Edward Steiner's vivid
description of a turn-of-the-century Cleveland cabaret is
quoted in full because of its valuable information on the
typical musical activities in such places. This particular
cabaret, "a combination of the Hungarian 'czardà' (inn) and
its American namesake, the saloon," was owned by a gypsy
and featured a band of two violins, cimbalom, and bass viol:

> The regular bar is supplemented by rickety
> chairs and tables and a clear space for the danc-
> ing floor, without which the Hungarian czarda [sic]
> does not exist. On Saturday night, the soot of the
> week washed away, the Hungarian is found here in
> all his native glory.... He differentiates himself
> from his neighbor, the Slav, by his agility of both
> temper and limbs, and to see him dance a czardas
> [sic], to hear him sing it and the gypsy play it, is
> as good as seeing that other acrobatic performance,
> a circus.... [The innkeeper] has ready a band of
> gypsies, who look shabby enough and very unprom-
> ising from an artistic standpoint. The leader, who
> plays the first violin, tunes it with remarkable
> care and tenderness, the second violin scrapes a
> few hoarse notes after him, the bass-viol comes

in grudgingly, and the cymbal-player exercises
his fingers by beating cotton-wrapped sticks over
the strings of his strange instrument.
One patriotic youth, who has had just enough
liquid fire poured into him, now lifts his voice
and sings a song of the puszta (the Hungarian
prairie), of the horses and cattle which graze upon it, and of the buxom maiden who draws water
from the village well. Slowly, pathetically, almost painfully melancholy, the notes ring out as
if the singer were bewailing some great loss.
The musicians follow upon their instruments as
sorrowful mourners follow a hearse. But all at
once the measure becomes brisk and the notes
jubilant; the singer and the musicians are caught
as by a fever, faster and faster the bows fly over
the strings, the cymbal is beaten furiously, and
the bass-viol seems in a roaring rage. [143]

Whether tiny coffeehouse or spacious cabaret, this
sort of entertainment place was widespread by the twenties.
Hundreds of immigrants had had experience operating them.
For this reason, when the days of Prohibition and the speak-
easy arrived, cabaret proprietors and their sons found it a
logical extension of their activities to cater also to customers outside the ethnic community. Immigrants would continue to demand their customary evening's relaxation with
music and drink; Americans who came discovered a novel
and exciting means for enjoyably passing the time. In this
manner did ethnic Americans help give birth to the American nightclub--a twentieth-century institution stemming largely from the earlier ethnic night spots.

Music in Everyday Life

Little by little, greater financial security and the lessening
of the working day allowed the devotion of off-hours to musical diversions. [144] By 1937 a Slovenian man was able to say
that the principal recreation of his countrymen living in Eu-
clid, Ohio, was music making. He claims that during a
visit to this Slovenian colony the sounds of Slovene music
made en famille inundated the neighborhood. [145]

The simplest musical amusements satisfied most settlers. Plucking a guitar at home, taking the entire family
to a social club to perform music with others, and singing

and dancing at picnics were all they attempted.[146] If men lingered too long on the ancient laments, the women insisted that they turn to sentimental ballads and dance-songs.[147] If musical instruments and lessons were unaffordable, some people made their own instruments and taught themselves to play. One young Italian-American writes: "My grandfather was self-taught on the mandolin and others [of my relatives] played home-made instruments--such as flutes made from hollowed-out wood. At the song fests all relatives participated and any makeshift instrument was welcomed."[148]

Regardless of ethnic origin, amateur instrumentalists were usually males. A few girls played the piano; all women sang. But at home the men normally provided the accompaniments to the singing. Occasionally to accompany singing, more often to accompany dancing, a woman assisted the men by snapping out rhythms on a hand drum or tambourine. Only with the weakening of traditional demarcations between what was appropriate for male and female, and the realization that homes without sons limited the family's potential for making music, did matters change. Regarding the event as unusual, Elizabeth May tells of meeting a Japanese-American girl, Chiye, who played in a family shakuhachi ensemble. The mother had prevailed upon the father to let Chiye play the instrument, "in spite of the fact that in Japan it is not played by a woman."[149]

A reason why ethnic Americans acquired player-pianos and phonographs is given by George Hardick. As an amateur instrumentalist, Hardick treasured his phonograph because he could play his clarinet along with recordings.[150] Other instrumentalists mention doing likewise to the backing of a player-piano. Music-lovers unskilled as performers looked forward to returning home at day's end to the comforting sounds of the phonograph.[151] Robert Merrill, for example, says his father, a tailor, liked his evenings with music: "To my father, life was a gift that needed no extra wrappings. You worked and you ate and you ... listened to some good music on your Victrola."[152]

Another reason for owning a phonograph was for the entertainment of guests. When conversation flagged, a typical resolution of the impasse was the playing of a recording or two. In several instances known to the author families purchased recordings only for the entertainment of guests, rarely for their own pleasure. On a few occasions where the author was present neither host nor guest was particularly interested in music. Nevertheless, at the first threat of dead air the host swiftly put on a recording and all listened politely for a half-hour or so before saying their good-byes. 153

On the other hand examples abound of the entertainment of guests in this manner, not as a crutch for the verbally crippled, but as a result of a shared enthusiasm for music:154

> Quite a few times there was only money enough for the food on the table, but the music still filled the house. It seems that my [maternal] grandparents had managed to hold onto their Victrola and a small assortment of records. Since this was the only record player in the immediate neighborhood [all the neighbors having little money], my grandparents' house became a natural gathering point for friends, relatives, and all of my mother's school friends. My grandfather [despite his poverty] was always inviting people to his house for a glass of wine or beer. The record player would naturally be brought out and the few records played. On the weekends a larger number of people would be invited to the house for informal parties. The rug would be rolled back and the record player brought out. Everyone danced and sang to their heart's content without fear of disturbing the neighbors, for the neighbors were almost always at the house. The children were always included in these weekend festivities and more often than not invited friends joined in the fun. 155

This report, by a young Italian-American, is one of many on the weekly open house with music, which ethnic Americans from the Mediterranean area, in particular, say was a constant feature of their lives.

A far greater number of reports describe the customary Sunday afternoon and evening gatherings of families only, at the house of the eldest and closest relative, usually grandparents or the eldest son. These meetings were unceremonious affairs. An Armenian-American, for example, mentions her paternal and maternal grandparents' houses as constantly full of relatives on Sunday afternoons--eating,

relaxing, dancing, singing, and playing dumbeg, tambourine,
flute, and lute. No one brought music. All played by
ear.[156]

In some instances the partying commenced on Saturday evening, because family members had to travel long
distances to the gathering place and a late Saturday arrival
was convenient. Suad Joseph claims that this was true for
Lebanese families in New York's Cortland County. Here
the Saturday-through-Sunday meetings were flexible enough
to embrace distant cousins and close neighborhood friends.[157]

In an earlier chapter we observed that these same
immigrants routinely sang at work, whether as owners of
their own shops[158] or as employees.[159] To this we add
that occasionally ethnic street musicians visited shops and
factories. Thus one day in 1903, amidst the wretched ambience of an East Side clothing factory, three street musicians began "playing Hungarian music on violins out of tune.
The men worked on. The musicians were as hopeless-
looking as the men at the machines."[160]

In at least one instance, related by Maurice
Marchello, music-on-the-job was a ploy to ensure continued
work: two Italian house-painters in Chicago advertised to
their paesani that, as they scraped and brushed, they would
sing the regional songs of any customer hiring them.[161]

Finally, the settlers had a constant diet of music
heard on the streets, particularly during the warm months.
Foremost were the ubiquitous concerts proffered passersby
by Italian organ-grinders. They could be heard plying their
trade among Saturday shoppers buying produce from push-
carts on New York's Mulberry Street, regaling all comers
with Neapolitan songs and tarantellas; or among Brownsville's Jews, executing hits from the Yiddish theater, like
"A Bis'l Libe"; or among New York City's other ethnic
Americans, cranking out Slovenian polkas, Hungarian gypsy
dances, and sentimental East European waltzes. During the
last two decades of the previous century and the first two
of the present, organ-grinders, bearing the light, portable
barrel organs or trundling the heavy street-pianos, wandered
through the city streets and along the rural lanes of a large
part of America.[162]

On hot days and evenings city-dwellers deserted their
stifling tenement flats for the comparative coolness of stoop

and sidewalk. Hearing the organ-grinder's music, groups of loungers sang or danced to the familiar tunes.[163] At other times, guitars, mandolins, and accordions were brought out to guide throats and feet.[164]

The improvised dancing and shrill game-songs of children were also a part of street life. Catherine Brody has written sympathetically about the play of Italian and Jewish children. She tells of listening to the half-song, half-wail of Italian children's voices "in a folksong, the tune of which had somehow come from the lands where they sang the 'Violetera.' It was a genuine folksong, expressing their hopes and their ambitions, their customs and their manners--and also their pronunciation of English:

> My mother ga' me a nickul,
> To buy a pickul.
> I didn't buy no pickul.
> I bought some--chew'n gum!"[165]

Also heard during warm summer nights were courting serenades of young men to their inamorate and wedding-night shivarees that friends aimed at the bedroom windows of bride and groom. These were customs common to most European ethnic societies.[166] Now and then, when an evening's party broke up early, relatives and other guests might adjourn to their homes for a moment, gather musical instruments and fresh supplies of food and drink, then return for a surprise serenade that awakened the inhabitants, reopened the doors to visitors, and recommenced the festivities. Italians and Portuguese, in particular, seem to have relished this kind of impromptu concert.[167]

A macabre incident involving a serenade took place in 1937. Amerika Domovina, Cleveland's Slovenian newspaper, printed an editorial on May 6 that read in part: "Cojecko Malkovic, from Grubisnega, Polja, and his wife did not live in complete harmony. The wife moved to her daughter's home and soon was taken ill. When the husband realized that his wife was on her deathbed, he ordered a gypsy band to play beneath her window. The woman died while the band played. The populace was furious at this. The people's resentment had such an effect that on the day of the funeral the man hanged himself. "

On balance, we must conclude that music played a role of considerable importance in most immigrants' lives.

Whether for consolation, sheer joyousness, or, in unbalanced moments, revenge, the settlers turned spontaneously to music, for music represented a significant dimension of their lives. To Americans this music may have been the sound of strangers. To immigrants the sound was an invigorating and life-sustaining force.

Chapter 4

MUSICAL ACCULTURATION AND THE CRISIS OF IDENTITY

●————————————————————————————————

Assuredly, cultural practices were modified in response to changes in the ethnic American's habitat, educational opportunities, economic status, interest in politics, and growing acceptance by other Americans.[1] It is obvious that adult settlers and their children heard an unfamiliar music when they attended school, worked among strangers, relaxed in American entertainment halls, listened to the radio, watched the movies (and, later, television), visited with nonethnic acquaintances, and witnessed family members marrying outsiders.[2] For these and other reasons the songs and dances, which at first had helped define each subculture's uniqueness within the American context, decreased their ethnic orientation and took on significant Americanisms in direct connection to the number of decades the immigrant group had lived in the United States.[3]

First- and second-generation ethnic Americans learned that they were by no means surrounded by a monolithic Anglo-Saxon culture. Nor was what existed outside the enclave necessarily to be rejected out of hand. A willingness to subsist on what musical activities the ethnic group approved was often supplanted by the concept that how a person acted and what a person enjoyed might just as well originate in the individual as in the community. Consequently, in the creation, performance, and listening to music, each person was free to follow the mandate of his or her own senses and feelings. The subculture's imperatives had no significance unless the person consented to them. Indeed, this was the first lesson taught by American democracy.

The New Cultural Choices

Unfortunately the freedom to choose without a stabilizing

force to guide the selection resulted in an unanticipated pre-
dicament. By electing to cross over the conservative boundaries of their ethnic enclaves, the adventurers had stepped
out into unmarked territory. As often as not they found
themselves gazing disconsolately over an empty no-man's-
land margined between what seemed to them to be the limited certitudes of their parents' walled-in existence and the
chaotic profusion in values of the open American civilization.

The musical result in many instances was an acceptance of a few compositions from their own subcultures, perhaps as many from other subcultures, and even more from
American popular music. Thus one Polish-American was
able to say of himself: "I found not all but a lot of the
stuff my parents listened to was pretty dull, always the
same thing. Maybe the music meant something to them,
not to me. So, on top of a few Polish songs, I went into
other things like Italian songs and tarantellas, and some
Slovak polkas, and flamenco. But mostly I went for the
Broadway stuff of people like Kern and Gershwin. "

Waverers might attempt to reconcile the culture of
their ethnic groups with that of the larger world beyond the
enclave. Many a polka, tarantella, hora, cabaret-gypsy
song, and theater air--written, performed, and enjoyed by
second-generation Americans--is a syncretic exercise of
this sort. Additionally, some nonethnic music was acceptable to Jews, because "it sounded Jewish"; to Italians, because "the melody was sweet and the words were like those
from home"; and to Slovenians, because "you could dance
to it like a polka. " Also, when a popular song originating
in the homeland or in a subculture achieved widespread
American acceptance, as did "O Sole Mio, " "Bei Mir Bist
Du Schön, " and "The Beer Barrel Polka, " the conflict between cultures seemed, to a few people, on the verge of
resolution.

On occasion ethnic Americans poised between two
aesthetic alternatives and undecided on their choice might
find an answer to their quandary in mental sleights-of-hand
that assumed a spiritual affinity with a specific musical literature. The radical Jew concerned with the laborer's
plight and delighting in workers' protest songs, the mystical
son of Italians fusing his spirit to Gregorian monody and
Palestrinian mass and motet, and the Hungarian-American
folklorist mining the Appalachian hills for Anglo-American
ballads and singing them with a new-found dedication provide
instances of resolutions of this sort.

Finally, there were the adults who remained insensate to musical beauty and estranged from every cultural activity. They contentedly dwelt in a vacuum and considered the aesthetic world outside of no consequence. Some of the saddest of the author's visits were to second-generation dwellings where, despite the parents' childhood exposure to music and the months of voice or instrumental lessons, no music quickened the leisure hours. "Sure, I like all kinds of music. But I don't get around to hearing much of it. And I've got to admit, when I'm tired, it can give me a headache" was the rejoinder to questioning of a successful Italian-American businessman and a former trombonist. The only compositions heard in his home were on the few recordings employed to provide unobtrusive background sounds for the cocktail parties he tendered business associates and their wives.

In short, while members of the immigrant generation might try to live in quasi-isolation, adhere closely to the music of their heritage, and feel slight need to reconcile what they treasured with what the rest of America offered, some adults and most children had to live in two cultural worlds, adjust to a dual heritage--ethnic and American-- and decide what music they would make their own, or give up and avoid all music altogether. It is with this process of musical acculturation that the chapter is concerned. [4]

The Disintegration from Within

An ethnic music underwent change in at least three ways: through the unconscious introduction of fresh sounds and a modification or elimination of traditional ones; through the deliberate borrowing of rhythmic and melodic patterns and subject matter from the host culture, which served to adulterate the old music (this influx of new music, one adds, did reflect the bicultural tendencies within every aging ethnic society); and through the acceptance of entire compositions originating outside the subculture, which were allowed to exist beside or supplant traditional works.

What induced these kinds of change? An obvious consideration was the necessity for adjusting to the American physical and social environment, in response to which old cultural patterns proved inadequate or outmoded. [5] The swift and varied pace of American life, for example, caused many Chinese-Americans to grow impatient with what seemed more and more to be the interminable length

and monotony of Chinese musical theater. [6] If not for the
first generation, this reaction was certainly true for the
second. For similar reasons the lengthy epics of the Middle East, sung to short, constantly repeated chant-like melodies, quickly disappeared. "Suhrab wi Rustan," the delight
of Syrian children and of idlers in Damascus's coffeehouses
and a road to profit for itinerant storytellers, did not survive transportation to America. No American-born children
willingly lingered to listen to the tragic tale of hand-to-hand
battle of father and son. Adults paid the balladeer so that
he would move on and bore somebody else with a story distant from their American concerns. Soon the balladeer found
it wiser to forsake the old profession for the steadier work
and higher profit of the factory. [7]

We must remember, too, that a large minority of
immigrants was eager to repudiate traits tagging it as belonging to an ignorant peasantry and equally eager to establish its worthiness to be considered as up-to-date American.
Whatever music it had known usually gave way to American
popular songs. [8] In addition, quite a few settlers with no
music in their backgrounds turned to American rather than
ethnic sources when they took up song for the first time. [9]
One or two of these ethnic Americans might attempt a desultory revival of a vaguely remembered song or two; little
caught on; nothing seemed congruous with their changed con-
ception of life. [10]

A not inconsiderable cause of cultural alteration was
the inevitable drift of like peoples into contiguous and even
sometimes the same neighborhoods. Side by side occasionally lived age-old enemies--Greeks, Albanians, Turks, and
Armenians, for example. Each became aware of the other's
humanity and similar cuisines, tastes, and habits. As the
years progressed into the thirties and beyond, ethnic Americans mingled their musicians and dancers. Typically, at a
1965 Lebanese hufle, an evening social, held in Miami on
New Year's Eve, nobody thought it unusual to have as entertainers an Armenian on violin (kabunja), a Syrian on lute
(oud), a Greek on flute (zumoora), and a Palestinian on lap-
harp (kanoon). The vocalist came from Egypt; the dancer,
Algiers. The Palestinian was Jewish; the Egyptian and Al-
gerian, Moslem; the rest, Christian. Similarly, at a 1973
international cultural fair sponsored by the Boston International Institute, both the Greek and Armenian folk-dance
groups were lacking sufficient male dancers. The director
of the Turkish troupe volunteered some members to help

out. First-, second-, and third-generation Greeks, Armenians, and Turks danced together and afterward partied together.

Concomitant with the intermixing of musicians and dancers was the gradual elimination of the boundaries demarcating one musical culture from another. Save for language, songs of different ethnic groups whose former homelands lay within the same supranational cultural area increasingly resembled each other. Soon obliterated from the melodies were those musical characteristics belonging exclusively to a single provincial region. As illustration, a young Armenian woman, who arrived here with her parents in 1970, tells of her surprise on first hearing what passed for Armenian music in the Boston area. Some big "hits" that "Armenians were wild over at the time" sounded to her family more like a blend of Turkish and Greek music set to Armenian words.

Nor did touring foreign musicians and imported recordings help reinstate the purity of a national style. Since the twenties, the cultivated and popular musics of all countries have exhibited strong international tendencies, while the lessening rural isolation, the move into cities, the increased opportunities for formal education, and the onset of phonograph, radio, motion pictures, and television have weakened folk practices. As a case in point, during a recent visit to Italy the author entered a café in a hill-town northwest of Rome and witnessed a largely local group of patrons, young and middle-aged, sitting at tables, eating confections, sipping coffee, and listening to recordings featuring Italian songs, to be sure, but also Italian vocalists' remakes of pieces originating in France, Spain, and Portugal. One or two were direct imports from these countries. Moreover, a surprising number of the Italian songs had borrowed liberally from current American popular styles.

Musicians from this contemporary Italy did not come to America solely to perform the compositions brought here by the first-generation Italians, whose musical preferences for the most part continued frozen in the era from around 1900. These musicians represented a different generation and taste. Although they placated the older people with durable Neapolitan classics and recent compositions descended directly from the old song-styles, they also performed Italian-language versions of contemporary works emanating from sundry countries, including the United States. If some

oldsters hesitated to accept these last songs, assuredly
their children enjoyed them.

As further illustration, when Fairuz, an extremely
popular Lebanese singer, toured Lebanese-American communities in 1971, she sang a few works from the old times.
But she was happier with the compositions of the Rahbani
brothers, music that often is indistinguishable from contem-
poraneous Italian, Greek, and Iberian songs.

Even from the first days of settlement no possibility
existed of keeping any subculture free from an extensive admixture of outside musical elements. The omnipresent
organ-grinders plied ditties for handouts along every urban
thoroughfare. City-dwellers daily heard a few, perhaps, of
their own native tunes. They received, however, a far more
thorough indoctrination in American and Italian music, insin-
uating tandems of "The Sidewalks of New York" and "O Sole
Mio," "Sweet Rosie O' Grady" and the "Miserere" from Il
Trovatore, "Give My Regards to Broadway" and "Addio del
passato" from La Traviata, and "My Gal Sal" and "Maria,
Mari."[11] We are therefore hardly surprised to hear of
Jews, among them the young Irving Berlin, "soaking up the
songs ... heard on the streets" and singing a song "in Yiddish one moment, and one in Italian the next,"[12] then following this with the music of Tin Pan Alley. Nor are we
surprised to learn that the Yiddish theater was soon supple-
menting its East European types of melody with tunes from
American and Italian sources.[13]

The radio in the 1920s, the movies in the 1930s, and
the children home from public school and from play with
youngsters of diverse backgrounds forced the settlers to
hear songs alien to their culture. A third-generation
Lithuanian-American writes:

> As my parents progressed in school, my father
> experienced more music by making new friends
> in the Italian neighborhood near where he resided.
> He heard Italian music such as "Fickle Women"
> and "O Sole Mio." He appreciated these songs
> because they were very beautiful. His mother
> and father couldn't understand why he liked that
> type of music. Yet, although his father couldn't
> understand the words to the songs, he would still
> hum to the music.[14]

The Cultural Defection of the Second Generation

Having neither nostalgia for a distant land they did not know nor longings to sing about faraway countrysides, villages, and peoples, the children growing up in America rapidly became Americanized.[15] What Samuel Ornitz writes of the Jewish boys he grew up with on New York's East Side and their attitudes toward their parents' way of life can apply to other ethnic children as well:

> An ocean separated us.... Many of us were transient, impatient aliens in our parents' homes. Then there was that strict, rarefied public school world. The manners and clothes, speech and point-of-view of our teachers extorted our respect and reflected upon the shabbiness, foreignness, and crudities of our folks and homes. Again, there was the harsh and cruel cheder life with its atmosphere of superstition, dread, and punishment. And then came our street existence, our sweet, lawless, personal, high-colored life, our vent to the disciplines, crampings, and confinements of our other worlds.[16]

Similar attitudes caused some young West Coast Chinese-Americans to insist on an American repertoire for the drum-and-bugle corps and other instrumental ensembles they joined. They found that their elders were entirely old-fashioned in musical taste, and they denominated recent arrivals of their own age as "squares" foolishly loyal to "song and dance presentations of traditional Chinese vintage." On the continent's Atlantic side, a Greek-American described herself and her friends as tired of the first generation's narrow tastes. The younger generation, she claimed, took "no real interest in" Greek music, which "represented something ancient and nothing which I felt could be of any value." Neither traditional Greek secular music nor church hymns and chants were considered worth "listening to as a musical experience."[17]

Though in some households strong family relationships continued to bind first- to second-generation members, in at least as many homes the authority of the parent deteriorated to such an extent that children ceased accepting their elders' guidance in cultural and other matters. After World War I the daughters of the first-generation women, who had been bulwarks against cultural change, started to repudiate the extreme restrictions circumscribing their activities. Instead of assuming their mothers' role of chief guardians of ethnic tradition, many, though not all, shaped their preferences after American models and found the crooning of an American singer backed by a smooth saxophone section more attractive than an ethnic oldster's rendition of outdated works in a half-understood language. [18]

When the thirties arrived, a general lament arose from ethnic cultural leaders over the children's refusal to attend national schools to study the language and customs of their forebears, over the spurning of membership in ethnically oriented choruses and other performing groups, and over the lack of enthusiasm for any community-sponsored cultural enterprise. [19]

Though enough control persisted for most parents to forbid their daughters the attentions of young men from outside the subculture, similar injunctions to their sons were frequently ignored. Some young men dated nonethnic women to satisfy their sexual needs; others, to go out with someone less closely supervised than the girls of the neighborhood. Bolder youths brought their "American" dates to social affairs in the enclave and insisted, if only as a matter of politeness, that American music appear alongside the ethnic songs. By the thirties the social evenings for the young held in the ethnic community had to feature American dancing to the music of American-type bands, usually with a singer or two performing the latest American hits. Thus were recognized the changed tastes of the second generation and the infiltration of the community by outsiders and outside ideas. [20]

A majority of the men dating outsiders did eventually marry a woman from their own subculture. But a growing minority took wives foreign to their group. For instance, citing a 1956 survey of Jews living in the Washington, D. C., area, Judith Kramer found 1. 4 percent of the first-generation, 10. 2 percent of the second-generation, and 17. 9 percent of the third-generation men married to outsiders. The largest incidence of such marriage (37 percent) took place among the college-educated. [21]

Few as they were in relation to the total number of marriages, weddings breaching ethnic barriers were remembered vividly for years thereafter by the community. With

intermarriage the dilution of ethnic culture was a certainty
and affected more people than just the bride and groom.
The first voluntary attendance of the most diehard of the
immigrant generation, particularly the women, at a function
that included nonethnic music was often at the wedding reception for a young man and his nonethnic bride. At such
a reception in Toledo, Ohio, for a Moslem youth and an
American girl: "There were over five hundred people invited, most of them Arabs. Many of the Toledo community
families attended. After the dinner, there was music and
dancing for the bride's people, and Arabic music with the
traditional Dabka dance for the Arabs. These two alternated
with each other."22

At several receptions of this sort (Syrian-Lebanese,
Greek, Armenian, and Sicilian) attended by the author some
first-generation women were to be seen huddled together at
one side of the hall, arms folded, studying carefully the an-
tics of the Americans and tut-tuting over the closeness of
their dancing postures, the several other little freedoms men
and women took with each other, and the musical gibberish
emanating from the orchestra--of which they understood little, but which they suspected lent itself to the minor infrac-
tions of morality taking place before their eyes. On one of
these occasions the author heard a woman mutter: "Better
that my son marry an ugly and simple girl of his own kind,
one that does not even own the underpants sticking to her
bottom, than one such as these." Nevertheless, it is significant that, whether approving or not, these women were
forced to sit and experience nonethnic customs, dancing,
and music. What is more, the event remained indelibly in
their memories. Their subsequent behavior altered in subtle ways because of what they had witnessed.

As for the newlyweds, in all probability their household would no longer stress the cuisine, customs, and music
of the subculture. Chances were the young couple would
choose to live away from the ethnic enclave. This decision
alone would cause a considerable loosening of cultural ties,
as it undeniably did with all other ethnic Americans residing
away from persons of like descent.23

The Widening Gap

Families headed by first-generation parents "lost touch with
their cultural heritage" and saw children grow up knowing

mostly the music of the host culture when they lived apart
from an ethnic community. The only Jewish family in Goffs-
town, New Hampshire, the only Italian family in Holbrook,
Massachusetts, and a solitary Ukrainian family on a prairie
homestead all experienced a swift loss in ethnic identity and
a diminishing interest in the music of their fathers.[24]

Now and again the taking on of American colorings
produced incongruous results. Pardee Lowe writes of an
Uncle Jack who escaped Chinatown's influence and grew up
in a Colorado town, where Lowe's maternal grandfather op-
erated a restaurant. Uncle Jack had taken up singing, developed a husky tenor, and decided to appear on the American stage. His debut was at the Silver Lyceum Theater in
East Belleville, California. Dressed as a mandarin and
drawn on stage in a jinriksha, Uncle Jack commenced singing songs by George M. Cohan and other American popular
composers. Next, accoutered with a bamboo cane and a
cigar, and wearing a theatrical Chinese costume, he cake-
walked around the stage to the rhythms of the "Dark Town
Strutter's Ball." Lastly he sang "Ireland Must Be Heaven,
For My Mother Came from There." "The audience was
stunned into silence," writes Lowe.[25]

A lesser knowledge of ethnic music and a decline of
interest in one's heritage were correlated not only with intermarriage and living outside the enclave, but also with higher
education, affluence, and professional employment. Especially when they entered professions necessitating lengthy and in-
tensive schooling amongst Americans, the educated ethnic
Americans had difficulty identifying with their parents' simple dances and songs.[26]

The cultural dissimilarity between the settlers and
their college-educated children is apparent in the following
statement of a middle-aged Polish-American manager of a
large book and record store in the Boston area:

> After I graduated from college, I went my own
> way. My parents couldn't forgive me for majoring
> in English literature. They thought I should have
> gone into business, become a lawyer or bank teller
> or something of that sort. I began to dislike ev-
> erything they stood for. Particularly irritating
> were what I saw as their silly Polish songs. I
> thought of them as symbols of their parochialism
> and as vehicles for their prejudices. My father

labelled the American songs I enjoyed as "crap, " and the concerts of the B. S. O. that I attended once in a while as my trying to prove I was above everyone. He was especially annoyed because I refused to speak Polish at home. From where I stood, his music was only an excuse for drinking. No cultural merit was to be seen in the music he cared for. 27

This statement should be compared with one by the poet Emanuel Carnevali on the musical taste of his grandmother. After his arrival in America in 1919 and his befriendment by American litterateurs Carnevali grew scornful of his grandmother's plebeian preferences:

> [My grandmother] had a cracked little voice with which she sang the same old song, always the same:
> Funiculi, funicula
> Yammo, yammo!
> It was the song of the celebration of the making of a rope railway up the side of Vesuvio. It was:
> Yammo, yammo in coppa va,
> Funiculi, funicula.
> A stupid song, the stupidest ever. Casella made it into a rhapsody, and it is bad, very bad music at that:
> Egghiuta Nannine, se n'e saliusta
> In coppa sta.
> (Do not let the student of Italian letters be dismayed at these quotations. They are not Italian. They are Neapolitan.)28

With the downgrading of the old culture came a relegation to limbo of the poets and musicians who remained loyal to, or unable to change from, old ways. Note the comment of Sol Liptzin on the fate of Eliakum Zunser, Yiddish poet, singer, and badchen, once in demand for weddings, circumcisions, and other important occasions. With overtones of bitterness and regret Liptzin writes:

> On the American continent ... Zunser shared the fate of all his contemporaries whose medium of expression was Yiddish. He became the victim of a growing apathy towards Jewish cultural values. The new, assimilationist generation that rose to dominance on the American scene between the two

World Wars cultivated a negative attitude towards
all manifestations of the Eastern European Jewish
heritage. It closed its ears to the melodies that
had brought tears to the eyes of its forebears. It
denuded itself of the folklore and the folk customs
that might have imparted warmth and beauty to
life. It strove to efface all distinguishing characteristics that set it apart from its non-Jewish
neighbors. [29]

The Pressures from Without

The ethnic community's musical culture also disintegrated in
its sense of common purpose and found its vitality depleted
as well, owing to the unrelenting assault of nativists appre-
hensive of the newcomers' impact on their civilization.
Typical with most American "reformers" was the complaint
about and a zeal to rectify what they perceived as the evils
besetting the nonnative society. Whether stated or not,
however, their final objective was not the correction of a
way of life but its eradication and supplantation by a different system.

The aggregate predilections of advisory books directed
at the new arrival tended toward this end. The warning contained in John Foster Carr's Guide for the Immigrant Italian
(1911) was the undersong written into the pages of most such
handbooks: "An Italian, like any other foreigner, is appreciated when he lives the American social life. Until then he
counts for nothing. Join American clubs; read American
papers. Try to adapt yourself to the manners and customs
and habits of the American people. "[30]

Because the stain of foreignism would not wash off,
numerous stalwarts of the American system offered the newcomer guidance along the purgative way, among them Protestant missionaries. The Protestant effort to convert Catholics, Eastern Orthodox Christians, Buddhists, and Jews,
though often futile, commenced early and persisted over several decades, since "some nativists viewed such conversions
as a crucial part of the process of Americanization. "[31] The
adult city-dwellers who did attend the missions may have
done so for want of a place to go to alleviate the monotony
of existence. Their children went attracted by the story
hours, modest plays and musicals, and other diversions
provided by the volunteer helpers. At the same time old

and young ethnic Americans learned of the Protestant road to salvation and sang hymns and uplift songs that, in effect, helped wean them from their own music.[32] It was this sort of impact the Morgan Memorial Chapel of Boston's South End had during the twenties and into the thirties. Boys and girls of Greek, Syrian, Jewish, and Chinese backgrounds were introduced to Lowell Mason's "Missionary Hymn" ("They call us to deliver/Their land from error's chain"), George Webb's "The Morning Light Is Breaking" ("The morning light is breaking/The darkness disappears/The sons of earth are awakening/To penitential tears"), and George Root's "The Battle Cry of Freedom" ("The Union forever, Hurrah! boys, Hurrah!/Down with the traitor/Up with the star/While we rally round the flag, boys, rally once again/Shouting the battle cry of freedom").[33]

This was the same mission Mary Antin attended in the first decade of the century and describes in The Promised Land. Every Saturday she went for the free entertainment, music, and recitations. "Beautiful ladies," she writes, "sang to us." "Clean gentlemen" also "sang or played." And Brother Hotchkins, "who managed these entertainments," made certain that "classics of the lighter sort were judiciously interspersed with the favorite streets songs of the days."[34]

Like the missions, the settlement houses that sprang up in urban America, including those specializing in music, had the Americanization of immigrants as an important reason for their existence. However much the new settlers' polyglot languages, customs, and musical traditions seemed to have merit, it was "felt necessary" that all foreigners "be assimilated, and what medium is stronger, or, if you will, easier, than the universal language of music?" Assimilationists regarded the sponsoring of instrumental and singing classes and the formation of chamber, orchestral, and choral ensembles as excellent means for acclimating the newcomers to the psychological world outside the ethnic enclave and for helping to "popularize, socialize, and democratize good music."[35] True, the children were most influenced; but music was one of the best methods the settlement worker knew for reaching the parents.[36]

In addition to musical instruction concerts were offered to the immigrants, either gratis or for a trifling entrance fee. In this fashion "the bad, cheap, and trashy music" heard on the streets might be countered with patriotic American songs; works of composers like Handel, Mozart, and Beethoven; Negro spirituals; and selected compositions representative of the "best" in every national repertoire.[37]

If the children performed, the parents were certain to attend. If concerts by professionals were given, the grownups were more likely to come if they heard some music reflecting their tastes. The philosophy underlying the attempts to involve the immigrants with music was best summed up by David Mannes, Director of the New York Settlement Music School from 1910 to 1915. In a 1912 interview he was asked why he wished to bring music to the several peoples of the East Side. Mannes replied:

> Our object in inaugurating ... concerts for the people of the neighborhood is to help make them good American citizens.... We are delighted at the way our audience received the patriotic airs and I hope to introduce a feature next year ... that will be the playing of the national airs of the various nationalities included in our audiences, arranged in a medley ... and close with the American songs. When our audiences are inspired by American patriotic songs they become better citizens of the United States, and when they absorb the refining qualities of good music they will become better citizens of the world.[38]

The Influence of the Public School

Surer than missions, settlement houses, and free concerts were the public schools in effecting cultural change through music. Most children had to attend them. Few settlers could afford parochial schools. Besides, the private schools intended for East European Jews were run by the German Jews; those for Italians, by the Irish; and as often as not these educators displayed less tolerance than the teachers in the public schools.

Unfortunately public-school attendance almost guaranteed the youngsters' eventual alienation from their parents, since before long the students ceased relying solely on them for guidance in their new experiences. Now the teacher, as surrogate parent, trained and refined their minds, taught them discipline, exposed them to a host of unfamiliar symbols, and encouraged them to participate in novel social activities not encompassed in their parents' world. Soon the youngsters were acknowledging and trying to convince their parents to accept the superiority of the host culture. 39 Frequently neither parent nor child seemed willing to meet the other halfway. The home at times resembled a battlefield where contenders fought to establish mutually exclusive ways of viewing life and living it. The music learned at the public school was profoundly involved in the conflict.

From first grade through high school the public-school system enveloped its learners with sounds different from those of the subculture. At the same time the lyrics to the songs and choral works studied by the pupils aired ideas unknown in the enclave. Without doubt the American educator saw a childhood and adolescence spent in school as an opportunity to tattoo indelible images of American right-thinking onto impressionable minds, and music as a ready and effective means to this end. The singing, general-music, and instrumental classes of the lower grades led to the choruses, bands, orchestras, and theater-arts music groups of the high school. American hymn and national anthem were integral to the daily morning exercises that began each day at school. Weekly assemblies, celebrations of American holidays, parents' nights, Christmas, visits by important people, graduations, and other school events called for music. Whether Jewish, Moslem, Buddhist, Roman Catholic, or Eastern Orthodox Christian, children were required to intone Protestant hymns like:

> What a friend we have in Jesus,
> All our sins and griefs to bear.

(This hymn and the songs that follow are samples of the music sung by the students of Boston's Quincy Elementary School and Abraham Lincoln Junior High School, in Boston's South End, during the late 1920s and the 1930s.)

With bemused expressions Italian boys and girls vocalized:

> Yankee Doodle went to town
> Riding on a pony,
> Stuck a feather in his cap
> And called it macaroni,

then asked their fellow-students what the verse really meant.

Greek youngsters, whose usual physical surroundings consisted of grimy brick tenements, narrow asphalt streets, and tall, light-denying factories and office buildings, dutifully chanted:

> O beautiful for spacious skies,
> For amber waves of grain,
> For purple mountain majesties
> Above the fruited plain!

Everyone had to pledge musical allegiance to the diverse regions of America:

> I wish I was in the land of cotton ...
> Oh, give me a home where the buffalo roam ...
> Meet me in St. Louis, Louis, meet me at the
> fair ...
> East side, West side, all around the town ...
> She was bred in old Kentucky ...
> Carry me back to Old Virginny ...

and confirm the homely sentiments appreciated by their mentors:

> Darling, I am growing older, silver threads among
> the gold ...
> Someone's in the kitchen with Dinah ...
> I'm a rambling wreck from Georgia Tech and a
> heck of an engineer ...
> Sometimes I feel like a motherless child ...
> When Johnny comes marching home again,
> hurrah ...
> I dream of Jeanie with the light brown hair ...
> Down by the old mill stream....

During recess the students shared songs in the schoolyard, songs considered too vulgar for the classroom:

> When the worms crawl in and the worms crawl
> out ...
> Ta-ra-ra-boom-de-re ...
> Oh, they don't wear pants in the southern part of
> France ...
> The game was played on Sunday in Heaven's own
> backyard, Jesus was the quarterback, the Devil
> was the guard.

Through these compositions the offspring of immigrants absorbed the American's devotion to country, brash jauntiness, confidence in oneself and the future, irreverent gaiety, longing for a dream-past, and sentimental attachment to old folks and to nubile maidens seemingly born and nurtured for love alone. Counteracted were the déjà vu pessimism, quiet and long-suffering submissiveness to authority, distrust of the future, and respect for all tried-and-true ways of thinking and acting that guided most of their parents. Several writers, the sons and daughters of immigrants, warmly second Ronald Sanders's comment on the importance of music in his public-school education:

> Singing was a much more central activity at P. S. 22½ and Flatbush High School, and had a much more educative role in these institutions, than its modest place on the syllabus might have led one to believe. I learned many academic things more effectively from singing at those two places than I did from such courses as geography and history. My first vivid sense of the real, Protestant America that stood outside the borders of immigrant Flatbush, for example, came not from textbooks but from the numerous songs I sang during the weekly assemblies at P. S. 22½. Many of them had a religious or quasi-religious character--so much so that the whole assembly program each week had the air of a slightly secularized Protestant service. When I sang things like
>
> Oh God, beneath Thy guiding hand
> Our exiled fathers crossed the sea,
>
> I obtained visions of worlds that were beautiful as well as strange to me, and that I wanted to learn a good deal more about. I liked the Pilgrims very much in those days; they were a means of reconciliation between us offspring of Jewish immigrants--our own exiled fathers who had crossed the sea--and the traditions of Protestant America. [40]

At first the youngest pupils reproduced the music in rote fashion and with limited comprehension:

Land-the-britches falling down ...

Columbia, the jam of the ocean ... [41]
Tree cheers for de Red Whatzam Blu! [42]
Silent night, holly night,
All's come, all's right,
Round John Virgin's mother and child.... [43]

From the beginning they recognized that what they
sang, though half-understood, had hardly any connection with
their parents' culture. As comprehension grew, cultural
loyalties whiffled between school and home. To their teachers, children tried to appear as nouveaux Americans, raw but
ready to learn; to their parents, as dependents heedful of
traditional values. Consequently the second-generation youngsters found their personalities divided into two distinct states
of being. The scission between the two was sometimes sharp.

War Service, Urban Renewal, and Change

America's wars had the effect of mandates requiring ethnic
youths to prove their prime allegiance to everything American. Here music also played a role. When the winter of
1916-17 brought the United States to the edge of war, the
Americanization movement reached full heat. New York's
East Side witnessed numerous demonstrations of loyalty,
"usually begun with someone singing 'The Story of Old
Glory,' 'Uncle Sam,' and 'Dixie.'" At these demonstrations Fiorello La Guardia, "wearing the now familiar Western hat and stringy bow tie, beat the drums for ... Americanization" before Italians and Jews. [44]

War began. First-generation men were promised
automatic citizenship if they enlisted. Those who were citizens and not volunteers were drafted. Whether boldhearted
or fearful, young men wrenched themselves away from their
communities and lived totally American lives for months.
The changed circumstances turned their world topsy-turvy.
Lads who had joined up barely knowing a dozen English
words eventually returned home experts in American slang,
diversions, and popular music. For the rest of their lives
they would recall and continue to sing the 1917 hits: "Good-
Bye, Broadway, Hello France!," "Good-Bye, Ma! Good-Bye,
Pa!" "Good-Bye, Mule," "Over There," "Smiles," "They Go
Wild Simply Wild over Me"; and those of 1918: "Come On,
Papa," "Good Morning, Mr. Zip-zip-zip," "Hinky-Dinky
Parley Vous," "K K K Katy," "Oui, Oui, Marie," and "Oh!
How I Hate to Get Up in the Morning." What is more, even

the first-generation citizens who resubmerged themselves in their ethnic society after release from the army still sang these songs for years thereafter. [45]

Similarly World War II would weaken the already-slender ties binding the second generation to the culture of their forebears.

After World War II another potent factor, urban renewal, accelerated the process of acculturation. Politicians and urban experts agreed on the necessity or renovating what they saw as the shabbier sections of the cities. Buildings housing ethnic minorities were condemned as examples of urban blight and torn down, their inhabitants forced to scatter. In Boston the entire West End and large parts of the South End and North End were demolished. Homes of Italians, Jews, Syrians, and Greeks were replaced by luxury apartments, expressways, hospitals, and high-rise commercial edifices. With the exodus ceased the physical sense of community and means for perpetuating a common heritage already enfeebled with Americanisms. Let one man of Italian descent tell of what happened to the Lawrence, Massachusetts, community he loved and saw bulldozed into extinction:

> The type of environment, the way of life and its music that I was raised in is ending. The urban-renewal relocation of families has virtually destroyed the ethnic communities. I feel these areas had a personality of their own that formed a musical attitude distinct to almost every city block [sic]. Now without it, the enthusiasm for parades is decreasing, summer band concerts may be cancelled, the elaborate Italian fiesta, "The Feast of the Three Sitting Saints," when Italian music is played for three days, is to be discontinued.... To me, all this means that this type of music is literally dying. [46]

The Marginal Culture

Second-generation ethnic Americans could not help but possess polycentric personalities that were shaped by an amalgam of influences. Inevitably their musical preferences reflected their several identities: American and ethnic, rebel and conformist, realist and sentimentalist. Withal they

remained diffident about participating in the world of Americans. An affecting illustration of this is provided by a
Jewish correspondent, who writes of her second-generation
father:

> My father is a rather shy, introverted sort of
> guy. He is much like his own father in many
> ways--old-worldish, religious, and dogmatic. Mu-
> sic served to liberalize him and open his eyes to
> the non-parochial world around him. In high
> school he played in all sorts of bands and groups.
> His participation in an all-state band (1943) is
> ample proof of his prowess. He related with
> special glee his forays with the band to strange
> cities and towns. It's interesting to hear him
> talk of marching bands and the white-legged, blue
> eyed, Waspy cheerleaders. I sometimes feel that
> this represents a world he would have liked to
> have had--but he is just too parochial in his out-
> look to attain it. His excitement [in talking about
> his musical past] is always nervous--an excite-
> ment that he feels somewhat uneasy with. He is
> not too sure of how he should like it [the "non-
> parochial world"].47

All things considered, the music to which second-
generation ethnic Americans turned failed to make them
whole. Their intercultural borrowings of song and dance
could not blend into a meaningful synthesis while they continued to hear and perform music in the company only of
like-thinking second-generation men and women. For the
most part their associates and whatever organizations they
joined continued to exist, and their cultural experiences to
occur, apart from the American mainstream--even when they
moved to the suburbs. The automobile and telephone bridged
the separation between them and their friends who had once
lived nearby in the central city.

Some second-generation men and women went on attending the traditional social functions of their subculture
but made clear their own independence from the old ways,
as did Pardee Lowe. He attended a time-honored Chinese
family "reception," listened to Chinese music that struck
him "as being totally alien," and underlined his reservations
about his father's taste by blurting out to him: "I like 'Yankee Doodle Dandy' much better!"48

Others never gave up "the old music" because they associated it with their childhood and loved elders. But they had difficulty understanding the language of the songs. Though they enjoyed the music, they rarely attempted to perform it, feeling more comfortable with American compositions. [49] By the 1930s reports were being issued that claimed only one-third of the ethnic households were employing a foreign language on a regular basis. By the 1950s and 60s the number had dropped to one-quarter or less. [50] As the immigrant generation died off, so also did knowledge of the language and the performance of the music it had brought to America. Ethnic cultural leaders tried to stem the erosion by issuing traditional songs with texts translated into English. [51] The situation only worsened.

Old tunes were also reissued with texts rewritten to center on American experiences. A few ethnic composers created new tunes and texts calculated to correspond to the new conditions. As early as 1922 one writer, Robert Park, was observing that the "young Italian composers" in America were using "melodies borrowed partly from Italian music and partly from ragtime, " which were set to words like "The American Workingman" and "Land of the Dollar. "[52] About the same time traditional Yiddish works lost their following, as Jews turned to the more modern songs of the Yiddish theater, then the Broadway theater. Ruth Rubin writes: "Though the songs of Abraham Goldfaden and Elyokum Zunser were still current, along with the old Yiddish folksongs, these could not long prevail against the commercial operetta, the popular song and the theatrical ditty. "[53]

The traditional songs that continued to be sung more and more corresponded to American melodies. They are usually in the major mode, have isometric rhythms, utilize intervals that lend themselves to a clear and simple I, V, and IV harmonization, and include melodic phrases whose counterparts are found in American music. Interesting in this regard is the major-mode tune that a Japanese-American girl from Los Angeles showed Elizabeth May, telling her it was one her parents had sung as children in Japan. The song persisted among the Japanese of the West Coast in the 1950s (Example 26). [54] Although its melodic phrases do not touch on the leading tone, the raised seventh (B-natural) is certainly implied as necessary in the harmony if one is to play the tune with Western accompaniment, which is what the young Japanese woman wished to do. In measure 4 the first phrase closes on a half-cadence requiring the harmonies of II-I$^6_4$-V, and the close (measures 6-8) employs a melodic commonplace that fits neatly onto the full-cadence formula, IV-I-I$^6_4$-V^7-I.

Also in the 1950s Bruno Nettl and Ivo Moravick collected Czech and Slovak folksongs still extant in Detroit. They discovered that the melodies they gathered had characteristics differing from those collected abroad. In particular they noticed the prevalence of the major mode. Of the eighteen melodies they reproduce in their study of folksong in Detroit most are in the major mode. What is more, although Czech and Slovak idioms are obviously present, some tunes have affinities with American traditional songs. Examples 27a-d reprint the beginnings of four of these melodies.[55]

One of the most fascinating reports on the preservation of elements of ethnic culture that correspond most closely to those of the New World is given by Robert Klymasz. Writing on the Ukrainian winter caroling customs, he distinguishes between their observance abroad and their alteration amongst the settlers here, owing to "tension and conflict" with the host culture. Klymasz found that less and less time could be assigned to traditional musical performances than had hitherto been the case. Instead of continuing over several days, caroling now (1970) took place only on Christmas Eve and Christmas Day. Moreover, the many secular types of carols once customarily sung during this season were eliminated. Favored were circumspect religious works, especially those consonant with the sounds and sentiments of favorite Western carols like "Silent Night." Ousted were all compositions with courting motifs, despite their having once been prominent in the repertoire. Eliminated also were the caroling parties of young bachelors, who had spent much of their time serenading the young women of the neighborhood. To "command respect," writes Klymasz, the carolers now constituted a mixed group of older people drawn from the church elders and ladies' "auxiliaries."[56]

An instance of the type of carol that disappeared in the New World is provided by "The Green Apple Tree" (Example 28).[57] Note the melody in the ancient Dorian mode and lacking the seventh tone. Note also the irregular meter and the uneven melodic phrases (5+3+5). The sound is related somewhat to the free parlando-rubato East European style described by Béla Bartók, in <u>Hungarian Folk Music</u>

(London, 1931). To be noticed, finally, is the completely secular text, and especially the sexual symbolism of the plucked apple.

Still popular is the religious carol-like "A Wondrous Event," which reveals similarities to Anglo-American traditional songs (Example 29).[58] Here the melody is in the major mode, the meter even, the phrases square-cut (4+4+ 4+4), the melodic movement stepwise and lyrical, and the form AABA--a common one in American popular song. The text is completely given over to Christ's birth in Bethlehem.

Of interest is a carol that once existed in two forms: one a jesting love song (Example 30a) and the other a sacred carol celebrating Christ's birth (Example 30b).[59] In both versions the melody is lyrical, isometric, and in the major mode--therefore in agreement with the music of the host culture. Nevertheless, the first version has been completely supplanted by the second owing to the former's inappropriateness within the New World context.

Secular song of all subcultures underwent a similar winnowing process. Richard Gambino, for example, in Blood of My Blood, The Dilemma of the Italian-American (Garden City, N.Y., 1974), writes that the frankly sexual and sensuous works brought to America by Italians, songs like "La Luna Mezzu O Mari" and "Comme Facette Mammeta?," "are no longer sung as freely as they once were."

Because members of the second generation made up a larger and larger portion of the ethnic community and demanded American popular music, gypsy orchestras learned how to play rhumbas and foxtrots for young Rumanians,[60] Japanese-American jazz bands and country-and-western groups entertained the up-to-date Nisei,[61] and Chinese-American young women belted out American dance-songs like "I Think I'm Goin' Out of My Head" as entertainment for seasonal celebrations like the Lunar New Year.[62]

Each ethnic society developed a special fondness for those American popular songs that pictured its way of life in nonderogatory terms. Humor was welcome. "A sure-fire hit in Jewish neighborhoods was 'Nathan, Nathan, Tell Me Vat For Are You Vaitin' Nathan?' or 'Put It On; Take It Off; Wrap It Up; Take It Home; Call Again; Call Again,' or 'Cohen Owed Me Ninety-Seven Dollars,'" writes Carrie Balaban.[63] The ethnic society had a special affection for

American musical performers originating from its membership. Thus a third-generation Italian-American writes that
her parents and relatives loved "listening to Perry Como,
Frank Sinatra, and Dean Martin, going 'wild' over Frankie
Laine's 'Pepino the Italian Mouse' records."[64] Furthermore, some vocalists belonging to one of the several subcultures (Italian, Jewish, Greek, and Armenian) told the
author that when they appeared before general American audiences, they sang American songs "straight" and employed
American mannerisms. On the other hand, when they performed these same compositions in their own communities,
they tried to endear themselves to their more particular audiences by deliberately becoming "ethnic." They sang with
hand gestures characteristic of their group, pronounced words
differently, and gave special twists to the sentences by in-
terpolating a non-English word or phrase, which often produced a sly deflection from the original meaning.[65]

The Amerethnic Community

Beginning with the late 1920s, when substantial numbers of
children born in America reached maturity, a mode of existence resulted that tried to accommodate itself to the dif-
ferences between parent and offspring. It also took cogni-
zance of the need for the reinterpretation of old, and the
creation of new, traditions and symbols.

While the oldsters desired traditional music and their
offspring placed a higher valuation on the contemporary musical productions of Tin Pan Alley and Broadway, both derived
pleasure from ethnically oriented popular songs imported
from the Old Country or composed by members of their subculture. These songs, it is important to remember, could
be performed in English or the foreign tongue with equal
felicity. A Portuguese-American, whose parents had migrated from the Cape Verde Islands, writes that most members of the Cape Cod Portuguese settlements regarded such
compositions and their singers with considerable affection:

> Many of these songs they sing every day at night
> clubs and parties can be purchased [in recorded
> form] at a local music store. "Gininha" (Jean),
> "Se oj e prete e doz" (Her Eyes Are Dark and
> Sweet), "Lola" (Lola), "Ai mar de lua cheau" (Oh
> Sea of the Full Moon), "Eu ojaba en crebu cheau"
> (I Saw You and I Loved You) are some of the more

popular songs [ca. 1970], which are sung in both English and Portuguese. Two of the important composers are Al Lopez and Jimmy Lomba; nearly every Portuguese knows them and their songs.[66]

A curious practice countenanced in Amerethnic communities was the introduction of nonethnic music into situations where it was decidedly inappropriate. From the early years of this century comes a description of a funeral procession in San Francisco's Chinatown led by solemn priests "in mortar board hats and black gowns, swinging rattles," followed by "three Chinese bands going on the trot" and hammering out ragtime tunes so as to be heard over the din of exploding firecrackers.[67] Into the same category of the incongruous falls the performance of the Bach-Gounod "Ave Maria" melody during a Reform-Jewish wedding service, and the Schubert "Death and the Maiden" melody during a Greek-Orthodox wedding service. The author was present at both events.

Fascinating to the cultural historian are the Amerethnic practices purporting to have traditional sanction but that in reality bear little relationship to transoceanic usages. To give an instance, Hanukkah, a minor celebration in the Jewish religious year, has become "popular among people who observe little else--because Jewish children are entitled to 'their Christmas.'"[68] As might be expected, a similarity exists between the sound of some Hanukkah songs and that of Christmas carols.[69] Also of interest is the elevation of the dubke, a local Lebanese circle dance, and its music, to widespread prominence in all Arabic-speaking communities, Christian and Moslem. In their study of the Syrian-Lebanese in America, Philip and Joseph Kayal state that the inspiration for the dubke's performance is "essentially Western," and the instruments and many of the musical inflections employed are also Western:

> The debke [sic] is actually a Lebanese folk dance primarily intended for weddings and has been refined and learned by all Arabic-speaking Americans. While it originated in Mount Lebanon, it is presently performed extensively by Syrians. However, the Syrians from Aleppo and Damascus had to learn it from the "Lebanese" after they arrived in the United States. The dance is hardly performed in modern Lebanon any more, and visitors from the Orient are amazed at its survival and the enthu-

siasm with which it is performed here. Undoubtedly, they miss the symbolic and emotional value
of the dance. [70]

The mélange of music and dance from heterogeneous
sources became a feature of every ethnic society. Though
the traditionalists realized that the true musical traditions
they wished to uphold and those the changing community
chose to stress as typical of their heritage were not always
the same, the modernists felt that not enough of the extran-
eous and exotic had been pruned away. Yet, both sides
sensed compromise was necessary. Concessions were made
to appease now one, now another of the conflicting musical
demands. Without plan the ethnic society drifted farther and
farther away from its original moorings.

The author was introduced about ten years ago to an
elderly Polish couple who once were active semiprofessional
musicians in the Greater Boston Polish community. [71] As
an experiment music popular among contemporary Polish-
Americans was played for them. While they listened, they
shook their heads again and again and said: "No, that is
not Polish." American tunes to Polish texts, songs by
Polish-American composers, dance-melodies performed by
Polish-American ensembles that the author had been assured
by others to be "very Polish" were presented. The reply
was consistent: "No, that is not Polish." Finally, a few
selections of recent popular and artistic songs imported directly from Poland were put on the phonograph. The two
old people wearily sighed: "No, that is not Polish." Their
musical day was a thing of the past. The author wondered
whether it was dead and beyond resurrection.

Chapter 5

THE CULTURAL COMMONWEALTH

●─────────────────────────────────────

Any consequential musical contribution to American culture
by the new immigration seems hardly possible at first glance.
If we examine the survival rate of ethnic music--what particular works continue to live--the conclusion is that few show
longevity. We have seen that ethnic music does change year
after year as the relationships of ethnic Americans alter vis-
à-vis the larger society and as educational levels and occu-
pational skills increase. Even when sociocultural status remains the same, the ethnic American goes from Leoncavallo's "Ridi, Pagliaccio" (1892), to Ted Fiorito's "Laugh!
Clown, Laugh!" (1928), to Bernie Wayne's "Laughing on the
Outside--Crying on the Inside" (1946), to ever-more-recent
works concerned with two-ply feelings.

A recent avenue of research has involved the question
of whether a reshaped ethnic identity has any chance of enduring divorced from a physically compact and omnipresent
community and articulated as a variation of the host culture.[1]
Prominent spokesmen for music have responded with an un-
qualified "No. " Virgil Thomson, a respected composer and
writer on the contemporary American scene, says of the
American composers of his generation:

> We have been less and less involved with the ex-
> pressive urgencies of continental Europe and more
> and more involved with our own heritage of feeling.
> This heritage has come to us mainly from England,
> Ireland, Scotland, and Wales. Our non-British
> settlers have relinquished their native poetry and
> tunes, preserving these in family or community
> use only so long as they have continued to speak
> the languages they spoke when they came here,
> which is usually just one generation. The melting-
> pot theory of American life is not, it would seem,

a true picture. Because the English-language
group has from the beginning absorbed to itself,
by means of language, all the others, giving to
them its ethics and customs and even going so
far as to lend them its racial memories, its folklore, legends, faiths, and aspirations. Our immigrants' eagerness for absorption is proved by their
constant [musical] preoccupation with Shakers and
Quakers, with Indians and cowboys, with black men
from the swamps and white Protestant mountain-
eers. Such composers, furthermore, though many
of them sons of immigrant parents, show a notable
lack of yearning toward their European origins. [2]

On the surface, if works of composers like Aaron
Copland, Walter Piston, and George Gershwin are examined,
Thomson's comments seem justified. Their descriptive compositions are centered mainly on American subjects. Sections of their abstract works seem kindred with hoedowns,
rags, blues, and the other musical styles denominated as
typically American. In truth their melodies and rhythms
are often borrowed from or patterned after established
American models, whether realized in more concrete fashion by Gershwin, or nonrepresentative fashion by Piston.
This chapter later will examine how keen Thomson's perception is.

The Decline of Ethnocentricism

Adding force to the argument that "try as the immigrants
may, in the long run they cannot perpetuate much of their
old culture, "[3] the aggregate of families headed by second-
generation parents that the author studied possessed only a
small fraction of the music once enjoyed by their forebears,
whether in their memory or in the form of sheet music and
recordings. What is more, the children who were music
students scarcely studied it, and few occasions saw it freely
performed.

As for households headed by third-generation adults,
the music heard was almost always entirely American. Some
homes contained a few recordings that could be considered
ethnic. These normally featured ethnic American performers. In as many homes one or two lonely foreign-language
recordings existed; but they were often shut away in the
limbo of cabinets and closets, among the family's forgotten
effects.

On the other hand, where the three generations lived together or close by, a sense of communal belonging lingered. Where the old language still rested on the tongue, as in Boston's Italian North End and a couple of New York City's Italian areas, old customs continued to surface and certain of the old music to sound. Whether this music will persist into the fourth generation remains uncertain. As yet few households include fourth-generation adults. Nevertheless, the several young people interviewed by the author demonstrate a diminished knowledge of their musical past-- save for what they, like any other Americans, hear fortuitously at the movies and on television. Little of the music that their great-grandparents tried to hand down is remembered. They may live in an ethnic enclave, see the elderly remnants of the pioneering generation about them, and encounter recent immigrants of varying ages. Yet ordinarily they conduct their own lives untouched by any of these. What ethnic music they overhear, as a rule, they listen to with inadvertence. American performers and works occupy their attention.

The complete jettisoning of ethnic music as cultural baggage seems only a matter of time. This sound is departing from the coffeehouses, restaurants, and bars. Radio, television, Muzak, and the coin-a-play phonograph hold sway. Now and again local or nationwide revivals occur; to be ethnic becomes fashionable again. Over the last two decades the author himself has participated in one cultural revival after another, those sponsored by individual ethnic groups, others by a confederation of Greater Boston societies. A few revivals may last longer than a year or two. But nostalgia, an attempt to fill a spiritual vacuum, and a yearning to allay a sense of loss cannot disguise the fact that the simple songs and dances from another era and another world fail to move to a contemporary beat. At first enthusiasm spurs on the renewed pursuit of the traditional music and dance of yesteryear. Performers rehearse faithfully and, at the end, present a cultural festival that, if the Muses are propitious, attracts a sizable audience. Regrettably, as often happens, each repetition of the festival finds less-enthusiastic participants and smaller audiences. [4]

Therefore, if we study the possibility for a reshaped ethnic identity, the answer as concerns music would seem to be that the chances are slender. The music brought to America from an extinct Old World has proved unmalleable. Additionally, ethnic American compositions in time have become so soggy with Americanisms that they are unsatisfac-

tory substitutes for the genuine article. Their erstwhile
proponents eventually abandon them altogether to take up the
musical pastimes of the American majority. One informative interview with a second-generation Italian-American
demonstrates this point. The speaker, a middle-aged grocer who had quit school when he was sixteen, was trying to
explain the music heard in his home:

> Sure we're your extended family and sure we live
> in East Boston with lots of other Italians, and we
> go to festas and all that stuff. But mostly we go
> to festas to eat and say "hello" to people you don't
> see all the time. My pa, he listens to his Franco
> Corelli records and goes wild over "Vurria Vasa!,"
> "Pecche'," and the rest of these Italian things.
> Me? I've gotten a kick out of Jerry Vale. He
> sings "Volare" and "Ciao, Ciao, Bambino" real
> good in English. And Perry Como, he's pretty
> good. A lot of the things he does sound Italian.
> But my kid? He used to like some things of
> Como and Sinatra and Prima. It's too bad when
> he got to be a teenager. He forgot all about them
> and went for that rock stuff. You know, with the
> electric guitars and noise. Nothing Italian about
> that. [5]

If the future travels along the cultural pathways just
delineated, then the son's son will almost certainly feel no
direct connection with the musical usages of his ancestors.
For this reason any exploration he may undertake of his
great-grandparents' music is likely to resemble an archae-
ological venture into a more or less remote period and
place. The music may embrace a significant part of his
family's past, but it remains closed off from his own present. Under such conditions any renaissance of ethnic music
involving him and his fellows will seem a trafficking in museum pieces. The sound offers a transitory enjoyment; it
scarcely can become part of a living tradition again.

Ethnic into American

Although allegiance to the old music has weakened, the in-
calculable contribution of immigrants to American musical
culture remains. The sheer numbers of first-, second-,
and third-generation ethnic Americans alone, their strength
concentrated in the influential urban centers of America, have

added weight to this contribution. Their preferences have affected the success and failure of every type of music heard in the cities, for audiences that once flocked to the Yiddish theater, Italian spettacolo, and Slavic and Magyar communal hall now comprise a huge portion of the crowds in attendance at American concert and stage productions. [6] In addition, and out of all proportion to their numerical strength in the total American population, the inhabitants of minority communities have supplied the world of music with dancers, singers, instrumentalists, and composers.

Though the music of the Old World disappears, some long-held attitudes toward life and the patterning of human activities continue even into the third generation. One that persists is the inclination to explore fully any present delights afforded by inconsistent fate. Scores of interviews have established the continuing existence of this guide to action. It was weakest among the Slavic-Americans interviewed, stronger among Greeks, Syrians, and Lebanese, and strongest among Jews, Italians, and Armenians. Undoubtedly these dwellers in the ethnic enclaves have reinforced the carpe diem attitude regarding the arts in America. At social functions the author has heard the admonition "Laugh; enjoy yourself" urged in all seriousness. The delights these men and women discover in music fully reflect a range of enjoyment reaching from eros to agape. Yet, however pleasureful the musical moment, lurking behind the gaiety we can detect a sad sensibility to human finiteness.

This is one view the new Americans have offered as an alternative to the self-denying Puritanism and optimism in the future that formerly shaped the American spirit but now seem defunct in the light of twentieth-century experiences. [7] The cities, where once was embraced a white Anglo-American Protestant outlook with some admixture of Irish-Catholic and German-Lutheran viewpoints, are slowly learning how to reconcile a mix of cultures and attitudes from many countries. [8] What is more, the ensuing cosmopolitanism and openness to a diversity of stimuli diffuse by almost imperceptible degrees into hinterlands where few foreigners reside.

America's music is vitally affected by the swirl of fresh ideas in the cities. In the first half of the present century recent immigrants and their descendants joined with black Americans to give popular music a mighty shove away from the sweet naivete and plain tunes, rhythms, and harmo-

nies of Anglo-Saxon America. When ethnic Americans ac-
ceded to the host culture, they desired and sponsored songs
that were more worldly-wise, passionate, and replete with a
zest for living. In part to please them, piquant rhythms,
sensuous melodies, and chromaticized harmonies replaced
the monoglot simplicity of the older style. Going some way
toward explaining the eventual dominance of this different
mode of expression is the fact that these men and women
made up a major portion of the auditors in the cities where
the music was first published, performed, and popularized,
and that their compatriots wrote and then publicized this music by repeated presentations in entertainment halls throughout the country, beginning with the years of World War I.
Moreover, the change took place at a moment in cultural
history when most urban Americans had become surfeited
with the existent sounds and wished a more varied musical
diet.

Further musical alterations introduced by ethnic Americans in conjunction with blacks were "blue" notes, rubato,
complex syncopations, polyrhythms, and improvisation.[9] All
one has to do is listen to a cantor "bend" notes as he sings
in one of the synagogal modes; a Hungarian violinist and
cimbalomist freely introduce flexible alterations of note values in a melodic phrase; a Greek vocalist persistently dis-
place metrical accents over the steady beat of an accompanist; a Syrian instrumental ensemble glory in the whirring
counterpoint of subtly inflected rhythms; or a Sicilian, Portuguese, or Armenian musician extemporize on traditional
melodic patterns to realize that black Americans have no
monopoly in these areas. In short, as ethnic music has
died out, several significant elements that characterized it
have been transferred into the music of the host culture.

Paradoxically, these humbly born people, many of
them the scions of unlettered peasants and impoverished
shtetl dwellers, helped articulate what Americans came to
accept as an up-to-date musical style representative of contemporary urban life and distinctive enough to dominate the
music of Tin Pan Alley, Broadway, and Hollywood musicals.
Moreover, the style was eminently exportable to the cities
of Europe. In America only the jazz and blues of blacks
and the country-and-western compositions of the rural South
and Southwest were able to carry on parallel existences and
command followings of any, though not always of equal, mag-
nitude.

Ethnic Americans have repeatedly asserted that the simultaneous excitement of mind and emotion is the sine qua non of all fine music. Here again is a standpoint many of the third generation, regardless of educational level, share with their grandparents. From 1966 to 1976 over a thousand college students from the Boston area, the descendants of immigrants, were canvassed on their musical preferences. About ten percent of them were music majors. All claimed that they attended operatic, symphonic, and chamber-music performances at least occasionally, some constantly. As expected, the highly charged symphonic compositions of Brahms and Tchaikovsky, the humanized operas of Verdi and Puccini, and the vividly colored descriptive works of Berlioz and Rimsky-Korsakov were favorites. Among twentieth-century composers, the striking Stravinsky of the early ballet suites; the romantically oriented Rachmaninoff; the melodious Prokofiev and Shostakovich; and the strong, emotionally vigorous, and folk-inspired Bartók pleased them. As for Americans, Gershwin, Copland, Bernstein, Menotti, and Hovhaness, all quite approachable composers, won easily.

In contrast, they voiced strong hostility toward twentieth-century neoclassicism, serialism, electronicism, musique concrète, and aleatory music. In experiments the author carried out over several years no amount of special instruction in, and repeated listening to, the dissonance in Ruggles's Sun Treader, the rational organization in Babbitt's Quartet No. 2, and the surprising juxtapositions in Cage's Fontana Mix could change the auditors' minds. [10]

Admittedly these reactions accord with the sentiments of most concert-goers. What makes the findings significant, however, is the much higher percentage of dissidents from the doctrines of the musical avant-garde, [11] when these young men and women are compared with young concert-goers of native American and northern and western European extraction, who also were asked their preferences. Owing to their concentration in cities and preferred attendance at urban colleges and universities, ethnic Americans like these have cast a pall on concerts of "difficult" music by being conspicuously absent from performances and compelling performers to serenade empty seats. Unconstructed romantics and relentless conservatives in their musical tastes, they may yet turn the cultivated-music picture around and encourage a wide return to personal feeling and recognizable melody in contemporary music.

Another facet of ethnic input into American culture is the repeated rise to general prominence of non-American songs that usually have had first currency in a minority group. The large number of these songs is extraordinary, especially when we discover that they are far more numerous than compositions favored by people from northern and western Europe. Most of these works have come to general notice, caught the fancy of a much wider public, and numbered among the "hits" of the day only after ethnic sponsorship and refitment with an English text. Nor is it altogether fortuitous that these songs first won extensive approval through interpretation by ethnic American singers. A correlation does exist, for example, between the high incidence of Italian works in American popular music and the multitude of successful Italian-American vocalists before the American public who are sympathetic to the music of their numerous compaesani--performers like Tony Bennett, Vic Damone, Perry Como, Mario Lanza, and Dean Martin. About forty percent of all foreign-language works that have become broadly accepted in America are Italian. Here follows a representative list of such compositions, enumerated by title, composer, author of the English text, and date of appearance as an American popular song:[12]

1. "April in Portugal" ("Caimbra e' una Lição de Amor"), Portuguese, m. Raùl Ferrão, Eng. w. Jimmy Kennedy, 1953.

2. "Beer Barrel Polka" ("Skoda Lasky"), Czech, m. Jaromir Vejvoda, Eng. w. Lew Brown, 1939.

3. "Bei Mir Bist Du Schön," Yiddish, m. Sholom Secunda, Eng. w. Sammy Cahn and Saul Chaplin, 1937.

4. "Botch a Me" ("Ba-Ba-Baciama Picina"), Italian, m. R. Morbelli and L. Astore, Eng. w. Eddie Stanley, 1952.

5. "Ciribiribin," Italian, m. A. Pestalozza, Eng. w. Rudolf Thaler, 1909.

6. "Don't Forget" ("Non Dimenticar"), Italian, m. P. G. Redi, Eng. w. Shelley Dobbins, 1953.

7. "Eh, Cumpari," trad. Italian, adapted Julius La Rosa and Archie Bleyer, 1953.

8. "For the First Time" ("Come Prima"), Italian, m. M. Panzeri, Eng. w. Buck Ram, 1958.

9. "Frenesi, " Spanish, m. Albert Dominquez, Eng. w. Ray Charles and S. K. Russell, 1939.

10. "Funiculî, Funiculà, " Italian, m. L. Denza, after 1880.

11. "Goodbye to Rome" ("Arrivederci Roma"), Italian, m. R. Rascel, Eng. w. Carl Sigman, 1955.

12. "I Want to Be Wanted" ("Per Tutta la Vita"), Italian, m. Pino Spotti, Eng. w. Kim Gannon, 1960.

13. "Lisbon Antigua, " Portuguese, m. Raul Portela, Eng. w. Harry Dupree, 1954.

14. "My Love, Forgive Me" ("Amore Scusami"), Italian, m. Gino Nescoli, Eng. w. Sidney Lee, 1964.

15. "Never on Sunday, " Greek, m. Manos Hadjidakis, Eng. w. Billy Towne, 1960.

16. "Oh, Ma-Ma" ("Luna Mezzo Mare"), Italian, m. Paolo Citorello, adapted Rudy Vallee and Lew Brown, n. d.

17. "On an Evening in Rome" ("Scott'er Celo de Roma"), Italian, m. S. Taccani, Eng. w. Nan Frederics, 1959.

18. "Play to Me, Gypsy, " Czech, m. Karel Vaček, Eng. w. Jimmy Kennedy, 1934.

19. "Return to Sorrento" ("Torna a Surriento"), Italian, m. Ernesto de Curtis, after 1905.

20. "Rose, Rose, I Love You, " Chinese, m. adapted Chris Langdon, Eng. w. Wilfrid Thomas, 1951.

21. "Santa Lucia, " Italian, m. Teodoro Cottrau, Eng. w. Thomas Oliphant, n. d.

22. "Tell Me That You Love Me" ("Parlami d'Amore, Mariu"), Italian, m. C. A. Bixio, Eng. w. Al Silverman, 1935.

23. "There's No Tomorrow" ("O Sole Mio"), Italian, m. Edoardo de Capua, m. adapted and Eng. w. Al Hoffman, Leo Corday, and Leon Carr, 1949.

24. "They Call It Love" ("Yala Yala"), Greek, m. adapted Dimitri Tiomkin, Eng. w. Ned Washington, 1961.

25. "Two Guitars," Russian Gypsy, adapted Harry Horlick, 1925.

26. "Vieni, Vieni," Corsican, m. Vincent Scotto, Eng. w. Rudy Vallee, 1937.

27. "Volare," Italian, m. Domenico Modugno, Eng. w. Mitchell Parish, 1958.

28. "What a Diff'rence a Day Made" ("Cuando Vuelva a Tu Lado"), Spanish, m. Maria Grever, Eng. w. Stanley Adams, 1934.

29. "Who'll Buy My Violets?" ("La Violetera"), Spanish, m. Jose Padilla, Eng. w. E. Ray Goetz, 1923.

30. "With All My Heart and Soul" ("Anima e Core"), Italian, m. Salve d'Esposito, Eng. w. Mann Curtis and Harry Akst, 1953.

31. "Yes, My Darling Daughter," Yiddish, w. and m. adapted Jack Lawrence, 1940.

32. "Yours" ("Quiérme Mucho"), Spanish, m. Gonzalo Roig, Eng. w. Jack Sherr, 1931.

The weight of the ethnic presence has materially assisted in carrying much of America's popular music in an altered direction. In the area of cultivated music it has encouraged the production of symphonic works and musical dramas that stress the human experience and attempt to meet their audience halfway. It has also contributed to the impasse binding the American avant-garde, unable to advance to bolder experimentation with scorn for the complaints of the uninitiated, unable to retreat to the more secure base of the acceptably familiar, which may win it the support of democratically oriented Maecenases and of auditors numbering more than a thimbleful. The question of whether humanity exists for music or music for humanity will eventually resolve in favor of the latter, if present ethnic opinion can sway the decision.

The Transmuted Teacher and Performer

From the beginning the immigrant community was a significant producer of musicians. Many of its members, unlike the majority of native white Americans, regarded music's pursuit as neither an enervating, nor a shiftless, nor yet a financially ruinous occupation. An intense enjoyment of song and dance was openly acknowledged. In contrast, a succumbing to the pleasure of music was oftentimes an uncomfortable admission to native white Americans, whose sensuously gratifying experiences had to be misrepresented as edifying and practical ones.

The inhabitants of the enclaves accepted the idea that musical success was achieved with difficulty. Yet to win a livelihood from music was a desired goal for the disadvantaged whose alternatives were the factory, the mine, or the other backbreaking jobs considered fitting occupations for them. Although children of immigrants expected to struggle to realize a musical calling, they felt that the effort was worth making. These youngsters flocked to music. Soon hundreds, then thousands of eager musicians spilled out into the greater American society.

Commentators repeatedly point out that several individuals from one family might become musicians. In a 1961 article Frank Hruby claims that most musicians from Cleveland who spread out into the rest of the United States came from the ethnic districts:

> Whole families were reared in the art. The Avellones, with innumerable cousins and nephews, fill half a page in the local musician's union book. The three Spitalny brothers got their start here before moving on to greater fame. The Hruby family, a father and eight children, toured ... in the early years of the century. Later, in the 30s, there were five Hruby brothers on the stage at one concert by the Cleveland Orchestra. So, too, with the Sholle family--a father and six children. Names like Hendershott, Fiore, and Patti are household words here, synonymous with music. [13]

Some families' commitment to music extended over two generations or more and to near and far relations. One of the most fascinating autobiographical reports submitted to the author came from a third cousin of Frank

Sinatra. She writes of a grandfather and his two brothers, who received musical instruction in Agrigento, Sicily; the grandfather on violin, mandolin, and guitar; one granduncle on violin; the other on cello. After emigrating to America all three played professionally--one granduncle in the Metropolitan Opera orchestra "under Toscanini." Among her parents' generation several became professional musicians. Her father, a composer, arranger, and pianist, had brothers and cousins who composed or arranged music for ballet, musical comedies, radio, television, and motion pictures. Several orchestras harbored other relatives, as instrumentalists and vocalists. Her generation of Sinatras numbered twenty-six, of whom eleven were already musicians. One was a member of the Baltimore Symphony, another of the National Symphony. At one time or another, cousins played in the bands of Stan Kenton, Woodie Herman, and Les Elgart, and in many New York musicals, including No Strings and Fiddler on the Roof. She and a cousin were guitarists specializing in folk and folk-blues performance; another cousin was studying to become "a classical pianist." None of the third generation, she adds, remembered much Italian music. Nor did it seriously interest them. Instead the Sinatras had penetrated into every area of American music, "popular, jazz, and classical," as instrumentalists, singers, arrangers, and composers. [14] Here certainly is an indication of the massive outflow of musicians from the ethnic community into the host society. In itself it amounted to a cultural contribution of awesome proportions.

The greater number of ethnic musicians, never wishing to venture far from their families, were satisfied with whatever modest rewards the local situation brought their way. They worked as music-teachers, performers in intra-urban ensembles, and managers of music stores. Thus Pasquale Armideo, born in Philadelphia in 1921, played and taught accordion locally and sold the instrument in his music store. Philadelphia-born Joseph Cavaliere taught piano; his son, violin. These three men, like other Italian-American musicians of that city, made a daily hegira from teaching room and music store to radio or television station, recording studio, theater pit, and nightclub. [15]

The odyssey of Frank Karas, a Bohemian-American from Chicago, charts several difficulties the ethnic musician encountered in the quest for a secure and satisfying position in music. When a boy, he studied violin with his father. But his first job was that of a meat-grinder in a cousin's

factory. An undaunted Frank Karas persisted in his efforts
to become a professional violinist. He yearned for a place
in a symphony orchestra. An installment loan permitted the
purchase of a fine violin. Formal lessons began. He continued to grind meat.

A "Wanted--Musicians for Army Bands" poster seemed
an "open sesame" into the music profession. Because he
was innocent in the ways of officialdom, he joined. His su-
periors ignored his talent for the violin and ordered him to
play the cornet and study reams of music he detested. His
enlistment ended, he married and returned to meat grinding.

Violin studies continued. Occasional employment with
small restaurant and theater orchestras came his way. At
one time he tried living as a full-time musician, turning to
cornet playing and private teaching to keep him solvent. Musical employment unfortunately proved irregular and unpredictable. Anxious for his wife and children, he finally gave
up the vision of himself seated in a philharmonic string section. Karas found a permanent position as high-school music-
teacher and band-director and concentrated on raising a family. One daughter eventually became a high-school voice-
teacher.[16]

Making Good in American Music

No simple explanation can encompass the motivations for en-
tering a music profession. Clarification begins with the reminder that no ethnic musician, from the most indifferently
trained popular singer who revels in a commonplace following to the intensively disciplined virtuoso for whom art is
life, can distance him- or herself altogether from background
and inner disposition, nor from the convictions issuing from
them. Assuredly the initial mover for some musicians was
a parent who loved or practiced music. In the instance of
Frank Karas, his father played trumpet; his mother sang.
Several important Jewish musicians claim cantorial fathers.[17]
Many Italian-American musicians had fathers and uncles who
sang or played violin, guitar, or mandolin.

Furthermore, an overwhelming number of these musicians were the dissatisfied offspring of parents not fully
settled in the New World or happy with their occupations
and surroundings. Malcontent impregnated young wills with
a drive for eminence. A few aspired to the highest musical

ranks and the adulation and speedy profits they hoped would
reward their struggles. These rising ethnic musicians,
more than most native Americans, had the capability and
choleric humor for abandoning self-restraint where the situation required it. They perceived that extravagant feeling
and its flamboyant display did help a performer catch the
public's attention.

Sammy Cahn, successful lyricist, says the ghetto was
"the cradle" of musicians, "because the struggle is to get
out of the ghetto, " whether the musician is Jewish or Italian. 18 Examining more particularly the Italian-American
singers who came from the urban enclaves, Gay Talese
states: "Many Italo-American boys of his [Frank Sinatra's]
generation were then shooting for the same star--they were
strong with song, weak with words, not a big novelist among
them ... yet they could communicate bel canto. This was
more in their tradition, no need for a diploma; they could,
with a song, someday see their name in lights ... Perry
Como ... Frankie Laine ... Tony Bennett ... Vic Damone
... but none could see it better than Frank Sinatra. "19

Successful young musicians usually were aggressive
strivers, hardened to fortune's knocks and accustomed to
self-display. During his growing years in the ghetto, Eddie Cantor recalls, he boldly pushed himself forward whenever the opportunity arose, at a bar-mitzvah, in a saloon,
and during amateur night at a local theater (where he and
other performers "got hardened to the hook and took it as
part of their performance"). 20 If his neighborhood crowd,
on New York City's Henry Street, needed a champion to
outrival an entertainer from another street, he was ready
to oblige:

> On Sunday, Henry Street needed somebody to be
> proud about. A neighboring but rival village
> called Jefferson Street was welcoming one of its
> famous sons. Roy Arthur had achieved greatness
> as a member of Bedini and Arthur, a team of
> jugglers and travesty artists that played the top-
> line theaters, and when he descended to the slums
> to visit old friends, the haughty Jefferson Street-
> ers paraded their man of renown along the length
> and breadth of Henry Street. Henry Street, deeply
> humiliated, almost buried itself with shame in its
> own ash-cans, for it had no one worthy of compar-
> ison. So they trotted me out. "Go on, Eddie, do

your stuff!" We were on a stone stoop overhung
with bedding, and the audience jammed the steps,
overflowing to the curb. I did not want to be
asked twice. I cast one swift appraising eye at
Arthur and went into my act as if he and the rest
of them had paid for admission. The crowd ap-
plauded and cheered lustily. It was a triumph for
Henry Street.[21]

Of the second-generation Italian singers Henry Gans
writes that exhibiting oneself to impress others was a trait
they acquired while youngsters. Its purpose, in the Italian
communities he studied, was "to create mild envy among the
rest of the group." Naturally the most talented became entertainers. No one objected to their boys becoming popular
singers, "for this is an opportunity for self-display. In
fact, most of the successful white singers today [ca. 1960]
are Italians, and it is no accident that they are purveyors
of songs. Italians have done well in contemporary popular
music, because it emphasizes the development of an individual image and style more than technical musical skill."[22]

Performers from whatever ethnic group learned to
think on their feet, to bluff things out if necessary. Eddie
Cantor says he and Jimmy Durante first won jobs as singing
waiters supposed to be able to reproduce any requested song.
Even when they had never heard of the requested work, they
brazenly improvised one on the spot in order to satisfy a
customer.[23]

As illustration of the self-attitude of ethnic performers, including many cultivated musicians, Wladziu Liberace
admits his own uncomfortableness over the word "artist,"
which suggested to him one who lives in isolation, indulging
himself, creating what he pleases, and believing the public
be damned. In contrast, Liberace tried to establish a rap-
port with others, for by pleasing an audience he pleased
himself.[24] His statement shows him true to his background,
as the ethnic household and community in which he and others like him grew up rarely permitted a faulty awareness of
reality. At home and on the streets people crowded all
around, denying the individual the luxury of a withdrawn self.
Escape into an ivory tower of aloofness from one's audience
was nearly an impossibility for musicians coming out of such
an environment.

This attitude also helps explain the demand for Hungarian instrumentalists in New York City and elsewhere and the success of bands led by Guy Lombardo, Carmen Cavallero, Teddy Powell (Alfred Paolella), and others. The Guy Lombardo Orchestra, for example, had a considerable public following as well as a pronounced influence on the makeup and playing style of other American bands. By 1970 some hundred million of the orchestra's recordings had been sold, despite the panning of critics who felt the ensemble should aim less at gladdening the spirits of vast audiences, more at artistry to satisfy the tastes of the discriminating. Typically, Guy Lombardo and his brothers, who played and sang with the orchestra, ignored the critics and continued to espouse "the sweetest music this side of heaven." It was a winning formula. [25]

A lesser number of ethnic instrumentalists breached the obstacles between them and permanent positions in symphony orchestras--long a German monopoly. The lack of financial means for study and the absence of fine music in many ethnic homes kept the numbers low. However, the anti-German feelings generated by World War I and the closing-off of immigration did much to open the ranks. Edward Ross, in 1914, already observed Italian players starting "to break the musical monopoly" of the Germans. [26] Jews, Italians, and Hungarians, first the immigrant generation, later the descendants, began to supply orchestras with personnel. [27] By the 1930s the New York Philharmonic's makeup was reflecting the huge Jewish and Italian presence in New York City; the Cleveland Orchestra, the considerable Hungarian presence in its area; and the more modest Utica Orchestra, the musical Italians in large local supply. [28]

A few fortunate ethnic Americans have won worldwide reputations as outstanding virtuosi. [29] Yehudi Menuhin, born in New York City in 1916, to penniless descendants of Palestinian Jews, surmounted all obstacles to become a renowned violinist. [30] Another eminent violinist, Ruggiero Ricci, was the son of an Italian immigrant, who had to struggle to cope with the expenses of a large family by working as a day laborer, fruit-picker, and foundry welder in California. Luckily, outside financial assistance arrived to help the talented young Ruggiero along the road to the stardom he eventually achieved. [31]

No less worthy contributions to American cultivated music came from opera and art-song singers born to recent immigrants. Robert Merrill, Maria Callas, and Rosa

Ponselle--Jew, Greek, and Italian--were three outstanding
vocalists. Their start was not easy. Robert Merrill says
that his singing career began with his wangling every kind
of entertainment job. He performed at Jewish weddings,
bar-mitzvahs, and other social affairs. Resort hotels provided him with summer work. During his hire at Schroon
Manor, an Adirondacks hotel, Merrill learned invaluable
lessons for the future: "I danced and acted and helped with
the scenery; I learned my trade there. The stage may have
been outdoors, and it may have starred burlesque comedians
and musical-comedy players, but I learned how to feel at
home in front of an audience. "32

A handful of promising musicians had the good fortune to win some financial support from their local community. For example, Lina Pagliughi, a coloratura soprano
born in New York City and brought up in North Beach, San
Francisco's Italian section, would have failed if her poor
father, a mattress-maker, had the sole expense of her training. But from her eleventh year, in 1919, she was considered una bambina prodigiosa and became the "darling of North
Beach. " Nine years later the Italian colony clubbed together
and collected money for her further education. At the end,
three thousand dollars was raised, which enabled her to continue study in Italy and eventually achieve her opera-singing
goal. 33

The instrumentalists and singers who found general acceptance revealed personalities and preferences to Americans
that were splinters from the ethnic experience. In popular
music, far more than in cultivated music, the injection of
self into performance is expected and deemed praiseworthy.
Inevitably the ethnic performer's successful appearances were
imbued with the colorations taken on in childhood and youth.
Irving Howe states: "Jolson's large-gestured sentimentalism,
Jessel's gritty wisecracking, Brice's yente grandeur, Cantor's
frantic shakiness: all these were spin-offs from immigrant
experience. "34 We read of Frank Sinatra's loyalty to several
aspects of Italian music making. He himself explains that he
always retained an Italian love for the sound of strings. Because he "was always crazy about strings for a vocal background, " he left the Harry James band in 1942 and joined
Tommy Dorsey, as the latter had "a vast band complete with
string section, which gassed me. "35 Sinatra's larger-than-
life gestures toward casual acquaintances, demand for respect, unwavering adherence to friendships formed in his
earlier years, sudden rages, and unstinting largesse have

been termed "real Italian" by many Italian-Americans.
These facets of his personality became part of the legend
endearing him to thousands of American enthusiasts, who
rushed to glimpse him and buy his recordings. During his
prime a lover's intimacy bathed his delivery of a song,
each note a token of limitless affection. This manner of
singing also can be denominated as "real Italian." When
hundreds of other singers started to imitate him, the manner was converted into a singing style perceived as truly
American.

The Ethnic American Composer

Composers writing for their ethnic society managed occasionally to win an audience beyond the confines of the subculture. In most such instances the composers introduced
Americanisms into their music that their ethnic group, at
least the second and third generation, accepted. One composer of this kind, Frank Yankovic, was the son of Slovenian immigrants. Born in Davis, West Virginia, in 1915,
Yankovic grew up in Cleveland. In childhood he learned
Slovenian songs from his mother. At the age of nine he
took up accordion playing and furthered his acquaintance
with Slovenian music. Seven years later he formed a
three-piece neighborhood band to play for Slovenian dances,
receptions, and community functions. At twenty-six years
of age he opened a café in Cleveland and serenaded his customers mainly with polkas, some of them his own compositions. He commenced recording his own works, which soon
won popularity among his own people--the "Rozica" polka
(Daisy polka) and the "Jutranja Zarija Valček" (Twilight
Waltz), to name two. While a few such pieces won American recognition, his biggest successes among Americans
were Slovenian-American dances more largely influenced by
American popular idioms, compositions like the "Just Because" polka and the "Blue Skirt" waltz.

Typical of most ethnic American writers on the history of their subculture, Gerald Govorchin, in Americans
from Yugoslavia (Gainesville, 1961), and Marie Prisland,
in From Slovenia to America (Chicago, 1968), devote a
great deal of printed space to musicians. Frank Yankovic
appears prominently in their pages.

The dilution of a native style with American idioms
is unexceptional in the music making of second-generation

musicians. Nor is Frank Yankovic's fame as the "American
Polka King" an isolated instance of a musician winning enthusiastic backing in a subculture then going on to gain a
larger support from the general American public.

More importantly the ethnic communities produced not
just one or two but many songwriters who succeeded in dom-
inating twentieth-century American popular music, as well as
cultivated composers who numbered among those appealing
most to the concert-going public. From the first decades
of the century the ascendancy of Jews, followed by Italian-
Americans, grew over every phase of popular-music production. They were the composers, lyricists, performers, im-
pressarios, publishers, and music-retailers. Other nationalities, though in lesser numbers, also participated in providing Americans with musical compositions--musicians with
Hungarian, Czech, and Polish backgrounds. Now and again
emerged a composer or lyricist from the less numerous
Armenian, Greek, and Syrian-Lebanese communities, who
would contribute a work or two destined to achieve considerable recognition.

Though the songwriters from these diverse cultures
might not employ the actual language of their ancestors, nor
consciously imitate the musical styles they had heard about
them as they grew up, implicit nevertheless in their compositions were the cadences and sounds of their heritage. The
juxtaposition of vulgarity and insight, the chattery interplay
of sardonic wit and feisty paradox, the inwardly felt com-
monplaces of existence, and the intense romanticism that
delineated the musical activities of the ethnic communities
were captured in countless works intended for the ears of
all Americans. Few pieces reveal a direct use of ethnic
material; more of them show an alchemization of things remembered so that every musical phrase seems to pulsate
with new life.

These composers were usually city-born and reared.
They thought in terms of the city and had no encumbering
connection with the older types of popular song rooted in
America's rural past and values. Their arrival on the music scene coincided with America's changing emphasis from
country to city, from national isolation to international cooperation. Because they tried to speak for the millions en-
trapped in brick, concrete, and asphalt, they won the affection of town-dwellers. Because their music sounded with
few overtones referring back to Anglo-Saxon tastes and in-

stead accommodated the desires of a motley constituency, these composers attracted a vast following amongst the millions of descendants of recent immigrants, who had felt themselves disenfranchised in the world of Yankee-dominated popular entertainment.

When these musicians created new works, they dipped into memories made up of the singing and dancing of the contemporary musical stage and dance hall, the "hot" playing of jazz musicians, the recent successes of Tin Pan Alley, and the rhythms and tones sounding in immigrant neighborhoods. Various writers on music have asserted that nothing escaped the notice of these composers: the noise of auto horns, the rumble of traffic, the peculiarities of speech common to different urban districts, the conversational rattle of passersby, vendors' cries, the wheeze of hurdygurdies, the raw entertainment of dives, the chants of synagogue and church, and the patter-songs of children. At one point or another these intonations inspired the melody, propelled the beat, and shaped the lyrics in the compositions offered to the twentieth-century American public.

The irony is that in finding their authentic, contemporary voice, these musicians alienated quite a few among their parents' generation, who sensed a betrayal of their traditions and beliefs. Their children, as some oldsters saw it, had helped themselves to whatever ethnic materials were congenial and gone on to fashion a separate kind of sound. They were certain the allurements of Broadway and the seductions of the dollar had led their sons and daughters away.

To elderly conservatives some American songs written by ethnic Americans extolled the selfish amorality and lasciviousness inherent in the city life beyond the enclave's barriers. Yet to their offspring these compositions spoke truly about modern life. The emancipated young woman might boldly sing an early Laska-Kern ditty, in which she invites a man to hug, squeeze, and kiss her.[36] The modern young man proved his contemporariness by delivering an ode to the American cocktail, contained in a second ethnic American composition where alcoholic indulgence, sensuous living, and constant love-making become concomitants of a tropical paradise.[37]

A reassurance of sorts was proffered the disturbed elders, when, in a third ethnic-American song, they were told that the liberated young woman might wear flapper's clothes, use heavy makeup, dance in cabarets to all hours of the morning, and flirt; yet, at heart, she was really very much like her mother, and as virtuous and sensible.38

Nevertheless, the divergence of taste remained. The young ethnic Americans writing the new music and those enjoying it did have a regard for their forebears' culture but found standing still an impossibility. Meanwhile, whether unknowingly or with intent, they introduced snatches of ethnic musical style into the works they wrote. Harold Arlen, trying to explain his songwriting manner and its possession of features seemingly common to blues and jazz, says that his father, a cantor, was his influence. His father had noticed a likeness between synagogal and black music. He himself heard elements similar to what his father sang when he listened to jazz and gospel song. Arlen regarded his father as one of the greatest improvisers he had ever heard and was certain that cantorial music "must have had some effect on me and my style."39

With regard to George Gershwin, Isaac Goldberg writes that the composer frequented the Yiddish theater during his youth, so naturally introduced a "Yiddish element" into his own music. Gershwin became "increasingly conscious of the similarity between the folk song of the Negro and of the Polish [Jewish] pietists.... In Funny Face there is a tune [that] begins Yiddish and ends up black. Put them all together and they spell Al Jolson, who is the living symbol of the similarity." Later Goldberg claims that the song "Swanee" "was born right in Our [Tin Pan] Alley, by pseudo-Dixie out of Judaeo-Gypsy Land.... It's Jewish, it's Gypsy, it's white, it's black."40

The Ethnic Composer's Contribution to American Popular Music

If we study Gershwin's music closely, Goldberg's meaning becomes clearer. For example, the first eight measures of the refrain in "My One and Only," from Gershwin's musical Funny Face, shows an undoubted connection with Hasidic song,41 as seen in the syncopated rhythm, the freely altered note values, the chant-like recitation on the repeated B-flats, the slide of a half-tone down to a', and the rise of a minor third to d"-flat, and the adherence to the Mi Sheber-ah mode (B-flat C D-flat E-flat F G-flat A B-flat).42

Again, "My Man's Gone Now," from <u>Porgy and Bess,</u> contains a keening wail on the word "ah" that resembles a <u>Kaddish</u> recitation. [43] And the well-known refrain of "Fascinating Rhythm" utilizes eight-note rhythmic patterns showing some enchantment with Hasidic dance. [44] Certainly Gershwin's close friend Isaac Goldberg believed such relationships were more than accidental.

Goldberg tells of meeting Gershwin one day. The possibility of Gershwin's writing an opera on a Jewish subject came up:

> A couple of years ago, shortly after he had contracted with the Metropolitan to write an opera, and he was considering <u>The Dybbuk</u> as a libretto, we were standing before his Steinway. He picked up one of his note books.... "Look this over," he said, pointing to a few melodic phrases unsupported by any harmonic structure; they suggested a slow lilt and might have been anything from a buck-and-wing to a dirge. He glanced at the notes and was soon constructing not only a music but a scene. This slow lilt gradually assumed a hieratic character, swinging in drowsy dignity above a drone. The room became a synagogue and this was the indistinct prayer of those to whom prayer had become a routine such as any other. The lilt had acquired animation; it was the swaying of bodies of the chanters. An upward scratch in the note book suddenly came to life as a Khassidic dance. And those who know what khassidic tunes can be like in their wild, ecstatic abandon, know also that the Khassid, like his brother under the skin, can grow wings and walk all over God's heaven. [45]

If we consider the works of Italian-American composers next, correspondences between some of their popular songs and Italian music are quite evident. Indeed they are sometimes too obvious. After Vincent Rose's "Avalon" (1920) became an American hit, the Italian publisher Ricordi sued this Italian-American composer for infringement of copyright, claiming that Rose's melody was lifted from "E lucevan le stelle," in Puccini's <u>Tosca.</u> Rose lost the case.

Ted Fiorito did not try to conceal what others readily perceived. His hit "Laugh, Clown, Laugh" (1928) he admitted was a free adaptation of the principal aria in Leoncavallo's <u>Pagliacci.</u>

We find, however, that most songs by Italian-American composers have no easily recognizable connection with Italian music. At first glance their style seems completely indigenous to America. But with careful scrutiny of the music, the relationship becomes manifest. Rather than take the easier path and show the link between ardent Neapolitan songs and American compositions like Russ Columbo's "Prisoner of Love" (1931),[46] a more instructive course is to study the kinship of the gentle, folk-toned southern-Italian songs with American works that are similarly featured.

What we have in mind are traditional pieces like "Se Fossi una Viola, " "La Capuana, " "Tiritomba, " and "Margarita. "[47] Their melodic phrases tend to move downward or in a balanced S curve with median resting places. Tessituras usually are low or medium. No phrase sweeps upward to a high climactic note. The tunes make considerable use of the third of the scale, which softens the force of the melodic passages. A further softness results when the harmony is obscured by movement back and forth between a major tonality and its relative minor, and when the music shifts to the flat side of the home key or to the tonic minor through the lowering of the third, sixth, or seventh of the scale.[48]

A similar impression of gentilezza is produced by Carmen Lombardo's "Sweethearts on Parade. "[49] The amiable mood of the work is established from the beginning when, as is typical of one class of Italian folksong, the melody begins on 5 of the scale, rises stepwise to 2, and closes with an understated feminine cadence, 2-1. A mild suspense results from the prolonged V^7 of the first three measures; but release comes gently in measure four with the tonic resolution on the second beat, as if a person in a moment of quiet contemplation had breathed slowly in and out.

By measure nine the music has moved temporarily to the flat side, with a modulation to the subdominant. Then, after a brief flirtation with the supertonic minor in measure thirteen, the music cadences on the dominant and introduces the refrain. Yet the sound continues benign. The refrain's start is a skip from the third to the sixth of the scale, followed by a downward step to five. Underneath, the supporting harmony is a tonic chord shaded by the intrusion of the submediant. A nicely calculated mood of graciousness results owing to the deemphasis of the

major tonality and the constant swing of the tune below and
above each long note--c", g', and a'. The edge of the passage is further blunted by the melody's stressing of the
third of the scale, finally even resting for almost two measures on this note. The nonaggressiveness of the music is
also conveyed by the downward movement of the melody.
Later the music modulates again into the subdominant, and
again into the supertonic minor, before closing in the home
key. For most of the piece the tessitura remains low or
medium.

Another work cut from a similar Italianate fabric is
"I Only Have Eyes for You, "50 by Harry Warren, an Italian-
American bootmaker's son. Once more a quiet gentleness is
achieved. The opening phrase of the refrain forms an S
curve that winds twice between d' and g' before dissolving
into triplets and coming to rest on b', the seventh of the
scale. Triplets of this sort, employed to add a lilting
gracefulness to the phrase's continuation, is a device well
known in Italian song. Indeed the triplets of measure three
are a simple variation on the melody of measure one, and
as such make up one of the standard vocal figurations of
Italian singing. The touching on the supertonic and the introduction of the flatted sixth and seventh of the scale aid
the music's easy flow and feeling of delicacy. It is fascinating to see the composer drain away the assertiveness of
the final b" by avoiding the expected dominant seventh and
inserting instead the mediant minor.

Another instructive passage begins in measure
eighteen of the refrain. Here a four-measure phrase is
repeated in mellower fashion by the addition of a flat before the a'. There follows a slide into the key of the tonic
minor, with the vocalist sounding a suspenseful sigh on b"
flat and a" flat, over an ambiguous altered chord (the augmented subdominant seventh, which is followed by the dominant seventh), an artifice straight out of Italian song.
Again the tune hews almost entirely to the vocalist's low
and medium range.

A final example by an Italian-American composer is
Henry Mancini's "Moon River. "51 The music is simplicity
itself; the texture translucent. A gently rocking accompaniment figure fills in the pauses of the melody. Again a
major-relative minor duality softens the tonality, in measures one and two and in measures eight and nine. Distinguishing the tune is the sweet poignancy of the seventh note

of the scale heard as an appogiatura above the subdominant chord in measures three and five, an expressive device already one hundred years old in Italian music. Also to be noted is the introduction of flats, beginning with measure ten. The highest note of the tunes is d". As expected the melodic passages move downward--from d", from b', from g', and from c".

Notwithstanding the several comments just made about the appearance of non-American features in their music, ethnic American composers did write indigenous works intended to have a general appeal, not narrowly conceived pieces based on a minority's tastes and traditions. Their most accepted songs did employ forms of expression characteristic of, and originating naturally in, the contemporary America they knew.[52] Yet, as one ethnic society or another nurtured these composers, the reference to the music favored in the foreign communities as the origin of some important and ostensibly American musical concepts is essential to understanding the new immigration's impact on New World culture. Moreover, it is a credit infrequently cited in the writings about twentieth-century music in the United States.

In contrast to composers growing up in America, musicians of European birth and training who came here did not always speak with the same consistent or assured American voice. Karl Hoschna, for instance, was a Bohemian composer who arrived in America during the operetta vogue. He immediately busied himself writing compositions exploiting the popularity of the song styles associated with these European-oriented musicals. A piece he wrote for the operetta <u>Madame Sherry</u> (1910) is one example. In triple time and a minor tonality (both exceptional in American popular song), the song "The Birth of Passion" might just as well have been written in Vienna or Prague. A novelty number written for the same operetta, "Every Little Movement Has a Meaning of Its Own," belongs less to the febrile American era then unfolding, more to the comfortable years with no hint of the vexatious that typified music in the earlier 1890s. The lyric provided by Otto Hauerbach is said to be provocative and suggestive.[53] But this is so only if a Victorian atmosphere is predicated and the text alone bears the burden of the proof--for the music, while pleasant, never "hots up" the listener. In another Hoschna work, "Cuddle Up a Little Closer" (1908), originally conceived for vaudeville, the composer tried to incorporate American musical elements. However, the song approximates an indigenous sound only through the syncopated inflections of American vocalists.

Ira and George Gershwin make an amusing commentary on the operetta song in their early "The Real American Folk Song" (1918), [54] in which the lyric states that however attractive and tuneful this importation may be, it has not the infectious swing, foot-tapping beat, or unconstrained abandon of true American song. It is devoid of the sounds that interested the Gershwins and other ethnic American composers attuned to the local scene. Somewhat naively, the lyric goes on to equate folksong with rag, praising its exuberant syncopations and cheerful energy and describing it as a pick-me-up to ward off depression and stimulate the spirit.

When ethnic composers first attempted to thrust themselves forward and win recognition, dialect songs were much sought after. Therefore they busied themselves in this area. [55] Typical is Al Piantadosi's "My Mariuccia Take a Steamboat." The composition was popular and encouraged Irving Berlin to capitalize on its fame by writing "Marie from Sunny Italy" in 1907. In other ethnically centered songs Berlin divided his attentions between Eastern Jew and Italian: "Yiddisher Nightingale," "Yiddle on Your Fiddle," "Goodby Becky Cohen," "That Kazzatsky Dance," and "When You Kiss an Italian Girl," "Antonia, You'd Better Come Home," "My Sweet Italian Man," "Dat's-A-My Gal." [56] Edward Marks, well-known music publisher, says the popularity of such songs was highest in the first two decades of the century. "The cycle closed in 1920" with the Morgan-Swanstrom piece "The Argentines, the Portuguese, the Armenians, and the Greeks." [57]

Distant cousins to these songs continued to appear from time to time, like the broken-English-inspired but highly sophisticated "'S Wonderful" (1927) of Ira and George Gershwin, and the good-humored burlesque of Armenian speech "Come On-A-My House" (1950), the brainchild of William Saroyan and Ross Bagadasarian.

Perhaps to exploit a subject of established popularity, prove how American they were, or repeat the musical lessons learned in public school, ethnic composers were also responsible for a host of songs that extolled one or another section of the United States: "How's Every Little Thing in Dixie" (1916), words by Jack Yellin, music by Albert Gumble; "San Francisco" (1936), words by Gus Kahn, music by

Bronislau Kaper; and "Oklahoma" (1943), words by Oscar Hammerstein II, music by Richard Rodgers. [58]

Only a short step needed to be taken to arrive at the patriotic song, a vein also worked most assiduously. Without question one of the most famous American songs of all time is Irving Berlin's "God Bless America," composed in 1918 but withheld from the public until Kate Smith took it up in 1938 and hurtled it to national celebrity. It helped resolve some of the political uncertainties of the time and gave succinct musical expression to the loving concern for one's country that so many Americans had found difficult to articulate for themselves.

For the quieter, profoundly personal feelings welling up in people during those unsettled years, composers provided mood pieces like Peter De Rose's "Deep Purple." Conceived in 1934 as a piano work, the music was arranged for orchestra by Domenico Savino in 1935. But only after Mitchell Parish wrote a lyric to the music in 1939 and the song received the sponsorship of Larry Clinton's orchestra and Bing Crosby's voice did the composition really become popular.

Because of their continuing appeal to Americans from different generations and their versatility as vehicles for singers of various attainments, several songs by ethnic composers have had an unexpected longevity. Thus James Monaco's "You Made Me Love You" was first sung by Al Jolson in 1913. Quickly the young Fanny Brice incorporated it into her repertoire; Ruth Etting did the same. The song brought Judy Garland to public notice in 1937; a few years later Harry James had his first great success with this composition. Later the song was featured in several motion pictures, among them the 1942 Syncopation, with Jackie Cooper and Connie Boswell, the 1942 Private Buckaroo, with the Andrews Sisters, and the 1955 Love Me or Leave Me, with Doris Day. Finally, in 1963, the piece was selected by ASCAP for its All-Time Hit Parade. It was pronounced one of the sixteen compositions which the public had most favored in the present century. [59]

The staple of the popular-song industry is the love ballad in its many varieties. In 1913 Al Piantodosi published his overly sentimental "Curse of an Aching Heart"; in 1925 Ted Fiorito, the affecting "I Never Knew That Roses Grew"; in 1926 Erno Rapee, the "schmalzy" "Charmaine";[60] in 1933 Harold Arlen, "Let's Fall in Love"; in 1937 Danny Di Minno and Carmen Lombardo, "Return to Me" ("Ritorna a Me"); in 1942 Phil Tuminello, "Can I Steal a Little Love?"; and in 1959 George Khoury and Phil Battiste, "The Sea of Love." Here, too, the ethnic composer was preeminent.

The ethnic American singers who popularized songs like the ones cited--such vocalists as Tony Bennett, Dean Martin, Tony Martin, Perry Como, Vic Damone, Al Jolson, Julius La Rosa, Al Martino, and Frank Sinatra--were specialists at manipulating all the emotional stops for putting over a song. Popular-song composer and performer--each was incomplete without the other. Together they formed a formidable alliance for the furtherance of their common interests.

As testimony to the importance of these composers to American musical culture, we should read the Variety Musical Cavalcade, 3rd edition, 1971, pages xii-xiii. These pages contain a list of all-time American "Golden 100" hits, which includes titles of songs from the nineteenth and twentieth century. "Continuing performance, longevity, and reactivation from time to time" were the tests for inclusion. Of these one hundred songs about sixty were composed in the twentieth century by ethnic Americans--an astonishing statistic that establishes beyond doubt the momentous significance of the new immigration in America's cultural life.

Art Music and the Ethnic Composer

The ethnic composer's entry into cultivated music was neither as easy nor as uncomplicated as into popular music. Training had to be more thorough and prolonged, therefore more costly and demanding of patience. Compositional guidelines remained befogged, since contemporary musical styles tended to be individually arrived at or free variations on internationally recognized practices. The questions of subjectivity versus objectivity, tonality versus polytonality, triadic harmony versus free note combinations, musical tones versus sounds of undefined pitch, traditional performing groups versus electronic machines and taped sounds, and perceptible compositional structures versus formal happenstance had to be resolved on a one-person basis. Then, when the composition was completed, it contended for attention with thousands of other works from the distant past to

present times and from every nation. The followings for
contemporary artistic works were usually sparse, the financial rewards niggardly. Most compositions, so painfully
gestated, experienced sudden deaths.

Given these problems, the surprising conclusion we
reach, after examining lists of twentieth-century American
composers, is that at least forty-five percent of these musicians came from the new immigration. [61] The largest
number had East European Jewish backgrounds; next, Italian.
A further surprise follows when we discover that predomi-
nant amongst the most successful contemporary works--in
terms of audience interest, sale of recordings, and frequency
of performance--were the compositions of ethnic Americans.

In attempting to explain the comparative success of
these works when compared with the creations of other American composers, the author offers several observations gar-
nered from published studies of ethnic composers; meetings
with prominent musicians like Aaron Copland, Alan Hovhaness,
and Walter Piston;[52] conversations with acquaintances of
Leonard Bernstein, Vittorio Giannini, Norman Dello Joio,
Paul Creston, and others; and interviews with young composers of ethnic descent living in the Boston area. There exists the possibility of oversimplification, of errors that may
loom if the main line is traveled upon and the branches of
inquiry ignored. Nevertheless, a summary of the major
sentiments of composers is attempted in the hope it will il-
lumine understanding. For the most part the following statements apply more to second-generation, less to third-
generation, composers. In addition, it should be noted that
a small but highly visible group of Jewish composers are
stalwarts of the experimental and unorthodox musical camp.

A first observation concerns how closely ethnic musicians continue to adhere to significant ways of thinking about
music and its purposes that for years have guided tastes in
their ethnic societies. On the whole the composers with
whom we are concerned see themselves as conservators,
creating music springing from ageless principles. Generally they object to the stance of segments of the avant-garde
that holds musical standards to be entirely relative to time,
place, and the individual--the result being, in the opinion of
ethnic composers, works of incomprehensible eccentricity.
To ethnic musicians the preoccupation with the unusual pro-
duces works replete with unnatural sounds that fail to communicate anything to their audience. In particular they find
the notion of "Art for Art's sake" abhorrent.

They themselves prefer subject matter of interest to their listeners, projected in understandable and enjoyable tones. The highly dissonant and experimental procedures of "advanced" composers they disavow. In contrast, their own works reveal compositional methods that have evolved from the cultivated music of the past, to which they feel bound by strong persuasions of its viability. They like writing well-ordered compositions articulated through intelligible structures, functional harmonies, and sensuously appealing melody. [63]

For reasons like these, Vittorio Giannini's works demonstrate an Italianate faith in melody's ability to touch an audience. His symphonies and his operas The Harvest and The Taming of the Shrew flare up with the emotions of a closet romantic. Another Italian-American composer, Norman Dello Joio, is an exponent of warm, expressive sound: "What I strive for most of all is the complete confidence, the lyric quality, the feeling for line we find in Verdi."[65] He believes strongly in tradition and the music he heard during his growing years. Therefore his style contains components derived from plainchant, Italian song, opera, colorful dance suites, Broadway, and jazz. These several elements converge in his 1949 New York Profiles: "The Cloister," "The Park," "Grant's Tomb," and "Little Italy." His cultural roots are also manifested in works like the Ricercari for piano and orchestra (1946), the opera The Triumph of St. Joan (1950), the cantata To Saint Cecilia (1959), and the Antiphonal Fantasy on a Theme by Vincenzo Albrici (1966) for organ, brass, and strings.

Paul Creston, another Italian-American composer, believes in the employment of lyrical melody, dance rhythms, and tonality in his works, as can be seen in his Symphony No. 2, op. 35 (1944). He reveals his Catholic affinity in the Symphony No. 3, op. 48 (1950), entitled "The Three Mysteries," which depicts the emotions arising in those who witnessed the Nativity, Crucifixion, and Resurrection of Christ. The thematic basis for the work is medieval plainchant.

In the 1970s a third-generation composer of Sicilian ancestry, Thomas Pasatieri, has won the acclaim of opera audiences in several large American cities distant from the Atlantic seaboard. The enmity of New York critics espousing the cause of one or another of the advanced composers has left him indifferent. Pasatieri grew up in Flushing, New York, and studied composition at Juilliard under Vittorio

Giannini. The composer states: "I learned from Giannini that the most important element of a successful opera is communication of the drama through an expressive line. "66 Descended culturally from the compositions of Puccini and Menotti, his operas The Seagull, premiered in Dallas, and The Black Widow, in Seattle, are praised by proponents as effective, lyrical, richly emotional, and entertaining theater. 67 Pleased with his reception by opera-lovers and aware of the criticisms directed at his conservative stance, Pasatieri has explained himself as follows: "I'm only continuing a musical and theatrical tradition that has already been plotted out for me--I'm not a revolutionary. I feel serialism and more recent avant-garde practices just don't work for musical drama. Now some of us are going back and starting on a different road, the one music was meant to travel. "68

Turning next to Walter Piston, in several conversations with the author this composer has said he feels little cultural connection with his Italian forebears. Nor had he any fondness for the rhapsodic emotionalism found in some works by contemporary ethnic composers. Yet the labeling of his own work as frigid neoclassicism by a few critics, he claims is a falsehood. He has gone the gamut from the popular-toned and sprightly The Incredible Flutist to the warmly ruminative Symphony No. 2. We discover his link with the other composers discussed here in his often-stated attempt to capture musically the dictates of his feelings, but subject to the discipline of his mind. His compositions are given an intelligible structure through harmony used functionally and based on a tonal center, and through permutations of melody and rhythm that are an outgrowth of a two-hundred-year-old symphonic tradition. He has had a tremendous influence on younger composers, as a teacher at Harvard University and as an author of admired textbooks on harmony, counterpoint, and orchestration.

Among the best-known Jewish musicians, Leonard Bernstein (a student of Piston) has written works pleasing to most concert- and theater-goers. Jazz, Broadway, Weill, and Gershwin are in the background of his highly successful stage works On the Town (1944) and West Side Story (1957). Acknowledgment of his Hebraic ancestry is found in his intensely emotional and orchestrally vivid Jeremiah Symphony (1944) and the Kaddish Symphony (1963). Both these compositions owe something to older Jewish composers--Mahler, Bloch, and Copland.

As for Aaron Copland, one of the handful of truly outstanding twentieth-century American composers, only his trio Vitebsk, Study on a Jewish Theme (1929) makes any overt reference to Judaism. Yet most of his works, even the so-called difficult and abstract compositions divorced from a jazz or folk framework, indicate a deep involvement with the concerns of a common humanity, which is so characteristic of liberal Jewish thinking and the motivating force for enlightened Jewish social action embracing Jew and non-Jew alike. Chiming with the observations of other music commentators, Marion Bauer has said of Copland's music in general: "The quality of his melodic line frequently is Hebraic [though] he seldom consciously seeks out Jewish folk melodies."[69] Of the Copland Piano Variations (1930), described by some as abstruse and puzzling, Richard Dobrin speaks with great insight:

> It is a work which gave expression to the same fierce emotions that so many writers were displaying in their new books. Some critics said that the work spoke of the thousands of alienated, homeless men now taking to the road. Others were reminded of the music of both the Negroes and the Jews, both dispossessed people who are symbols of uprootedness. The elements of Copland's work to which they referred were the ambiguous thirds, sixths, and sevenths of the Negro blues as well as the declamatory leaps of Jewish synagogue music. The moods evoked by this work change swiftly from the fierce and angry to the naive, warm, and tender.[70]

Indicative of Copland's real feelings, when Agnes de Mille first asked him to write the Rodeo ballet music, he demurred and asked: "Couldn't we do a ballet about Ellis Island? That I would love to compose." Her thoughts distant from the millions of recent migrants to America, Agnes de Mille rejoined: "You can go to hell!"[71]

Nevertheless, in Rodeo (1942), Appalachian Spring (1944), A Lincoln Portrait (1942), Fanfare for the Common Man (1944), Symphony No. 3, and other works written after the mid-thirties Copland appears as a creative writer intent on capturing humankind's "deepest feelings about life," through works that engage successfully with an audience. Indeed for him "every move toward logic and coherence in composing is in fact a move toward communication."[72] The

orientation and some of the melodic materials employed in
these five works are American. The themes, however, are
peculiarly Jewish--the yearnings of the rejected cowgirl for
acceptance, the visions of a martyred fighter against human
oppression, the socio-religious rituals of an isolated society,
the ode to brotherhood, and the grand summation in symphonic form of the nobility inchoate in humanity. More conjec-
tural is Dobrin's suggestion that "Copland's music speaks
also of the longing for the open country felt by a people who
were for centuries forbidden by law from ownership of
land."73

Perhaps the American composer manifesting the greatest ethnic consciousness is Alan Hovhaness. Though his
mother was of Scottish descent, Hovhaness identified with the
culture of his Armenian father, especially after 1940, when
he became organist at the St. James Armenian Church in
Watertown, Massachusetts. His music derives from the
liturgical chants based on ancient Armenian melodic formu-
las and from the complex Armenian rhythmic system with
its subtle organization of extremely small note values into
traditional patterns. His works also contain a plenitude of
sounds akin to Armenian secular song and dance. Instead
of striking listeners as music of interest only to Armenians,
his symphonies, Armenian rhapsodies, Avak, the Healer,
and The Mysterious Mountain have met with wide audience
approval. This response supports the argument that music,
however restricted its references, is unlike a specific ver-
bal language, which requires a rendering into one's own
tongue to be understood. Rather, music consists of more
generalized and exceedingly pliant matter that is more uni-
versally possessed and enjoyed.

During the twentieth-century hundreds of compositions
have employed discordant sounds that strike the large majority of listeners as hideous or ludicrous. Few of these
works have helped men and women to realize themselves
and to define their place in the several worlds of fantasy
and reality they inhabit. Without meaning to disparage the
quality of the music making, certainly Roger Sessions, Carl
Ruggles, and Milton Babbitt cannot claim many partisans of
their formidable idioms. Montezuma, Sun Treader, and
Composition for Synthesizer please only a limited clientele.
On the other hand, some compositions by composers of
ethnic descent, like Porgy and Bess, And God Created Great
Whales, and Quiet City, have prospered, while most of the
remainder have at least received respectful hearings from

audiences. Though popular acceptance in itself is not necessarily a measure of quality, it does indicate the impact that
ethnic composers have had on the general American public.

Music in the Ethnic Society of the Late Twentieth Century

What are the chances for survival of any sort of musical
ethnicity? Earlier in this chapter a continuous decline in
musical ethnocentricism was noted. The conclusion reached
was that the music brought to America by the immigrants
had gradually ceased to play a vital role in ethnic American
lives. A study of the state of the ethnic American society in
the late twentieth century permits several further observations.

Recent migrants from isolated transoceanic rural
areas and a few remaining first-generation ethnic Americans
who continue to associate with each other exclusively, it is
true, still seek out the traditional music of their birthplace.
In contrast, the second- and third-generation men and women
who have penetrated into the host society have turned to
American popular music (or, for some of the highly educated,
to Western cultivated music) for their entertainment needs.
For a minority of today's second-generation Americans,
neither an ethnic nor yet an American music appears capable
of producing pleasure.

As for some third-generation young men and women,
they search constantly for music that can arouse and gratify
them completely. Each new style in popular music is pursued intensely, like an ephemeral beauty to be relished immediately before it dies. Every new singing star is granted
a moment's worship before being supplanted by another:
Elvis Presley, Bob Dylan, Paul Anka, The Drifters, The
Four Seasons, Ricky Nelson, Bobby Vinton, Jimi Hendrix--
the list is endless.

After examining the recent autobiographical reports of,
and the record of interviews with, young people of this type,
we reached several conclusions concerning their upbringing.
Most of them claimed parents who no longer spoke the language of the immigrant generation. Their fathers and
mothers had uprooted all connection with ethnic culture and
paid attention to none of the arts. An Italian-American
youth, who had immersed himself "in rock and pot" and
surfaced to find his life a shambles, describes his growing

up in an "empty" house where the Italian language and customs had been given up, where music was regarded as noise and a "waste of time and money." His brothers and sisters all felt cheated and denied ties with any sort of social community. Possibly owing to anger, they had ceased being Catholics and left home as soon as they were able.[74]

A young man of Russian-Jewish descent says that his parents and other Jews he knew, in their ardor to become Americans, had tried to cleanse their homes of most vestiges of "Jewishness," without the substitution of anything else. At the same time they forced their children to take music lessons and study "classical music," because this was "the thing to do," not because anyone had a love for music. "To this day [1969], I have yet to hear any Jewish music in any Jewish home, with the exception of religious rites such as the Sadir [sic]." He and his friends grew up in "a musical void," came to dislike cultivated music, and turned to modern jazz and rock, both because their parents hated these sounds and because an outlet for restlessness was needed. Each year something different in popular music won their allegiance.[75]

A third-generation Lithuanian-American provides a final example. Again ethnic music remained unheard at home. The parents presented no other music as an alternative. "With a flick of a [radio] switch," the children sought their own music. "We immediately began to form our own points of view concerning music, which led farther and farther beyond the Lithuanian culture of songs." A strident, overamplified rock sound was the only music they wished to hear.[76]

Other threads running through the accounts of today's third-generation men and women who are completely cut off from ethnic music and entirely into rock compositions are parents of divergent cultural backgrounds, childhood homes outside the ethnic community, growing years without grandparents, fathers (and usually mothers) who worked long hours and spent little time with the children, and days on end of their family receiving visits from and calling on no one. Owing to such conditions the young people were culturally displaced persons seeking haven in whatever musical port would welcome them.

Nevertheless, the group just described remains only a minority of the total number of third-generation ethnic Americans studied by the author. Most young people growing

up in the 1960s and 1970s claim families held together by
shared affection. Grandparents lived with them or nearby.
Family social gatherings that included grandparents, parents,
and relatives were frequent. Their parents' homes were
located either in an urban ethnic community or in a suburb
where many "of their own kind" also resided.[77] The enjoyment of food and music were common. Heard were traditional and popular ethnic compositions, selections from
Broadway musicals, and nonabrasive American popular music. Sometimes they listened to opera and other works from
the cultivated repertoire.

One Jewish woman who came from such an environment writes that her grandparents loved the Yiddish theater;
her parents, American "operettas and Broadway shows"; and
she, any music but rock.[78] Though brought up during the
rock-music era, several other correspondents state they
could scarcely abide this kind of sound. For example, a
young man of Portuguese descent writes of the Portuguese
popular music and the Broadway musicals like The Sound of
Music that he had heard at home and continued to listen to.
Now (1970), he states, he finds pleasure in some "classical"
works. Rock music he dislikes.[79]

A like antagonism to "rock and roll" and other forms
of "jungle music" is expressed by a young woman whose
grandparents and parents loved and exposed her to Armenian
and cultivated music. Secure in her family's affections and
brought up among Armenians, she had learned to enjoy the
culture of her community. She spoke its language, sang its
songs, and performed its folk dances. At the same time,
she had taken piano lessons and studied artistic music.[80]

An inability to speak the grandparents' language was
not always a deterrent to an enjoyment of ethnic music.
One woman observes that though she had difficulty understanding Italian, she had learned at an early age to love
opera from her grandparents' example, and, later, Broadway musicals like those of Rodgers and Hammerstein. She
remained indifferent to rock music. Undoubtedly the closeness of her relationship with her family more than compensated for her mother's refusal to have Italian spoken at
home:

> My earliest recollections involving music are wed-
> dings and family gatherings overflowing with wine
> and Italian folk songs. Although I never knew quite

what they were all about, I remember my grandfather's laughter at the gesturing singers and the
tears in his eyes over the ballads. Italian music
always conjures up a nostalgic feeling in me. My
childhood was spent mostly with my grandparents
who lived with me. From them I learned of opera:
Pagliacci, Madame Butterfly. Since my mother
insisted that her parents speak English, I never
knew the language--but the music said enough without words. 81

Although the examples just cited make no reference to
them, the ethnic American popular singers and the mixture of
American and ethnic music they performed had a strong at-
traction for many of these young people. This was especially true for youths who passed most of their daily lives in one
of the ethnic enclaves still persisting in the late twentieth
century: "Young Italians always seem to be talking about
their favourite Italian artist. They go out of their way to
see such performers as Enzio Stuarte, Connie Francis, Ser-
gio Franchi, Louis Prima, Al Martino, and Jerry Vale whenever they come to Boston. "82

Not all young people who fancied ethnic music, Broadway musicals, and the sweeter love ballads were averse to
rock compositions. Though none expressed a great attachment to the more raucous compositions, a few confessed to
having lived through a "rock phase, " and even more mentioned a continuing enjoyment of the less assertive popular
songs of their own day. Describing her precollege years,
an Italian-American from the North End of Boston says that
her entire family encouraged her to take music courses,
sing in choruses, and join musical-theater clubs while she
was in public school. At the same time parents and grandparents coaxed her into studying the accordion. During her
adolescence many happy evenings passed with her playing,
and the adults singing, Italian songs: "I got the greatest
pleasure of all out of watching the expression of pride on
my grandfather's face as he sang along with my playing. "
But departure to attend a distant college and the influence
of new non-Italian friends caused her to spurn the music of
her childhood in favor of the latest rock works. She tried
to model herself after her friends. She also felt psychologically alone and "longed to return home. " After living away
for two years she transferred to the Boston campus of the
University of Massachusetts in order to return to her life in
the North End. She still liked the milder rock compositions,

particularly those modeled after folksongs, but had contentedly resumed playing the music dear to her family. [83]

Concerning most third-generation men and women, we
conclude that while they felt sympathetic toward their grandparents' traditional songs and their parents' musical favorites from the thirties and forties, they themselves had grav-
itated toward the popular and jazz works of recent times.
Normally the conservative rather than the farfetched sounds
of their own age prove most attractive to them. For family
reunions and communal celebrations, however, they still re-
vert to the music that had permeated their growing years.
Typically, two youths have written that mainstream jazz and
the smoother rock works of the 1970s are what they volun-
tarily listen to, although they also remain proud of their
Italian musical heritage. [84] They consider operatic arias
and Neapolitan songs pleasant concomitants of their early
lives, which they fondly remember and occasionally bring
to life. Their regular fare is American music.

A regard for historic truth necessitates a consideration of several countercurrents that have gathered strength
in the latter half of this century. Without question a sense
of ethnic identity still persists in America's cities. In part
it feeds on the continuing experiences of racial, economic,
social, political, and cultural discrimination in the United
States. One instance is the Japanese-American community's
feeling of outrage at the treatment accorded its members
during and after World War II. A music different from
what the Issei had known, but still an ethnically delimited
one, arose to encompass their recent experiences and to
remind Americans of their professed regard for democracy.
Thus was born the Japanese-American Citizen's League
Hymn, with a lyric written by Mr. and Mrs. Larry Tajiri:

> There was a dream my father dreamed for me
> A land in which all men are free--
> Then the desert camp with watch towers high
> Where life stood still, mid sand and brooding sky.
> Out of the war in which my brothers died--
> Their muted voices with mine cried--
> This is our dream that all men shall be free!
> This is our creed, we'll live in loyalty,
> God help us rid the land of bigotry,
> That we may walk in peace and dignity. [85]

Another instance is provided by the passions that

continue to be aroused among Italian-Americans over what
they see as the rank injustice of the Sacco-Vanzetti execution. In the summer of 1977 Michael Dukakis, the Greek-
American governor of Massachusetts, issued a proclamation
questioning the fairness of the court procedures that led to
the death penalty. Yankees rose up to excoriate the governor for his action; Italian-Americans, to upbraid the Yankees
for their obstinate defense of legalized murder and their persistent intolerance toward the new immigrants. In September
the author came upon a gathering of Italian-American students on the campus of the University of Massachusetts at
Boston. An emotional discussion of the Sacco-Vanzetti case
was taking place. One youth, guitar in hand, began singing
the following words to a singsongy, modal-minor tune:

> Do not think that I'm still stupid,
> Kissing ass at every chance.
> To you I'm still that unwashed Dago,
> Give'm a monkey, make'm dance.
> You don't love me, I don't love you,
> So we're even, it's o.k. with me.
> This land is yours, it's also mine,
> So don't mess with my liberty. [86]

In part the persistence of ethnicity is owing to transoceanic conflicts. The strife between Greek and Turk over
the island of Cyprus has encouraged at least a few Greek-
Americans to update the old klephtic songs that commemorate
the struggle for independence from the Turks. Among the
Jews the rise of Zionism and the establishment of the Israeli
state despite adversity is depicted in numerous musical compositions. This had led in recent years to the substitution
of contemporary Israeli works for the formerly prevalent
Yiddish songs and dances. [87] While Jews turn to Israel, the
once-culturally-somnabulant Arab-Americans, aroused in
some measure by the Middle East conflict and in greater
measure by the abusive racial jokes aired on television and
the denigratory racial cartoons in American newspapers,
have awakened to their own traditions. They vigorously
dance the modernized steps of a remodeled dubke, attend
hufles (evening musicals featuring one or two musicians
from Lebanon and Syria, and American vocalists of ethnic
descent singing in a manner best characterized as Arab-
american), and travel to national pan-Arabic conventions,
which combine ethnic camaraderie with musical entertainment. [88]

For similar reasons Ukrainians and Lithuanians, embittered by the Soviet rule of their homelands and anxious over what they see as the cultural genocide threatening their people, doggedly persist in trying to convince their young to join dance and music ensembles that keep alive their special identities.

Three other factors encourage continuance along ethnic ways. First, a pride in non-Anglo-Saxon ancestry and traditions is now considered compatible with American patriotism. The shame and dread of ridicule that caused many settlers to conceal their customs from American eyes no longer inhibit the grandchildren from enjoying what music they will. Furthermore, acculturation has not led to complete integration. Places of worship, clubs, business partnerships, and social circles still tend to divide along ethnic lines. [90] Finally, the host culture provides frequent reminders of one's non-Anglo-Saxon heritage that are positive in tone--like the celebration of Columbus Day, musicals on ethnic subjects (such as Fiorello! and Fiddler on the Roof), opera performances, imported films and domestically sponsored films with foreign settings, the political pundit's and newspaper editor's constant references to the voting habits of hyphenated citizens, advertisements of travel agents and international airlines, and news reports of worldwide goings-on.

A few respected writers on ethnic matters claim that America has filled the stomachs of the descendants of the new immigrants but left their souls empty. Therefore for considerable numbers of these people the maintenance of ethnicity continues in order to provide a warm sense of belonging to something. At the same time they fend off the feeling of social isolation and personal disorientation that has spread like a sickness throughout the entire American society in recent years. [91]

Participation of some third-generation ethnic Americans in cultural activities underlines a selfsameness that bolsters morale. The "One World" outdoor fair sponsored annually by New York City's Armenians and the St. Vartan Church; the renewed Japanese interest in celebrating Buddha's birth and the Buddhist All Soul's Day (the Obon festival) in costume, song, and dance on the San Francisco streets; and the return of Croatian-Americans to the observance of their wine festival (the Berba), complete with kolo dancers and tambouritsa orchestras, can serve as examples of this renewed interest in one's background. [92] In New England there is enthusiastic Polish sponsorship of the Boston-based Krakowiak Polish Dancers, 110 men and women with their own thirteen-piece orchestra. A striving for authenticity in costume, dialect, ways of producing tones, and choreography has won this group the unstinting praise of the Polish government and the highest awards that Polish cultural committees can bestow. [93]

Commenting on the renewal of ethnic roots, Irving Howe, in a 1977 issue of Newsweek, interprets the movement back as a "last hurrah" of ethnic sentimentalism, because it romanticizes the color and ignores the suffering in early immigrant life. On the other hand an array of analysts of the contemporary ethnic scene discover a new ethnicity arising among the third- and fourth-generation Americans, one that will "express the experience of their generation, not of an earlier generation," and will treat "past history only as a means of illuminating the present, not as an ideal to which they must return. The new ethnicity is oriented toward the future, not the past."[94]

A description of one Armenian-American's experiences helps put this new ethnicity into perspective. In an autobiographical report and an interview[95] the young man states he was born and brought up near Boston and outside the Armenian community. His family had little to do with its American neighbors, possibly because his mother spoke English with difficulty and the family's religion, cuisine, and "good times" were different. Family members looked different, too. His school acquaintances made him uncomfortably aware of his sallow complexion, black curly hair, and other physical characteristics that set him apart from his classmates. He took up the trumpet and joined the school band to satisfy his love for music and to gain some measure of acceptance. But as time passed he and the rest of his family felt increasingly isolated, outsiders to the American life surrounding them.

Suddenly, in a moment of extreme exasperation, they gave up suburban living and moved to a house located in the midst of the Waltham-Watertown Armenian community. Immediately they involved themselves in Armenian-church affairs and the social and political activities in their new neighborhood. Friends were made. "The feeling of isolation" disappeared.

He and a few other young musicians formed an up-
dated Armenian band made up of a clarinet, trumpet, guitar, and drum. They performed both "American songs"
and modernized versions of traditional Armenian songs and
dances, in order to give pleasure to themselves and the
people they knew. Often they met with other "Mid-Eastern
players, Greek, Syrian, and Lebanese." On occasion, all
the players would make up a large ensemble to perform for
functions in each other's community. The young man claims
his prime motivation was not the preservation of Armenian
music. "I do it for myself," he explains. "If later on my
children want to buy what I'm doing, o.k. If not, that's
o.k., too. They'll have their own lives to lead."

Some government officials and social workers are
still concerned over the mental and emotional confusion of
immigrants who feel cut off from the majority of Americans,
and continue to try to help them bridge the gap between an
ethnic and American way of life, thinking that the encouragement of pride in one's culture would ease the continuing
problems of transition. One result is that in various cities
folk festivals that invariably include the music and dance of
the several nationalities in their municipalities are still
held. The more enlightened educators still introduce songs
of ethnic origin into the public-school curriculum to help
stem the drift of children from parents, a practice that had
begun early in the century.

In the 1980s it has become clear that present-day
Americans of ethnic descent do have unmet psychological
and cultural needs, which the larger American community
fails to satisfy. Nor can today's ethnic communities always
provide a means for easement, since these settlements have
diminished in number and size. The fact that most men and
women of ethnic extraction no longer live compactly together
has made the continuance of cultural institutions difficult.
Nevertheless, some music and dance groups have been
formed that draw their membership and support from ethnic
Americans living in widely scattered areas. This is the
case with Boston's Krakowiak Polish Dancers, whose members rehearse weekly, though they must drive in from Rhode
Island, New Hampshire, and western Massachusetts. The
participants realize that what they do is not part of a living
tradition. They regard themselves as caretakers of long-
gone customs. More important, participation in the ensemble's activities links members not merely with each other
but also with a psychologically useful past. "After all,"

said one member, "my ancestors weren't ... dancing square
dances. They had their own dances." Asked whether nostalgia had brought him back to Polish music and dance, he
replied, "Sure it has. But it's a lot more than that. I see
the empty living around me; everyone going their own way,
doing not too much; you know, getting into a beer and television routine and that sort of thing. But I'm where I belong, with people I belong with [sic]. Besides, I want to
remind all Americans of what we Polish people have that
we're proud of."[97]

Today the inner barrenness felt by Americans of
every description has encouraged a good many of them to
join umbrella organizations where an exploration of worldwide cultures is the principal objective. The Mandala ensemble, which draws members from the Greater Boston
area, is one of these organizations. The Arabic, Bulgarian,
Scottish, English, Greek, and Philippine music and dance
that the group studies and performs mirrors the cosmopolitanism aspired to by the participants. "Everyone comes
from a culture of some kind. And if you haven't one or
can't remember one, you can share someone else's. When
you come down to it, we're all Greeks and Bulgarians and
English and what have you!" went the conversation with members on a February evening in 1972.[98]

That the investigation of ethnic cultures not one's own
also goes on outside the Boston area is made evident in a
1960 article on a French-Canadian ensemble, Les Feux Fol-
lets, from Montreal. The group was to present a program
of Bulgarian dances and songs at the seventeenth annual con-
vention of the American-Bulgarian League, in Toronto. The
earlier verdict of a Bulgarian audience in Montreal had been:
"Incredibly well done." Michael Cartier, the group's founder
and director, was said to have made a thorough study of the
cultures of a number of countries.[99]

The complete sociocultural boiling-down of all new
immigrants in the American melting pot so that a uniform
hundred-percent Americanism is the only part that remains
has proved a false theory. What has actually resulted is a
stew-like mixture of heterogeneous ingredients, none of them
ready to dissolve yet all of them adding to the flavor of the
whole. Nor has the doctrine of cultural pluralism proved
tenable, as the various ethnic cultures have neither continued
in an untouched state nor discovered a way of stopping their
change into forms so unlike their transoceanic antecedents

that complete alteration may be a question of time.[100] For that matter neither has the dominant Anglo-American culture remained static; an immense aesthetic distance separates the present age from that of Washington, Franklin, and Jefferson.

Cultural changes in the last half of the twentieth century take place at a time when the old certainties from which consensus was derived have crumbled. Among the problems awaiting resolution are the divergences in culture and outlook of the American citizenry. The need exists for propitiating a variety of heretofore neglected constituencies. Fortunately a start has been made in reconstituting American cultural expression so that it includes a greater number of human perceptions and modes of aesthetic expression. The many ethnic Americans active in popular and cultivated music have made vital contributions to this reformation.

What has already been accomplished fails to satisfy a small but determined group of third- and fourth-generation Americans. In recent conversations with scores of them-- college students, amateur participants in the cultural activities sponsored by several of America's International Institutes, and professional musicians--there is agreement that almost all the published studies of American musical culture they have read either ignore, give passing mention to, or denigrate the cultural impact of the new immigration. They concede that the musical traditions brought here by the settlers are vanishing. They insist that the remembrance of these men and women and what they valued and accomplished must not also disappear.

Moreover, they see their grandparents' and parents' mental and emotional shock, experienced during the years of absorption into American society, as past history. They themselves feel confident they occupy rightful places in the American scheme. If Americans can celebrate their Plymouth Rock and Colonial Williamsburg, why then can't they also celebrate their Ellis Island and the tragicomic Lower East Side? A diversity of roots has nourished the civilization growing in the New World. An honestly restated nationhood, they claim, must valuate impartially all origins, all lines of development, without judging the quality of one from the standpoint of another.

What seems undisputable is that American civilization, at least in the foreseeable future, is still in the grip of a cultural dynamism that can be explained only in terms of

the interaction of a huge array of forces. Every ethnic
group retaining a more or less distinct identity exerts its
influence on the whole. Through today's men and women of
ethnic descent, as through their predecessors, proceeds a
ceaseless transmission of musical traits and ideas into the
American mainstream, resulting in ever-new configurations
in the way Americans as a whole express themselves.

Nostalgia and a search for self-identity have often
been cited as reasons for a reexploration of one's musical
heritage. They have also led to a restatement of those
qualities that distinguish the present-day descendants of the
new immigrants from their fellow Americans. To these two
reasons must be added the determination to make certain
the ethnic component is never again excluded from any narration of America's cultural history. For almost a century
many old-time Americans have belittled, and some ethnic
Americans have blushed over, the nonconformist ways of
life of the millions who arrived in the United States around
the turn of the century. Those times are over. An increasing number of ethnic Americans are adamant about
discovering their own set of cultural artifacts that truly
articulate their relation to the past and their place in the
present. What is more, whatever position they carve out
for themselves they expect all Americans to honor. They
recognize the importance of music in the lives of their ancestors. They expect that it will remain an essential but-
tress to their concept of themselves.

NOTES

●───────────────────────────────────

Chapter 1

1. These conclusions are based on the interviews conducted by the author and on the autobiographical reports submitted to him by students at the University of Massachusetts at Boston. See also "A Century of Immigration," Monthly Labor Review, 17 (1924): 4; William S. Bernard, "Indices of Integration into the American Community," International Migration, 11 (1973): 96.

2. H. C., American, "Autobiographical Report," May 1972, p. 2. In this regard see Gerald R. Leslie, The Family in Social Context, 3rd ed. (New York: Oxford University Press, 1976), p. 340.

3. Louis Adamic, "The Bohunks," American Mercury, July 1928, p. 324.

4. An explanation volunteered by a second-generation Polish man who worked beside the author in a Hampden Street factory owned by the author's father. On the same point see William I. Thomas and Florian Znaniecki, The Polish Peasant in Europe and America, 2nd ed. (New York: Knopf, 1927), Vol. I, p. 123.

5. This was related by a student at the University of Massachusetts at Boston during a private discussion of his autobiographical report for Music 242, January 1969. He was of Albanian descent. The Irish-American woman had married his uncle.

6. The young man reported this as his uncle's response. The student had been asked by the author to question the older man about this episode, which had taken place the previous summer.

7. Isaac Goldberg, George Gershwin, supplemented by Edith Garson (New York: Ungar, 1958), p. 18.

8. Hutchins Hapgood, Types from City Streets (New York: Funk & Wagnalls, 1910), pp. 283-84.

9. Rev. Enrico C. Sartorio, Social and Religious Life of Italians in America (Boston: Christopher, 1918), pp. 20-21.

10. Henry Pratt Fairchild, Greek Immigration to the United States (New Haven: Yale University Press, 1911), pp. 62-63.

11. Peter I. Rose, "Foreword," in Joseph Lopreato, Italian Americans (New York: Random House, 1970), p. viii.

12. Nathan Glazer, in White Ethnics, ed. Joseph Ryan (Englewood Cliffs, N.J.: Prentice-Hall, 1973), p. 169.

13. Konrad Bercovici, It's the Gypsy in Me (New York: Prentice-Hall, 1941), p. 75. In The Children of the Poor (New York: Scribner, 1892), p. 10, Jacob Riis writes: "Irish poverty is not picturesque in the New World. . . . Italian poverty is."

14. Zona Gale, "Robin Hood in Jones Street," The Outlook, 26 June 1909, pp. 439-46.

15. Margaret Blake Alverson, Sixty Years of California Song (Oakland: Author, 1913), pp. 162-66.

16. Bill Hosokawa, Nisei, the Quiet Americans (New York: Morrow, 1969), p. 77.

17. Daniel Chauncey Brewer, The Conquest of New England by the Immigrant (New York: Putnam, 1926), pp. 169-71.

18. College Songs, new and enlarged ed. (Boston: Ditson, 1887), pp. 44-45.

19. The words and music are by Emma Washburn; Irwin Silber, Songs America Voted By (Harrisburg, Pa.: Stackpole, 1971), pp. 146-47.

20. For further information on this song see Lester S. Levy, Flashes of Merriment (Norman: University of Oklahoma Press, 1971), pp. 129-30; the music is reproduced on p. 158.

21. The corner was close to the dividing line between the Greek and Jewish settlements and the then general business area of Boston. The song's text is the author's reconstruction, based on his father's and uncle's recollection of similar verses they had heard on the streets of the South End. What was actually taken down was more like:

Greasers one and all,
Greasers peeing downstairs hallway,
Wetting the wrists with the head
And smelling up the place, maybe you think its flowers
    in a bed.
Greeks and Jews are stupid and slimy,
Speak a noise, "Itchy Koo";

No one speaks right worth a damn,
Who needs you, get out of the country of Uncle Sam.

Reluctantly, the author admits he was one of the children who, on at least one occasion, was thrown a few pennies and chased after someone not of his own extraction, chanting a derogatory verse of this sort.

22. Musical America, 15 October 1898, p. 6. The more usual reaction was to move away quickly.

23. Emil L. Jordan, Americans (New York: Norton, 1939), p. 372.

24. The words and music are by Charles B. Lawler and James W. Blake (New York, 1894).

25. The words are by Blasee, music by Albert Harry (Philadelphia, 1868); see Levy, Flashes, pp. 59, 88-89.

26. Jacob A. Riis, Out of Mulberry Street (New York: Century, 1898), p. 44.

27. The Immigrant Jew in America, ed. Edward J. James et al. (New York: Buck, 1907), p. 241.

28. Musical America, 8 July 1911, p. 8.

29. Musical America, 17 May 1913, p. 13; 31 May 1913, p. 13; 9 August 1913, p. 19.

30. Alter F. Landesman, Brownsville (New York: Bloch, 1969), p. 58; Rudolph J. Vecoli, in Divided Society, ed. Colin Greer (New York: Basic Books, 1974), p. 229. The criticism of the Italian peasants as uncultivated boors was offered by a Florence-born and -educated resident of Boston, who was an amateur pianist and a member of the Dante Society.

31. Though some truth resides in the accusation made in Peter Roberts, Anthracite Coal Communities (New York: Macmillan, 1904), p. 53, from which the quotation comes, that Slavic miners visited saloons after church on Sunday, where they gambled freely, sang ribald songs, danced, and got drunk, similar conclusions were unfairly reached concerning the way most immigrants enjoyed Sunday with music, dance, and socializing.

32. Constantine Panunzio, The Soul of an Immigrant (New York: Macmillan, 1921), p. 144; Maurice Hindus, Green Worlds (New York: Doubleday, 1938), p. 215; Ravage, An American, pp. 247-49.

33. C. T., Italian, third generation, "Autobiographical Report," May 1969, pp. 2-3.

34. D. V., interview of December 1949. When questioned, few of the older immigrants spoke objectively. Most injected some emotion into their description of their American experiences. The "Americans" making fun of the "Khris-

tos Anestes" were apparently of Irish extraction.
35. R. S., Italian, third generation, "Autobiographical Report, " May 1971, p. 3.
36. See Charles F. Marden and Gladys Meyer, Minorities in American Society, 3rd ed. (New York: Van Nostrand Reinhold, 1968), pp. 20-22.
37. The chewing tobacco was supposed to catch the free lint in the air and keep it from getting into the lungs.
38. He is possibly referring to the klephtic songs that became widespread in Greece during and after the struggle for independence from Turkey.
39. D. V., Greek, first generation, Interview, December 1949. The name is fictitious.
40. Michael Novak, The Rise of the Unmeltable Ethnics (New York: Macmillan, 1972), pp. 36, 47-48.
41. Abraham Mitrie Rihbany, A Far Journey (Boston: Houghton Mifflin, 1914), p. 154.
42. Maxine Adams Miller, Ali, A Persian Yankee (Caldwell, Ida.: Caxton, 1965), p. 123.
43. S. N., Italian, third generation, Interview, April 1969. E. R., a third-generation Portuguese-American, in an "Autobiographical Report" he wrote in April 1971, states on page 8: "When my mother ... was a teenager she recalls having bought a record that she liked very much, 'It Ain't Gonna Rain No More.' The first time her stepfather heard it he tore it from the Victrola, smashed it, and said, 'If it don't rain no more you ain't gonna eat.' He had many of the supersititions of the old country and thought modern music a disgrace. For many years after the incident my mother never sang or played records in his presence. "
44. E. G. Stearn, My Mother and I (New York: Macmillan, 1918), p. 47.
45. Ibid., pp. 50-51.
46. Lou D'Angelo, What the Ancients Said (Garden City, N. Y.: Doubleday, 1971), p. 77.
47. H. J., Armenian, first generation, Interview, December 1949.
48. M. K. Argus [Mikhail K. Jeleznov], Moscow-on-the-Hudson (New York: Harper, 1951), pp. 23-24.
49. This was, for example, certainly true of Boston's South End settlers. Concerning the conservatism of immigrants see Maldwyn Allen Jones, American Immigration (Chicago: University of Chicago Press, 1960), p. 231; for one explanation of the peasant mind see Louis Adamic, Laughing in the Jungle (New York: Harper, 1932), p. 12.
50. Bruno Roselli, "The Italians, " in Immigrant Backgrounds, ed. Henry Pratt Fairchild (New York: Wiley,

1927), pp. 98-99. Some of these traits, of course, were common to Jews and Asians. For example, Jade Snow Wong, in No Chinese Stranger (New York: Harper & Row, 1975), p. 22, writes: "Grandfather Wong believed that a person who could work with his hands would never starve."
51. Monica Sone, Nisei Daughter (Boston: Little, Brown, 1953), pp. 44-45.
52. Francis L. K. Hsu, Americans and Chinese (Garden City, N. Y.: Doubleday, 1970), p. 47.
53. S. G., Ukrainian, first generation, Interview, October 1971.
54. Rudolph J. Vecoli, The People of New Jersey (Princeton: Van Nostrand, 1965), p. 230; Adamic, Laughing, p. 11. See also Arthur Evans Wood, Hamtramck, Then and Now (New York: Bookman, 1955), p. 230; Lopreato, Italian, pp. 87-88; Panunzio, Soul, p. 18. Direct questioning of immigrants has confirmed the conclusions summarized here.
55. Lopreato, Italian, p. 90; see also Vecoli, People, pp. 232-33.
56. For example, see Rihbany, Far, pp. 12-13; Leonard Covello with Guido D'Agostino, The Heart Is the Teacher (New York: McGraw-Hill, 1958), pp. 10-11; Mary Antin, The Promised Land (Boston: Houghton Mifflin, 1912), pp. 181-87.
G. E. Pozzetta, "The Italians of New York City, 1890-1914" (Ph. D. diss., University of North Carolina at Chapel Hill, 1971), pp. 3-5, describes the levels of society in southern Italy in the late nineteenth century as:
a. The dons or galantuomini: nobles, landed gentry, professionals, and higher clergy, who constituted the thin uppermost layer of society.
b. The artigiani: small shopkeepers, clerks, and craftsmen, who were few in number and not highly paid. They kept themselves apart from what they considered the lower elements of society.
c. The contadini: peasants leasing or owning small plots of land, who were never allowed to participate in local affairs. Traditionally they were apathetic to the events taking place around them. Their living standards usually were low. They had little hope for bettering their lot and often experienced great economic need.
d. The giornalieri: day laborers, who were penniless and always seeking work. They were looked down upon as social outcasts. This group made up a majority of the population in the rural South.
57. See, for example, Thomas Burgess, Charles Kendall Gilbert, and Charles Thorley Bridgeman, Foreigners or Friends (New York: Department of Missions and Church

Extension, 1921), p. 25.
      58.   The padrone's exploitation of the Italian organ-
grinder is discussed in Jacob A. Riis, The Children of the
Poor (New York: Scribner's, 1892), pp. 144-146.
      59.   The factory was moved to Kendall Square, Cam-
bridge, toward the end of the thirties. Some of the Polish-
Americans left their jobs and were replaced by Jewish men.
      60.   Cesidio Simboli, "When the Boss Went Too Far,"
in A Documentary History of the Italian Americans, ed.
Wayne Moquin and Charles Van Doren (New York: Praeger,
1974), pp. 148-49.
      61.   For a discussion of Jewish traits, the shtetl
experience, and the ready adjustment to American conditions
see W. Lloyd Warner and Leo Srole, The Social Systems of
American Ethnic Groups (New Haven: Yale University Press,
1945), pp. 54-55; Selig Adler and Thomas E. Connolly, From
Ararat to Suburbia, The History of the Jewish Community of
Buffalo (Philadelphia: Jewish Publication Society, 1960),
p. 214; Antin, Promised, p. 32; and Carolin F. Ware, Greenwich Village, 1920-1930 (Boston: Houghton Mifflin, 1935), p. 224.
      62.   A description of the relationship of Jews to
Italian opera is given by Rudolf Glanz, Jew and Italian (New
York: N. p. , 1971), p. 98. Regrettably he does not clearly
distinguish between the activities of the German Jews, who
had arrived earlier in the nineteenth century, and those of
the East European Jews, who came after 1880.
      63.   A. J. , Lebanese, first generation, Interview,
November 1949. Until the post-World War II period most
natives of present-day Lebanon described themselves as
Syrians. After Lebanese independence was won in 1941,
however, they have insisted on being called Lebanese. An
overwhelming majority of Syrian and Lebanese immigrants
are Christians, not Moslems.
      64.   Carla Bianco, The Two Rosetos (Bloomington:
Indiana University Press, 1974), p. 36.
      65.   George J. Prpic, The Croatian Immigrants in
America (New York: Philosophical Library, 1971), pp. 106-
07.
      66.   Wife of D. V. ; see note 39. The information
comes from a conversation between her and the author in
November 1972. As regards the relationship of immigrants
to their homeland, Humbert Nelli's comment about Chicago's
Italians is illuminating. He writes that they idealized the
Old Country and yearned to return. But when they did, they
found themselves changed, their attitudes altered, and their
habits different. The struggle for life in the rural villages
was depressing. The Italians, in turn, saw them clearly as

200 • A Sound of Strangers

"Americani." Humbert S. Nelli, Italians in Chicago, 1880-1930 (New York: Oxford University Press, 1970), p. 10.
67. Panunzio, Soul, pp. 7-8. An almost identical description is given of the activities in a small Sicilian town, in L. S., Italian, third generation, "Autobiographical Report," April 1976, p. 2.
68. E. R., Portuguese, second generation, "Autobiographical Report," April 1971, pp. 2-5.
69. H. R., Polish, third generation, "Autobiographical Report," April 1971, pp. 2-3.
70. Ruth Rubin, Voices of a People (New York: Yoseloff, 1963), p. 45.
71. Antin, Promised, pp. 39-40, 74, 108. See also Rubin, Voices, pp. 245, 264.
72. The author recognizes that this conclusion contradicts the usual assertions about the Italian's "natural" affinity for music and love of opera. After rechecking the evidence of the interviews and reports, however, the conclusions stated in the text received even greater substantiation.
73. Erik Amfitheatrof, The Children of Columbus (Boston: Little, Brown, 1973), p. 236.
74. Konrad Bercovici, On New Shores (New York: Century, 1925), pp. 14-15.
75. L. S., "Report," p. 2.
76. Argus, Moscow, p. 3.
77. Ivan Narodny, "Music of the Poles in America," Musical America, 3 May 1913, p. 27.
78. Thomas Burgess, Greeks in America (Boston: Sherman, French, 1913), p. 127.
79. Adler and Connolly, From Ararat, p. 187; Thomas and Znaniecki, Polish, II, pp. 1468-69; Nelli, Italians, p. 258; Maurice R. Davie, "Our Vanishing Minorities," in One World, ed. Francis J. Brown and Joseph Slabey Roucek (New York: Prentice-Hall, 1945), p. 541.
80. Nelli, Italians, p. 6; also Jones, American, p. 317.
81. Andrew F. Rolle, The American Italians (Belmont, Calif.: Wadsworth, 1972), p. 59; Bercovici, Gypsy, p. 42; Robert I. Kutak, The Story of a Bohemian-American Village (Louisville, Ky.: Standard, 1933), p. 13; Jones, American, pp. 214-15.
82. See Novak, Unmeltable, p. 67; and W. Lloyd Warner, American Life, Dream and Reality, rev. ed. (Chicago: University of Chicago Press, 1961), p. 7, for a general discussion of cultural conservation and of cultural symbols, respectively.
83. B. C., Italian, third generation, "Autobiographi-

cal Report, " May 1969, p. 3.

84. A few years ago the Krakowiak Polish Dancers
of Boston toured Poland and astonished audiences there with
the excellence of their performances and their authentic
rendition of a traditional dance repertoire that was all but
forgotten in many parts of Poland itself.

85. A. J. , Italian, first generation, "Autobiographical Report, " April 1970, p. 4.

86. Angelo P. Bertocci, "Memoir of My Mother, "
Harper's Magazine, June 1937, pp. 9-10.

87. E. R. , "Report, " p. 11.

88. See, for example, James D. Bratush, A Historical Documentary of the Ukrainian Community of Rochester,
New York, tr. Anastasia Smerychynska (Rochester: Christopher, 1973), p. 197.

89. George Papashvily and Helen Wait Papashvily,
Anything Can Happen (New York: Harper, 1945), pp. 40-41.

90. Y. D. , Armenian, third generation, "Autobiographical Report, " April 1975, pp. 1-2.

91. Jeremiah W. Jenks and W. Jett Lanck, in The
Immigration Problem, 6th ed. , rev. and ed. Rufus D. Smith
(New York: Funk & Wagnalls, 1926), p. 35, write that of the
men and women admitted between 1899 and 1909 at least 54%
of the southern Italians, 68% of the Portuguese, 59% of the
Turks, 54% of the Syrians, and 51% of the Ruthenians (from
the western Ukraine) were illiterate.   The percentage of il-
literates among Greeks is given as 27%, Armenians 24%,
and Jews 26%.

92. Robert E. Park and Herbert A. Miller, Old
World Traits Transplanted (New York: Harper, 1921), p. 152.

93. Jerre Mangione, Mount Allegro (New York:
Knopf, 1952), p. 219.   Similar sentiments were expressed by
Greek, Polish, and Syrian mothers.   They feared books as
bringing on madness, and saw culture as centered on language, religion, food, and music.

94. The christening took place in Medford, a town a
few miles north of Boston, in the spring of 1952.   The author's father stood as godfather.   The baby's father had been
a semiprofessional singer and lute player in Beirut.   The
song, he stated, was his own composition, created in honor
of the event.   The "daughter of Libnan, " he said, had a
double reference--to the land of his birth and to his daughter.   The translation from the Arabic is by the author.

Chapter 2

1. Abraham Mitrie Rihbany, A Far Journey (Boston: Houghton Mifflin, 1914), p. 11.

2. Two examples of such descriptions are found in L. S., Italian, third generation, "Autobiographical Report, " April 1976, p. 1; and M. M., Italian, second generation, "Autobiographical Report, " April 1976, p. 2.

3. Jerome Davis, The Russian Immigrant (New York: Macmillan, 1922), p. 84.

4. Alex Simirenko, Pilgrims, Colonists, and Frontiersmen (London: Free Press of Glencoe, 1964), p. 133.

5. Harry Manuel Shulman, Slums of New York (New York: Boni, 1938), p. 8.

6. Mario Puzo, "Choosing a Dream, " The Immigrant Experience, ed. Thomas C. Wheeler (New York: Dial, 1971), p. 35; Pietro Di Donato, Naked Author (New York: Phaedra, 1970), p. 3.

7. The author arrived at this conclusion after studying the attitudes and habits of Italian residents of Boston's North End and East Boston.

8. Simirenko, Pilgrims, p. 133.

9. Mary Heaton Vorse, A Footnote to Folly (New York: Farrar & Rinehart, 1935), p. 348. Similar accounts are found in Mary Mellish, Sometimes I Reminisce (New York: Putnam, 1941), pp. 61-62; George Schiro, Americans by Choice (n. p., 1940), p. 122; W. Lloyd Warner and Leo Srole, The Social Systems of American Ethnic Groups (New Haven: Yale University Press, 1945), p. 79; M. D., Italian, third generation, "Autobiographical Report, " January 1969, p. 7; A. C., Jewish, second generation, "Autobiographical Report, " May 1973, pp. 1-3; D. J., Italian, third generation, "Autobiographical Report, " May 1973, p. 1.

10. A. C., Jewish, "Report, " p. 1; A. R., Albanian, second generation, "Autobiographical Report, " January 1969, pp. 1-2; Arnold Shaw, Sinatra (New York: Holt, Rinehart & Winston, 1968), p. 8.

11. T. M., Polish, third generation, Interview, December 1965; D. D., Greek, third generation, "Autobiographical Report, " May 1974, p. 2.

12. The History of the Finns in Minnesota, ed. Hans R. Wasastjerna, tr. Toivo Rosvall (Duluth: Minnesota Finnish-American Historical Society, 1957), pp. 295-96.

13. See, for example, William I. Thomas and Florian Znaniecki The Polish Peasant in Europe and America, 2nd ed., Vol. I (New York: Knopf, 1927), pp. 760-61, the letters dated 28 July and 2 November 1913, sent by Aleksander

Wolski from Union City, Connecticut, to his mother in Poland.

14. Virginia Yans McLaughlin writes, in "Like the Fingers of the Hand: The Family and Community Life of First-Generation Italian-Americans in Buffalo, New York, 1880-1930" (Ph. D. diss., State University of New York at Buffalo, 1970), pp. 288-89, that when Italian boys reached working age they were expected to find a job. And this included about eighty percent of the children from the homes of professionals. She writes that the same expectations were held by Buffalo's Polish parents (p. 322).

15. The author attended the Quincy School with him.

16. Florence Kelly, in The Italian Experience in the United States, ed. Silvano M. Tomasi and Madeline H. Engel (Staten Island, N. Y.: Center for Migration Studies, 1970), p. 84.

17. Two such accounts are given in R. A., Italian, third generation, "Autobiographical Report," May 1972, pp. 6-7; and S. W., Chinese, second generation, Interview, November 1973.

18. E. S., Syrian, first generation, Interview, November 1974. A similar attempt at becoming cultured, involving a Greek man, is given in D. D., Greek, third generation, "Autobiographical Report," May 1974, p. 6. For a time the Greek man took up opera, because "he felt there had to be something more to life than work and sleep."

19. Pascal D'Angelo, Son of Italy (New York: Macmillan, 1924), pp. 149-50, 153-55.

20. S. F., Italian, third generation, "Autobiographical Report," April 1975, pp. 1-2; M. M., Italian, second generation, "Autobiographical Report," April 1976, p. 4; M. J., Italian, third generation, "Autobiographical Report," May 1973, p. 1.

21. Puzo, "Choosing," p. 37; A. B., Hungarian, second generation, Interview, October 1974.

22. David Ewen, Leonard Bernstein (London: Allen, 1967), p. 19.

23. These Italians and Jews apparently felt some guilt over their lack of interest in music.

24. See Herbert J. Gans, The Urban Villagers (New York: Free Press, 1962), p. 83, for his comments on the Italians who once lived in Boston's West End.

25. Joseph Wilfrid Tait, Some Aspects of the Effect of the Dominant American Culture upon Children of Italian-Born Parents (New York: Teachers College, Columbia University, 1942), p. 46.

26. A. R., Albanian, "Report," pp. 4-5.

27. See, for example, the complaint of Z. B. Dybowski, in Cleveland's Polish-language newspaper, Wiadomosci Codzienne, 9 July 1937, as reprinted in the Cleveland Foreign Language Newspaper Digest, 1937, Vol. IV, Annals of Cleveland, Newspaper Series (Cleveland: W. P. A. Project 18881-C, 1940), p. 525; also Robert I. Kutak, The Story of a Bohemian-American Village (Louisville, Ky.: Standard Printing, 1933), pp. 120-21. The village is Milligan, Nebraska.

28. For a fuller discussion of this point as concerns all minority communities see Judith R. Kramer, The American Minority Community (New York: Crowell, 1962), pp. 58-59.

29. Caroline F. Ware, Greenwich Village, 1920-1930 (Boston: Houghton Mifflin, 1935), pp. 339-40.

30. Musical America, 24 September 1910, p. 15.

31. An early organizer of folk festivals, Dorothy Gladys Spicer, is the author of Folk Festivals and the Foreign Community (New York: Woman's Press, 1923), which gives a description of some of these events and makes suggestions about dance and song material and procedures to follow in staging performances before a general audience. For several years now the author has assisted the International Institute of Boston in the music and dance programming of its Whole World Celebration, which in 1977 attracted an audience of sixty thousand people.

32. This did not mean that they all pursued music with singleminded devotion. Some did. Most enjoyed it in relaxed fashion, as a delightful diversion.

33. Michael Novak, in The Rise of the Unmeltable Ethnics (New York: Macmillan, 1972), pp. 47-48, insists that there exists an "ethnic memory" among members of every subculture, which at least in part consists of "patterns of emotion." Music plays an important role in articulating these patterns.

34. For example, see Joseph Remenyi, "The Hungarians," in Immigrant Backgrounds, ed. Henry Pratt Fairchild (New York: Wiley, 1927), p. 71.

35. August Mark Vaz, The Portuguese in California (Oakland: I. D. E. S. Supreme Council, 1965), p. 231.

36. Rodney Gallop, "The Fado (The Portuguese Song of Fate)," Musical Quarterly, 19 (1933): 200, 212.

37. Harry M. Petrakis, "The Ballad of Daphne and Apollo," in Pericles on 31st Street (Chicago: Quadrangle, 1965), pp. 56-59.

38. C. M., Syrian, "What Music Means to Us," December 1949. The writer had completed high school,

attending classes at night. Until his death in 1966 he was
an assiduous reader of books on historical subjects and of
the works of the English Romantic poets, though he never
really enjoyed Western music. He was also an adept in
several languages, able to speak and write in Greek, Turkish, French, English, and, of course, Arabic. The oud is
the Arabic lute; arrac, an alcoholic beverage; mazza, various little dishes of vegetables and fishes in a variety of
sauces. These dishes are meant to complement alcoholic
drinks. It should be added that at the insistence of the
wives and children, and perhaps just as frequently, entire
families went to the farm. However, for two or three
hours the men customarily sat apart from the women and
children in order to enjoy their music, sip arrac, and nib-
ble at the mazza.

     39. See Charles Angoff, Journey to the Dawn (New
York: Beechhurst, 1951), pp. 329-40; Alfred Kazin, A Walker in the City (New York: Harcourt, Brace & World, 1951),
pp. 62-63.

     40. Samuel Chotzinoff, Day's at the Morn (New
York: Harper & Row, 1964), pp. 15, 19-21.

     41. Eddie Cantor, My Life Is in Your Hands, as
told to David Freedman (New York: Harper, 1928), p. 6.

     42. Peter Roberts, The New Immigration (New
York, Macmillan, 1912), p. 274.

     43. The author had been sent there by his parents
for a four-week summer vacation.

     44. Charles Angoff, The Bitter Spring (New York:
Yoseloff, 1961), p. 195.

     45. See also the account in Philip V. Mighels, "A
Music-School Settlement," Harper's Monthly Magazine, 111
(November 1905): 837.

     46. In Chotzinoff's A Lost Paradise several in-
stances of weeping are cited. See the explanation of
the impact of Boris Thomashefsky's singing on Jewish audiences, in Irving Howe, World of Our Fathers (New York:
Harcourt Brace Jovanovich, 1976), p. 465: "He had a vi-
brating, crackling voice, somewhere between baritone and
tenor, going into falsetto in the upper ranges. When he
sang 'A Brivele der Mamen' ["A Letter to Mother," enor-
mously popular on the East Side], the whole audience found
it impossible to hold back their tears. No matter if the
scene was laid in the hot sandy desert or the Halls of the
Inquisition, Thomashefsky always managed to get in a song
about Mama."

     47. A version of this song is printed in Leonard
Deutsch, A Treasury of the World's Finest Folk Song (New

York: Crown, 1967), pp. 226-27. However, it bears little resemblance to the music I once played the accompaniment for at two Polish picnics around 1940.

48. M. K. Argus [Mikhail K. Jeleznov], Moscow-on-the-Hudson (New York: Harper, 1951), p. 57.

49. Jo Pagano, Golden Wedding (New York: Random House, 1943), p. 13.

50. The author attended the dinner, given at an East Boston restaurant.

51. Kazin, Walker, pp. 63-64.

52. For a discussion of culture as "social heredity," and the necessity for each succeeding generation to learn it anew, see Robin M. Williams, Jr., American Society, 2nd ed. (New York: Knopf, 1967), p. 22.

53. Peter M. Fekula, as quoted in the Cleveland Foreign Language Newspaper Digest, 1937, Vol. I (Cleveland: W. P. A. Project 18120, 1939), pp. 66-67.

54. After describing the pride of his family and community in his musicality one Italian-American writer states: "As an example of the importance my music career was to my parents, they took out a five hundred dollar loan (which incidentally they could not afford) when I was eight years old to buy me a one hundred and twenty bass accordion [sic]. My father drove me every Saturday morning for five years to the music school for my private lessons. He used to take great pride in watching me play for relatives on Sunday afternoon when we went visiting" (C. T., Italian, third generation, "Autobiographical Report," May 1969, p. 2). In the interview following the submission of the report C. T. explained that his grandfather worked part-time and his grandmother contributed some of the money she had set aside for their old age in order to help on the loan.

55. Arthur Mann, La Guardia: A Fighter Against His Time, 1882-1933, Vol. I (Philadelphia: Lippincott, 1959), pp. 31-32.

56. Booton Herndon, The Sweetest Music This Side of Heaven, The Guy Lombardo Story (New York: McGraw-Hill, 1964), p. 19. Jo Pagano, in Golden Wedding, pp. 163-64, writes that an Italian father started his son on violin lessons with a Professor Alessandro Berardi, a Piedmontese. Every day the mother stood over her son as he practiced; if he proved reluctant, she lashed out with: 'If you think I'm going to spend a dollar every week for your lessons for nothing, you're very much mistaken. Now then--start practicing, and be quick about it!"

57. Chotzinoff, Days, p. 2.

58. Ronald Sanders, The Downtown Jews (New York:

Harper & Row, 1969), p. 199.

59. Renee B. Fisher, Musical Prodigies (New York: Associated Press, 1973), p. 98.

60. Ibid., p. 142.

61. Max Wilk, They're Playing Our Song (New York: Atheneum, 1973), p. 150.

62. Ibid., pp. 27-28.

63. Jerre Mangione, Mount Allegro (New York: Knopf, 1952), pp. 218-19.

64. Konrad Bercovici, It's the Gypsy in Me (New York: Prentice-Hall, 1941), p. 49.

65. See Allan Schoener, Portal to America (New York: Holt, Rinehart & Winston, 1967), p. 128.

66. Arthur Evans Wood, Hamtramck, Then and Now (New York: Bookman, 1955), pp. 201-02.

67. This conclusion is derived mainly from the reports of and interviews with Boston's ethnic Americans.

68. Moses Rischin, The Promised City (Cambridge: Harvard University Press, 1962), pp. 205-06, 217-18; Constance D. Leupp, "Climbing Out Through Music," The Outlook, 26 October 1912, pp. 403-09; Mighels, "Settlement," pp. 832-33.

69. Esther G. Barrows, Neighbors All (Boston: Houghton Mifflin, 1929), p. 126; Claire P. Peeler, "Where Music Moulds the Future Citizen," Musical America, 24 July 1915, p. 15.

70. Herndon, Sweetest, p. 18.

71. E. G. Stearn, My Mother and I (New York: Macmillan, 1918), p. 75.

72. Jade Snow Wong, Fifth Chinese Daughter (New York: Harper, 1950), pp. 34-35.

73. George Jellinek, Callas (London: Gibbs & Phillips, 1961), pp. 5-7.

74. B. C., Italian, third generation, "Autobiographical Report," May 1969, p. 2.

75. T. C., Italian, third generation, "Autobiographical Report," May 1971, p. 5.

76. Ibid., p. 2.

77. Cleveland Foreign Language Newspaper Digest, 1937, Vol. II (Cleveland: W. P. A. Project 18120, 1939), pp. 29-30.

78. Kazuo Ito, Issei, A History of Japanese Immigrants in North America, tr. Shinichiro Nakamura and Jean S. Gerard (Seattle: Japanese Community Service, 1973), p. 815.

79. The program for the concert of 18 November 1923 is printed in James D. Bratush, A Historical Docu-

mentary of the Ukrainian Community of Rochester, New York, tr. Anastasia Smerychynska (Rochester: Christopher, 1973), pp. 191-93.

80. In this regard see Arnold Shaw, Sinatra, p. 10.

81. See, for example, Gerald Gilbert Govorchin, Americans from Yugoslavia (Gainesville: University of Florida, 1961), p. 122. In an "Autobiographical Report," May 1969, pp. 2-3, B. R., Lithuanian, third generation, writes about the formation by a Mrs. Ivaska of a Boston group of junior, and another of senior, dancers, who performed in costume and made appearances as far away as Chicago and Washington, D. C.

82. Samuel Rosenblatt, Yossele Rosenblatt (New York: Farrar, Straus & Young, 1954), p. 94.

83. Chotzinoff, Lost, p. 202. For further information on the Jewish cantor see Rosenblatt, Yossele, pp. 5, 90; A. Z. Idelsohn, Jewish Music (New York: Holt, 1929), p. 183; Fisher, Musical, p. 58; Morris Clark, "America as Cradle of Jewish Music," Musical America, 28 June 1913, p. 25.

84. The musical history of Jan Peerce, Richard Tucker, and other synagogue singers may be found in Morris N. Kertzer, Today's American Jew (New York: McGraw-Hill, 1967); a most valuable source for information on Jewish music, its forms, and performers is Macy Nulman, Concise Encyclopedia of Jewish Music (New York: McGraw-Hill, 1975).

85. To this sort of event the author can attest, having been almost suffocated by the throngs filling the Syrian St. John of Damascus Church, on Hudson Street in Boston, on several occasions during his childhood. Until about fifteen years ago the entire congregation, except for the old and infirm, stood for all of the service, which sometimes lasted for two hours. The author was also present at receptions like the one described.

86. Several publications that take up the role of the choir director and the establishment of the first choruses are Bratush, Ukrainian, p. 187; Wasyl Halich, Ukrainians in the United States (Chicago: University of Chicago Press, 1937), pp. 127, 133-35; Myron B. Kuropas, The Ukrainians in America (Minneapolis: Lerner, 1972), p. 73; One World, ed. Francis J. Brown and Joseph Slabey Roucek (New York: Prentice-Hall, 1945), p. 218; Josef J. Barton, Peasants and Strangers (Cambridge: Harvard University Press, 1975), p. 153; Selig Adler and Thomas E. Connolly, From Ararat to Suburbia, The History of the Jewish Community of Buffalo (Philadelphia: Jewish Publication Society, 1960),

pp. 271, 375; The Poles of Chicago, 1837-1937 (Chicago: Polish Pageant, 1937), p. 72; Ivan Narodny, "Music of the Poles in America," Musical America, 3 May 1913, p. 27.

87. See Barton, Peasants, p. 159; the quotations from the Yugoslav Amereska Domovina and the Slovenian Enakoprovnost, in the Cleveland Foreign Language Newspaper Digest, 1937, Vol. V (Cleveland: W. P. A. Project 18881-C, 1940), pp. 289, 545.

88. Emil Lengyel, Americans from Hungary (Philadelphia: Lippincott, 1948), p. 188.

89. Robert Merrill with Sandford Dody, Once More from the Beginning (New York: Macmillan, 1965), p. 48. H. J., Armenian, first generation, Interview, December 1949, mentions a similar exchange that took place between an Armenian mother and her daughter. The girl in the end was also made to go to choir. Later the girl became a well-known concert singer.

90. Konrad Bercovici, Around the World in New York (New York: Century, 1924), pp. 379-80; item by B. R., in Musical America, 4 April 1914, p. 13; Hungarian Szabadság, quoted in Cleveland Digest, 1937, Vol. IV, p. 61.

91. Govorchin, Americans, p. 122.

92. Poles in Chicago, pp. 157-58; see also the Polish Wiadomosci Codzienne, quoted in Cleveland Digest, 1937, Vol. IV, pp. 352, 493.

93. Mentioned variously in Cleveland Digest, 1937, Vol. IV.

94. Ivan Narodny, "Music of the Poles," p. 27.

95. See Poles in Chicago, p. 72; Cleveland Digest, 1937, Vol. IV, p. 61.

96. Poles in Chicago, pp. 68-69.

97. William Henry Bishop, "San Francisco," Harper's New Monthly Magazine, 66 (May 1883): 831; see also Wong, Fifth, p. 216.

98. Halich, Ukrainians, p. 75.

99. The author writes from experience. However, much the same thing is described in Jessie Freemont Beale and Anne Withington, "Life's Amenities," in Americans in Process, ed. Robert A. Woods (Boston: Houghton Mifflin, 1903), p. 233. Unmarried young women were infrequently seen at these performances.

100. Cleveland Foreign Language Newspaper Digest, 1938, Vol. II, p. 35.

101. Henrietta Straus, "Music Students in New York," The Century, 108 (May 1924): 33.

102. See Rischin, Promised, p. 134, for further information.

103. Rischin, Promised, p. 74. Hutchins Hapgood, The Spirit of the Ghetto, ed. Moses Rischin (Cambridge: Harvard University Press, 1967), pp. 113-35, contains a great deal of information on this phase of the Yiddish theater.

104. Cleveland Digest, 1938, Vol. III, pp. 278-79.

105. Chotzinoff, Lost, pp. 106-07; Hapgood, Spirit, pp. 69-70.

106. See Allan Sherman, A Gift of Laughter (New York: Atheneum, 1965), p. 26.

107. Chotzinoff, Lost, pp. 101-05.

108. Merrill, Once, p. 104.

109. "Cantor Yudele Appel will give a concert on Apr. 11.... He made a big name for himself by his interpretation of prayers and Jewish folk song" (Cleveland Digest, 1937, Vol. III, p. 132).

110. "Cantor Glinkovski will give a concert in the Temple, Nov. 14.... His concert will consist of Jewish love songs" (ibid., p. 252).

111. Cantor Yossele Rosenblatt was so famous for his rendition of operatic arias that in 1918 Cleofonte Campanini, director of the Chicago Opera Association, offered him $1,000 a performance to appear on the stage. The director even promised him Jewish leading ladies if he objected to Gentiles. The cantor refused (Rosenblatt, Yossele, pp. 141-42).

112. Samuel Rosenblatt writes that the actors in the Yiddish theater loved to imitate his father's style of singing cantorial music. His father, in turn, "incorporated into his secular repertoire their theatrical airs and folksongs" (Rosenblatt, Yossele, p. 119).

113. See the report on the Cleveland concert by the Slovenian tenor Louis Belle, "consisting of 18 numbers of national and operatic songs" (Cleveland Digest, 1937, Vol. V, p. 7); and on the New York concert by A. Chah-Mouradian, consisting of Armenian songs and opera arias sung before an Armenian audience (Musical America, 20 May 1916, p. 11).

114. Many singers who fit this description are Italian and are to be found on festa evenings close to the bandstand, ready to stride up onto the platform and regale their neighbors with arias from the favorite operas. See also Joseph William Carlevale, Americans of Italian Descent in Philadelphia and Vicinity (Philadelphia: Ferguson, 1954), pp. 113-14, on a Luigi Cresta, barber for sixty years, possessor of a natural tenor voice and "very popular in his younger days as a singer." He sang both Italian popular songs and opera arias.

115. William J. Hoy, "Chinatown Devises Its Own Street Names, " California Folklore Quarterly, 2 (April 1943): 73. Hoy writes here of the 1890s. He concludes with: "The songs and laughter of singsing girls ... have long since vanished. "
116. Ito, Issei, p. 138. Ito is describing Seattle's Japanese section at the turn of the century.
117. Cleveland Digest, 1937, Vol. IV, p. 327.
118. A. H. Gayton, "The 'Festa da Serreta' at Gustine, " Western Folklore, 7 (July 1948): 259.
119. Petrakis, Pericles, pp. 54-55.
120. Straus, "Music, " p. 30.
121. R. W. , Polish, third generation, "Autobiographical Report, " May 1973, p. 2.
122. Thomas and Znaniecki, Polish, Vol. I, pp. 968-69.
123. D. C. , Italian, third generation, "Autobiographical Report, " May 1972, pp. 13-14.
124. János Makar, The Story of an Immigrant Group in Franklin, New Jersey, tr. August J. Molnár (Franklin: Makar, 1969), pp. 102-04.
125. Chotzinoff, Lost, p. 261.
126. Musical America, 3 December 1910, p. 4.
127. For a description of the instruments see Govorchin, Americans, p. 122; see also George J. Prpic, The Croatian Immigrants in America (New York: Philosophical Library, 1971), p. 372.
128. Kuropas, Ukrainians, p. 75.
129. The orchestra consisted of ten mandolins, two guitars, and a contrabass (Musical America, 6 April 1912, p. 34).
130. Cleveland Digest, 1937, Vol. I, p. 135; Vol. IV, pp. 129, 192.
131. Jacob A. Evanson, "Folk Songs of an Industrial City, " in Pennsylvania Songs and Legends, ed. George Korson (Baltimore: Johns Hopkins Press, 1949), pp. 451-52.
132. Ibid. , pp. 429-30.
133. J. H. , Greek, first generation, Interview, January 1950.
134. See Cleveland Digest, 1937, Vol. IV, pp. 13, 16, 41, 61, 96, 118, 120, 126; Ruth Rubin, Voices of a People (New York: Yoseloff, 1963), pp. 270-71, 353; David Lifson, The Yiddish Theatre in America (New York: Yoseloff, 1965), p. 69; Halish, Ukrainian, pp. 138-40; Spicer, Festivals, pp. 21, 89.

Chapter 3

1.   The two Hungarian songs, recorded in the town
of Franklin, New Jersey, are published in János Makar,
The Story of an Immigrant Group in Franklin, New Jersey,
tr. August J. Molnár (Franklin: Makar, 1969), pp. 124-25,
136-37.
2.   The music is reproduced in Harriet M. Pawlowski, Merrily We Sing, 105 Polish Folksongs (Detroit: Wayne
University Press, 1961), pp. 8-9, 20-21.
3.   Folk Songs of Greece, ed. and tr. Susan and Ted
Alevizos (New York: Oak, 1968), pp. 18, 95. Similar compositions about priests' wives were sung by Albanians in
America. A. R., Albanian, second generation, "Autobiographical Report, " January 1969, p. 8, writes: "Along with the
love ballads, the people enjoy singing humorous songs. One
such song can be loosely translated as 'The Priest's Wife.'
This song tells of a priest's wife who doesn't like the priest
because he has long whiskers and as a result she chases
after the young men who were clean shaven. ... It is quite
a sight to see the people at the [church] picnic form a large
circle and sing to the song of 'The Priest's wife' in front of
the priest of their own church. Much laughter is caused
when the song is sung to the priest and his wife, and often
times a blush will come over the face of the priest or his
wife due to the subject matter of the song. "
4.   The author himself knew of these occurrences.
5.   Echoes of Naples, Thirty Neapolitan Songs, ed.
Mario Favilli (Boston: Ditson, 1909), pp. 8-10, 38-40.
C. T., Italian, third generation, "Autobiographical Report, "
May 1969, p. 3, states that the Italians who hired him to
play accordion for special occasions always requested the
old Neapolitan songs, in preference to any other music. He
then goes on to name over a dozen of them, including the
two reproduced in Examples 5 and 6. M. D., Italian, third
generation, "Autobiographical Report, " January 1969, p. 2,
writes that his "peasant" grandparents and their friends continued to enjoy most "the agrarian song types that revolved
around the seasons. " In "the splendor of summer" they sang
"Ah com' e' bell' la stagione, Vicino al mare, relieved now
and then with stornelli on the problems of love, like Cuor'
ingrato. "
6.   Jacob A. Evanson, "Folk Songs of an Industrial
City, " Pennsylvania Songs and Legends, ed. George Korson
(Baltimore: Johns Hopkins Press, 1949), pp. 439-40.
7.   The song was sung by the author's uncle in 1949.
"Souria" is both the Arabic name of Syria and of the author's

grandmother. It may be only coincidence, but two Lebanese songs with similar texts were collected in Cortland County, New York; see Suad Joseph, "Where the Twain Shall Meet-- Lebanese in Cortland County, " New York Folklore Quarterly, 20 (September 1964): 183-84.

8. Ruth Rubin, Jewish Folk Songs (New York: Oak, 1969), p. 61.

9. Maud Cuney Hare, "Portuguese Folk-Songs from Provincetown, Cape Cod, Mass. , " Musical Quarterly, 14 (1928): 35-53; sung by Joseph Jorge, formerly of San Jorge, the Azores.

10. Rubin, Jewish, pp. 46-47. The words are by Morris Rosenfeld. The composer is unknown.

11. Evanson, "Folk Songs, " pp. 437-38. The song was notated from the singing of Andrew Kovaly, at McKeesport, in 1947.

12. See Ruth Rubin, Voices of a People (New York: Yoseloff, 1963), p. 39.

13. Evanson, "Folk Songs, " pp. 429-30, 437.

14. Russian Folk Songs, ed. Florence Hudson Botsford (New York: Schirmer, 1929), pp. 22-23, 28-29.

15. The music was notated by the author during a December 1950 performance in Boston.

16. The author notated the song in 1950. The exact translation of the text obtained from the singer was so disjointed, the author has rendered the English in a paraphrase (Example 16).

17. V. S. , Armenian, first generation, Interview, November 1976. She can be characterized as a cultural leader in the Armenian community, a great lover of cultivated music, and an excellent pianist. It should also be added that she was born in Vienna.

18. Christie W. Kiefer, Changing Cultures, Changing Lives (San Francisco: Jossey-Bass, 1947), pp. 17-22.

19. Dorothy Gladys Spicer, Folk Festivals and the Foreign Community (New York: Women's Press, 1923), p. 2.

20. August Mark Vaz, The Portuguese in California (Oakland: I. D. E. S. Supreme Council, 1965), p. 130.

21. Arthur Evans Wood, Hamtramck, Then and Now (New York: Bookman, 1955), pp. 40-41.

22. Christine A. Galitzi, A Study of Assimilation Among the Roumanians in the United States (1929; reprint ed. , New York: AMS, 1968), p. 138.

23. James D. Bratush, A Historical Documentary of the Ukrainian Community of Rochester, New York, tr. Anastasia Smerychynska (Rochester: Christopher, 1973),

pp. 21-22.
    24.   Makar, Story, pp. 95-96.
    25.   S. L., Portuguese, second generation, "Autobio-graphical Report, " April 1970, pp. 4-5.
    26.   These conclusions were drawn after questioning University of Massachusetts students of Greek, Lebanese, and Syrian extraction, and, of course, from the author's own observation. Theodore Saloutos, The Greeks in the United States (Cambridge: Harvard University Press, 1964), writes that Greeks celebrated not Christmas but New Year's Day or St. Basil's Day.
    27.   Jo Pagano, "Signor Santa, " in Within Our Gates, ed. Mary B. McLellan and Albert V. De Bonis (New York: Harper, 1940), p. 288.
    28.   Ibid., pp. 294-95.
    29.   The translation is taken from the sheet-music edition of the song, published in New York by Bibo, Bloe-don & Lang, in 1927.
    30.   Rocco Fumento, Tree of Dark Reflection (New York: Knopf, 1962), p. 33. The novel is an accurate slice-of-life depiction of actual immigrant experience.
    31.   Ralph Corcel, Up There in the Stars (New York: Citadel, 1968), pp. 58-59, writes of Easter among Italian relatives and friends, where all joined together to sing songs like "Santa Lucia, " to the accompaniment of mandolin and accordion, flooding the street with the sound pouring out of the open windows. See also, Hare, "Portuguese, " p. 42, on the Portuguese observance of the "Imperio de Espirito Santo," from Easter until St. Peter's Day, with singing and dancing.
    32.   This is a description of Easter practices that the author himself, living in Boston's South End, experienced as a young boy, in the late twenties and early thirties.
    33.   See Chapter 2, note 38.
    34.   C. M., Syrian, first generation, "What Music Means to Us, " December 1949. On Saturday, about 11 p. m., the entire congregation vacated the church, still dimly lit and draped in black. They waited on the street until mid-night, when the priest knocked on the door with his staff and the doors opened. The congregation, standing in the dark, could see the inside transformed with bright lights and flowers everywhere.
    35.   Spicer, Folk, p. 20, writes that festive holidays furnished outlets "for the pent-up creative ability of the foreigner ... crushed under our modern industrial system" and gave him "opportunity for spontaneous self-expression" through the presentation of "the well-loved songs, dances, and customs of the homeland. "

36. Hare, "Portuguese, " pp. 42-44.
37. S. L. , "Report, " p. 3. A. H. Gayton, "The 'Festa da Serreta' at Gustire, " Western Folklore, 8 (July 1948): 258, speaks of the street procession for "Nossa Senhora dos Milagres" as including a thirty-piece band, a festival "queen" singing in antiphony with a choir of girls, and followed by four male accordionists, "who, like the band, played the hymn of Nossa Senhora dos Milagres continuously."
38. Ibid. , p. 44; Gayton, "Festa, " p. 262. Gayton (p. 251) writes that the most popular festival of the Azorean Portuguese from Serreta was that honoring Our Lady of Miracles ("Nossa Senhora dos Milagres"), held in September.
39. Hare, "Portuguese, " pp. 45-46.
40. Jacob A. Riis, The Children of the Poor (New York: Scribner, 1892), p. 25.
41. See Robert E. Park and Herbert A. Miller, Old World Traits Transplanted (New York: Harper, 1921), pp. 154-55; George Schiro, Americans by Choice (Utica, N. Y. : N. p. , 1940), pp. 126-27.
42. "Festa, " The New Yorker, 5 October 1957, p. 35.
43. Oscar Handlin, Immigration as a Factor in American History (Englewood Cliffs, N. J. : Prentice-Hall, 1959), p. 80.
44. "Festa, " pp. 35-36.
45. N. M. , Spanish-Italian, third generation, "Autobiographical Report, " April 1972, p. 2.
46. See, for example, the statement of Marie J. Concistre, in Francesco Cordasco and Eugene Bucchioni, The Italians (Clifton, N. J. : Kelly, 1974), p. 224; Alan Schaffer, Vito Marcantonio, Radical in Congress (Syracuse, N. Y. : Syracuse University Press, 1966), p. 8.
47. The author, a boy of eight or nine years of age, was visiting relatives in North Bergen at the time. He was taken to the Hoboken festa by an older cousin intent on "showing him the sights. "
48. Pietro Di Donato, Three Circles of Light (New York: Messner, 1960), pp. 112-15.
49. These are from the operas Il Trovatore, La Traviata, and Rigoletto, respectively.
50. The best-known aria in Pagliacci.
51. The drinking song in Cavalleria Rusticana.
52. Songs of Italy (London: Boosey, ca. 1892), pp. 52-53.
53. See Spicer, Folk, pp. 1-2, for a discussion of the festival's place in rural Europe and peasant consciousness.

54. Konrad Bercovici, On New Shores (New York: Century, 1925), pp. 95-99.

55. Folklore in America, ed. Tristram P. Coffin and Henning Cohen (New York: Doubleday, 1966), pp. 214-17.

56. S. L., "Report," pp. 5-6; Makar, Story, pp. 97-99.

57. This description is based on statements provided by several ethnic Americans. See also the account of Hungarian "Harvest Festivals," in the Cleveland Szabadság, and of a Polish "Harvest Festival," in the Cleveland Wiadomosci Codzienne, reprinted in the Cleveland Foreign Language Digest, 1937, Vol. IV (Cleveland: W. P. A. Project 18881-C, 1940), pp. 51-52, 93, 470.

58. The Nisei from whom the tune was obtained says that his mother remembers "Chochai Bushi" as becoming prominent in Japanese circles after Puccini used the melody in Madame Butterfly; Y. M., Japanese, second generation, Interview, November 1973.

59. Kiefer, Changing, pp. 38-39; Kazuo Ito, Issei, A History of Japanese Immigrants in North America, tr. Shinichiro Nakamura and Jean S. Gerard (Seattle: Japanese Community Service, 1973), pp. 805-09.

60. Idwal Jones, "Cathay on the Coast," The American Mercury, 8 (August 1926): 459-60. William Hoy, "Native Festivals of the California Chinese," Western Folklore, 8 (July 1948): 240-50, claims that seven festivals are still celebrated "as a source of familial and communal joy and, more important, as a spiritual tie with their ancestral culture." The festivals are New Year's (Sun Nien), Pure Brightness Festival (Ch'ing Ming), Dragon Boat Festival (Wu Yueh Wu--the Fifth day of the Fifth Moon), Spirits' Festival (Whiu Yi--Burning Paper Clothing), Moon Festival (Ch'ung Chiu), Ninth Day, Ninth Moon Festival (Chung Yang), Winter Solstice (Tung Chih). In 1946 China only the first, second, and fifth festival were still observed.

61. Pardee Lowe, Father and Glorious Descendant (Boston: Little, Brown, 1943), p. 43.

62. In Charles Angoff, Journey to the Dawn (New York: Beechhurst, 1951), p. 265, one Jewish man tells another: "I want to tell you that you have a treat coming in the moosaaf [the chief part of the Saturday prayer, the occasion for the cantor and the choir to exhibit their art]. We have a cantor who is a diamond, a real diamond, out of this world."

63. See Alter F. Landesman, Brownsville (New York: Bloch, 1969), p. 209, for a description of the growth of the Congregation Oheb Shalom and its hiring of cantors, including

the famous "David Roitman and Leove's Choir at a cost of the then huge sum of eighteen thousand dollars a year to the congregation. "

64. In Robert Merrill with Sandford Dody, Once More from the Beginning (New York: Macmillan, 1965). Merrill speaks of his first cantorial engagement for the High Holidays at $300, and of the increasing demand for his services as his fame grew.

65. Moses Rischin, The Promised City (Cambridge: Harvard University Press, 1962), pp. 138-39. See also Samuel Chotzinoff, A Lost Paradise (New York: Knopf, 1955), pp. 201-02; Samuel Rosenblatt, Yossele Rosenblatt (New York: Farrar, Straus & Young, 1954), p. 110.

66. Macy Nulman, Concise Encyclopedia of Jewish Music (New York: McGraw-Hill, 1975), s. v. "Kol Nidre. "

67. A Treasury of Jewish Folklore, ed. Nathan Ausubel (New York: Crown, 1948), pp. 675-76.

68. S. I., Jewish, second generation, Interview, Summer 1971.

69. Ausubel, Treasury, p. 724.

70. Nulman, Encyclopedia. s. v. "Hassidic Song. "

71. Ruth Rubin, A Treasury of Jewish Folksong (New York: Schocken, 1950), pp. 142-43. Eighteen holiday songs are printed on pp. 139-74.

72. Hutchins Hapgood, The Spirit of the Ghetto, ed. Moses Rischin (Cambridge: Harvard University Press, 1967), p. 22. The book was first published in 1902.

73. Landesman, Brownsville, p. 78.

74. Thomas Burgess, Greeks in America (Boston: Sherman, French, 1913), p. 89.

75. A claim made by several well-educated Italian professional men of the Boston area, but which the author was unable to prove without doubt.

76. See, for example, the report of 24 April 1938, in Cleveland's La Voce del Popolo Italiano, reprinted in Cleveland Digest, 1938, Vol. II, p. 20; also Lou D'Angelo, What the Ancients Said (Garden City, N. Y.: Doubleday, 1971), p. 19.

77. For example, all of these activities might take place when the Poles celebrated their Constitution Day, on May 3; see Wood, Hamtramck, pp. 35, 197; The Poles of Chicago, 1837-1937 (Chicago: Polish Pageant, 1937), p. 63; Carl Wittke, We Who Built America (Cleveland: Western Reserve University Press, 1939), passim.

78. Edward Steiner, The Immigrant Tide, Its Ebb and Flow, 2nd ed. (New York: Revell, 1909), pp. 303-04.

79. Monica Sone, Nisei Daughter (Boston: Little,

Brown, 1953), pp. 66-70.
    80. Jeanne Wakatsuki Houston and James D. Houston, Farewell to Manzanar (Boston: Houghton Mifflin, 1973), p. 78.
    81. Paul Nettl, National Anthems, 2nd ed., tr. Alexander Gode (New York: Ungar, 1967), p. 168, states that the melody, which begins:

was composed by Hayashi Hironokami, in 1880, and revised by Franz Eckert, a German, in 1916.
    82. Landesman, Brownsville, pp. 77-78.
    83. Allan Schoener, Portal to America (New York: Holt, Rinehart & Winston, 1967), p. 67.
    84. Cleveland Digest, 1937, Vol. III, p. 218.
    85. Di Donato, Three, pp. 49-51.
    86. Cleveland Digest, 1937, Vol. V, pp. 111, 113.
    87. B. R., Lithuanian, third generation, "Autobiographical Report," May 1969, p. 2: "In America, the Lithuanians worked long hours. The only means of entertainment that was looked forward to were the weekly picnics. ... My maternal grandparents would take the streetcar from South Boston to Dedham (a distance of about 10 miles). Picnics would last from 12 noon to 12 midnight. They would dance and sing the hours away."
    88. Mari Tomasi, Like Lesser Gods (Milwaukee: Bruce, 1949), p. 76.
    89. Schiro, Americans, pp. 127-28.
    90. Cleveland Digest, 1937, Vol. V, p. 99.
    91. Cleveland Digest, 1938, Vol. III, pp. 256-57.
    92. Cleveland Digest, 1937, Vol. I, p. 296; 1938, Vol. I, p. 353.
    93. Ito, Issei, p. 97.
    94. Sone, Nisei, p. 71, writes of the Seattle Japanese looking forward to the undo-kai, the Nihon Gakko picnic held in June, and of the children practicing Japanese songs and dances to perform at the picnic.
    95. Ibid., p. 77. For some other references to ethnic picnics see Joseph, "Where," pp. 180-81 (on Lebanese picnics); Burgess, Greeks, pp. 92-93, and J. P. Xenides, The Greeks in America (New York: Doran, 1922), p. 90 (on Greek picnics). H. R., Armenian, second generation, "Autobiographical Report," April 1972, pp. 2-3, describes the annual picnic at Camp Ararat, in Maynard, Massachusetts,

enjoyed by the Armenians from Watertown, Massachusetts. The occasion was also an observance of the Apostolic Festival of the Grapes. A. R., "Report, " pp. 58-59, describes an Albanian picnic in some detail.

96. S. L., "Report, " p. 6.

97. R. V., Armenian, second generation, "Autobiographical Report, " April 1969, p. 3. The songs are found in The Botsford Collection of Folk Songs, ed. Florence Hudson Botsford, Vol. I (New York: Schirmer, 1930), pp. 115-16, 118-20. R. V. himself brought in handwritten copies of the two songs, taken from Botsford. Regrettably his brother could not remember exactly what was sung that day; but he and his wife also endorsed the examples.

98. S. S., Armenian, third generation, "Autobiographical Report, " April 1976, pp. 2-3.

99. See, for example, Caroline F. Ware, Greenwich Village, 1920-1933 (Boston: Houghton Mifflin, 1935), pp. 365-66. Sidney Meller, Roots in the Sky (New York: Macmillan, 1938), pp. 365-66, describes a Sicilian homecoming party.

100. Clement Lawrence Valletta, A Study of Americanization in Carneta (New York: Arno, 1975), p. 128.

101. A. R., "Report, " p. 10.

102. Harry M. Petrakis, Pericles on 31st Street (Chicago: Quadrangle, 1965), pp. 47-48. Though invented by Petrakis, Leontis typifies the behavior of some actual Greek fathers at the christening parties for the firstborn son that the author has attended.

103. William Carlson Smith, Americans in Process (Ann Arbor, Mich.: Edwards, 1937), p. 9.

104. Jacob A. Riis, Out of Mulberry Street (New York: Century, 1898), pp. 34-35.

105. Rubin, Voices, pp. 107-08; Hapgood, Spirit, pp. 91-95.

106. A. R., "Report, " p. 9.

107. M. S., Greek, second generation, Interview, October 1971.

108. The author witnessed several such processions on their way to the St. John of Damascus Church, on Hudson Street in Boston. See also Abraham Mitrie Rihbany, A Far Journey (Boston: Houghton Mifflin, 1914), pp. 53-54.

109. Galitzi, Study, pp. 140-41.

110. Wood, Hamtramck, p. 42.

111. Makar, Story, p. 90, as sung by Mrs. Joseph P. Kovacs.

112. See Pietro Di Donato, Christ in Concrete (Indianapolis: Bobbs-Merrill, 1939), pp. 252, 255, 258-59, 263-65; Pietro Militello, The Italians in America (Philadelphia:

Franklin, 1973), p. 26.

113. For a description of a Slovak wedding in a
Pennsylvania mining town see Edward A. Steiner, On the
Trail of the Immigrant (New York: Revell, 1906), pp. 207-
08.

114. The kazatzke was "a familiar dance at all Jewish weddings" (Charles Angoff, In the Morning Light [New
York: Beechhurst, 1952], p. 213); see also Beatrice Bisno,
Tomorrow's Bread (Philadelphia: Jewish Publication Society,
1938), p. 65.

115. Example 32a was provided the author by his
uncle-in-law, Fortunato Sordillo. Sordillo was a professional trombonist, music educator, and bandmaster. Example
32b was provided by S. W., Chinese, second generation, Interview, November 1973.

116. Mary Mellish, Sometimes I Reminisce (New
York: Putnam, 1941), pp. 67-68. For other references to
the use of bands at funerals see Riis, Children, p. 24;
Chotzinoff, Lost, p. 131.

117. Wood, Hamtramck, p. 42; Carla Bianco, The
Two Rosetos (Bloomington: Indiana University Press, 1974),
pp. 118-19; B. R., "Report," p. 3, describes these songs as
characteristic of the type sung by Lithuanians at funerals.

118. B. P., Greek, third generation, "Autobiographical Report," April 1967, p. 4.

119. For example, George J. Prpic, The Croatian
Immigrants in America (New York: Philosophical Library,
1971), p. 374, writes that tambouritsas, manufactured by a
few factories in America and advertised in Croatian newspapers and other publications, were being sold "all over
America."

120. See, for instance, Rischin, Promised, p. 138,
on the Yiddish songs issued by Katznellenbogen and Rabino-
witz, in New York; and Cleveland Digest, 1937, Vol. I,
p. 29, on A Songbook, 1000 Slovak Gems, issued by Michael
Sincak, of Monessen, Pennsylvania.

121. Poles in Chicago, p. 16.

122. Chotzinoff, Lost, p. 41.

123. The Life Stories of Undistinguished Americans,
ed. Hamilton Holt (New York: Pott, 1906), pp. 27-28.

124. Robert E. Park, The Immigrant Press and Its
Control (New York: Harper, 1922), p. 133; Leong Gor Yun,
Chinatown Inside Out (New York: Barrows Mussey, 1936),
p. 22; Sol Liptzin, Eliakum Zunser (New York: Behrman
House, 1950), p. 226.

125. The History of the Finns in Minnesota, ed.
Hans R. Wasastjerna, tr. Toivo Rosvall (Duluth: Minnesota

Finnish-American Historical Society, 1957), pp. 298-99;
Cleveland Digest, 1938, Vol. II, pp. 3-4; Ito, Issei,
pp. 814-15.
126. Cleveland Digest, 1937, Vol. IV, p. 61; Ralph
Foster Weld, Brooklyn Is America (New York: Columbia
University Press, 1950), p. 217; Prpic, Croatian, p. 279;
Marie Prisland, From Slovenia--To America (Chicago:
Slovenian Women's Union of America, 1968), p. 130; Chotzinoff, Lost, p. 115; Landesman, Brownsville, p. 79.
127. Landesman, Brownsville, p. 152.
128. On this matter see Gunther Barth, Bitter
Strength (Cambridge: Harvard University Press, 1964),
p. 125; Stephen Graham, "The Bowery," Harper's Monthly
Magazine, 154 (February 1927): 335.
129. Giuseppe Cautela, "The Italian Theatre in New
York," American Mercury, 12 (September 1927): 111.
130. Lou D'Angelo, "What," pp. 104-15; see also
Frank Mele, Polpetto (New York: Crown, 1973), pp. 86-90.
131. C. T., "Report," p. 2, 4.
132. Helen Ware, "The American-Hungarian Folk-
Song," Musical Quarterly, 2 (July 1916): 435-38.
133. Park, Immigrant, pp. 153-54; Barth, Bitter,
pp. 124-25.
134. See, for example, Konrad Bercovici, Dust of
New York (New York: Boni and Liveright, 1919), p. 234;
Bercovici, Around the World in New York (New York:
Century, 1924), pp. 257, 356; Emil Lengyel, Americans
from Hungary (Philadelphia: Lippincott, 1948), p. 226; M.
K. Argus [Mikhail K. Jeleznov], Moscow-on-the-Hudson
(New York: Harper, 1951), pp. 4-5.
135. The author has stayed at several such hotels
and can vouch for the bountiful supply of food and music.
The daytime activities are ones he has witnessed.
136. A. V., Italian, second generation, "Autobiographical Report," April 1972, p. 5. For a description of
entertainment at Jewish resort hotels see Chotzinoff, Days,
p. 141; Harry Gersh, "Kochalein: Poor Man's Shangri-la,"
in Commentary on the American Scene, ed. Elliot E. Cohen
(New York: Knopf, 1953), pp. 161-77.
137. William Saroyan, My Name Is Aram (New
York: Harcourt, Brace, 1940), p. 198.
138. Saloutos, Greeks, pp. 78-81; see also Harry M.
Petrakis, The Odyssey of Kostas Volakis (New York: McKay,
1963), p. 76.
139. Cautela, "Italian," pp. 106-12; Hutchins Hapgood, "The Italian Theater of New York," in A Documentary
History of the Italian Americans, ed. Wayne Moquin and

Charles Van Doren (New York: Praeger, 1974), pp. 317-20.

140. Bercovici, Dust, pp. 54-55.

141. Michael Gold, "East Side Memories, " American Mercury, 18 (September 1929): 98. Other Jewish gathering-spots are mentioned in Zelda F. Popkin, "The Changing East Side, " American Mercury, 10 (February 1927): 171-72; and in Alfred Kazin, A Walker in the City (New York: Harcourt, Brace & World, 1951), p. 91.

142. Ivan Narodny, "Two of Hungary's Leading Composers Now in America, " Musical America, 17 May 1913, p. 13.

143. Edward Steiner, "The Hungarian Immigrant, " The Outlook, 29 August 1903, pp. 1041-42.

144. Most members of the first generation state that they had no time for music during their first few years in America.

145. Letter of M. F. Intihar, appearing 22 May 1937, in the Slovenian newspaper Enakopravnost, reprinted in Cleveland Digest, 1937, Vol. V, p. 521.

146. D. P. , Italian, third generation, "Autobiographical Report, " April 1972, pp. 2-3, writes that his grandfather worked long and hard for little money. Unable to afford recreations like attending the opera, he played his guitar and sang Italian songs with his family; also he often took his entire family to the Italian-American Social Club of East Boston, where some pleasant musical evenings were passed together with friends.

147. George H. Eckhardt, "What Do People Listen to on the Radio?, " Etude, 50 (July 1932): 517, writes that a Philadelphia poll found that eighty-four percent of the women and forty-six percent of the men spoken to favored dance music. M. J. , Italian, third generation, "Autobiographical Report, " May 1972, p. 1, says that his Sicilian grandmother always demanded lively dances like the tarantella and sentimental songs like "Come Back to Sorrento. "

148. L. S. , Italian, third generation, "Autobiographical Report, " April 1976, p. 2. Much the same thing is said in B. R. , "Report, " p. 1; however, instead of a violin the Lithuanians whom B. R. writes about taught themselves to play the harmonica and accordion.

149. Elizabeth May, "Encounters with Japanese Music in Los Angeles, " Western Folklore, 17 (July 1958): 192.

150. P. B. , Czechoslovakian, third generation, "Autobiographical Report, " April 1972, pp. 2-3.

151. Bill Hosokawa, Nisei, the Quiet Americans (New York: Morrow, 1969), p. 153.

152. Merrill, Once, p. 14. For further information

on Jewish use of phonographs, see Morris Clark, "America as Cradle of Jewish Music," Musical America, 28 June 1913, p. 25; Anzia Yezierska, Red Ribbon on a White Horse (New York: Scribner, 1950), p. 199.

153. The resorting to recordings when people had nothing to say to each other was more characteristic of men than of women.

154. Militello, Italians, pp. 16-17; Wladziu Valentino Liberace, An Autobiography (New York: Putnam, 1973), p. 63.

155. D. L., Italian, third generation, "Autobiographical Report," April 1970, p. 3.

156. S. S., "Report," pp. 3-4. Similar accounts are in Gene Fowler, Schnozzola (New York: Viking, 1951), p. 14; D. JA., Italian, third generation, "Autobiographical Report," April 1969, pp. 3-4; W. E., Italian, second generation, "Autobiographical Report," April 1976, pp. 6-7.

157. Joseph, "Where," p. 179.

158. Further evidence for music making at work may be found in Bercovici, Around, pp. 142-43; Bercovici, Dust, pp. 164-65. From 1937 through 1940 the author had his hair cut at a Washington Street barbershop on Boston's Dedham line, where two Italian barbers, father and son, sang continuously and played guitars when idle.

159. Andrew F. Rolle, The American Italians (Belmont, Calif.: Wadsworth, 1972), p. 171; Maurice B. Marchello, Crossing the Tracks (New York: Vantage, 1969), p. 37; Stoyan Pribechevich, "In an American Factory," Harper's Magazine, 177 (September 1938): 372; Di Donato, Christ, p. 190; Bisno, Tomorrow's, pp. 195-96; Rischin, Promised, p. 70. As the subject of music at work was taken up in Chapter 1, detailed discussion here is unnecessary.

160. Lillian W. Betts, "Child Labor in Shops and Homes," The Outlook, 18 April 1903, p. 922.

161. Marchello, Crossing, pp. 54-55.

162. Caroline Singer, "An Italian Saturday," The Century, 101 (March 1921): 592; Phyllis H. Williams, Southern Italian Folkways in Europe and America (New York: Russell and Russell, 1938), p. 33; Wop!, ed. Salvatore J. La Gumina (San Francisco: Straight Arrow, 1973), pp. 32-38, 50-51; Adriana Spadoni, "Cecco Remains," The Century, 102 (October 1921): 883; Rudolph Glanz, Jews and Italians (New York: N. p., 1971), p. 17; Marie Hall Ets, Rosa, The Life of an Italian Immigrant (Minneapolis: University of Minnesota Press, 1970), pp. 214-15.

163. Griffin Barry, "Where Music Lightens the

Toilers' Burdens, " Musical America, 22 (May 1915), p. 4.
164. More often than other ethnic groups, southern
Italians are mentioned as singing and dancing in the streets;
see, for example, William E. Davenport, "The Italian Immigrant in America, " The Outlook, 3 January 1903, p. 32;
Di Donato, Three, p. 174; Jessie Fremont Beale and Anne
Withington, "Life's Amenities, " in Americans in Process,
ed. Robert A. Woods (Boston: Houghton Mifflin, 1903),
pp. 225-26; D. C. , Italian, third generation, "Autobiographical Report, " May 1972, pp. 12-13.
165. Catherine Brody, "A New York Childhood, "
American Mercury, 14 (May 1928): 59. See also Hutchins
Hapgood, Types from City Streets (New York: Funk &
Wagnalls, 1910), pp. 134-35.
166. See, for example, Marie J. Concistre, in
Cordasco, Italians, p. 227; Mele, Polpetto, pp. 234, 239-44.
167. An excellent description of a Sicilian serinata
of this type is found in Jerre Mangione, Mount Allegro (New
York: Knopf, 1952), pp. 23-24.
168. Cleveland Digest, 1937, Vol. V, p. 563.

Chapter 4

1. Milton M. Gordon, Assimilation in American
Life (New York: Oxford University Press, 1964), p. 47.
2. For a more general discussion of this statement,
as it applied to Jews, see C. Bezalel Sherman, The Jew
Within American Society (Detroit: Wayne State University
Press, 1961), pp. 24-40.
3. In this regard see Neil C. Sandberg, "The Changing Polish American, " Polish American Studies, 31 (Spring
1974): 10; also I Am An American, ed. Robert Spiers Benjamin (New York: Alliance, 1941), p. 92.
4. Gordon, Assimilation, p. 71, gives a valuable list
of all the "assimilation variables" that effect cultural change
in the ethnic communities.
5. Oscar Handlin, The Uprooted (New York: Grosset & Dunlap, 1951), p. 5; William Carlson Smith, Americans
in Process (Ann Arbor, Mich.: Edwards, 1937), p. 211;
Joseph A. Wytrwal, America's Polish Heritage (Detroit:
Endurance, 1961), p. xvii.
6. Leong Gor Yun, Chinatown Inside Out (New York:
Barrows Mussey, 1936), pp. 189-90.
7. When the author met one of these former storytellers in 1947, the sixty-year-old man had already been an

employee in a bakery for thirty years. He still remembered the verses of "Suhrab wi Rustam" and sang a half-hour's portion of the epic.

8. Philip M. Kayal and Joseph M. Kayal, The Syrian-Lebanese in America (Boston: Twayne, 1975), pp. 125-26; Clement Lawrence Valletta, Americanization in Carnata (New York: Arno, 1968), p. 363; D. S., Jewish, third generation, "Autobiographical Report," April 1976, p. 2.

9. L. S., Italian, third generation, "Autobiographical Report," April 1976, p. 3; R. D., Polish, third generation, "Autobiographical Report," January 1969, p. 2; Elin L. Anderson, We Americans (Cambridge: Harvard University Press, 1937), p. 153.

10. Robin M. Williams, Jr., American Society, 2nd ed. (New York: Knopf, 1967), p. 119; D. M., Albanian, third generation, "Autobiographical Report," April 1970, p. 4; E. B., Lithuanian, second generation, "Autobiographical Report," April 1972, p. 3. For mention of the Italians' failure to transplant their culture see Caroline F. Ware, Greenwich Village, 1920-1930 (Boston: Houghton Mifflin, 1935), pp. 172, 364; of the Syrian-Lebanese failure see Kayal, p. 202.

11. Harriet Lane Levy, 920 O'Farrell Street (Garden City, N. Y.: Doubleday, 1947), p. 10; Myra Kelly, Little Aliens (New York: Scribner, 1910), p. 231; Charles Angoff, Journey to the Dawn (New York: Beechhurst, 1951), p. 207; Samuel Chotzinoff, A Lost Paradise (New York: Knopf, 1955), p. 69; Rudolf Glanz, Jew and Italian (New York: N. p., 1971), p. 120.

12. Michael Freedland, Irving Berlin (London: Allen, 1974), p. 12.

13. Moses Rischin, The Promised City (Cambridge: Harvard University Press, 1962), p. 138.

14. B. R., Lithuanian, third generation, "Autobiographical Report," May 1969, p. 10. Much the same thing is stated by S. S., Armenian, third generation. "Autobiographical Report," April 1976, pp. 5-6.

15. Cleveland Foreign Language Newspaper Digest, 1937, Vol. IV (Cleveland: WPA Project 18881-C, 1940), p. 193; Maldwyn Allen Jones, American Immigration (Chicago: University of Chicago Press, 1960), p. 298; Alter F. Landesman, Brownsville (New York: Bloch, 1969), pp. 236-37.

16. [Samuel Ornitz], Haunch, Paunch and Jowl, An Anonymous Autobiography (New York: Boni & Liveright, 1923), pp. 30-31.

17. Milford S. Weiss, Valley City, A Chinese Com-

226 ● A Sound of Strangers

munity in America (Cambridge: Schenkman, 1974), pp. 199-
200; D. D., Greek, third generation, "Autobiographical Report, " May 1974, p. 4.   See also Jeanne Wakatsuki Houston
and James D. Houston, Farewell to Manzanar (Boston:
Houghton Mifflin, 1973), p. 77, for young Japanese-American
reactions to traditional Japanese music.
   18.   For more on the subject of this paragraph see
W. Lloyd Warner, American Life, Dream and Reality, rev.
ed. (Chicago: University of Chicago Press, 1962), pp. 183-
84; Paul J. Campisi, in American Minorities, ed. Milton M.
Barron (New York: Knopf, 1962), p. 310; Ware, Greenwich,
pp. 191, 340; W. Lloyd Warner and Leo Srole, The Social
Systems of American Ethnic Groups (New Haven: Yale University Press, 1945), pp. 131-34.
   19.   Cleveland Newspaper Digest, 1937, Vol. V,
pp. 494-95, 618; Alex Simirenko, Pilgrims, Colonists, and
Frontiersmen (London: Free Press of Glencoe, 1964), pp.
114-15; Maud Cuney Hare, "Portuguese Folk Songs from
Provincetown, Cape Cod, Mass. , " Musical Quarterly, 14
(1928): 35; D. P. , Italian, third generation, "Autobiographical Report, " April 1972, p. 5.
   20.   See, for instance, Suad Joseph, "Where the
Twain Shall Meet--Lebanese in Cortland County, " New York
Folklore Quarterly, 20 (September 1964): 188-89; J. P.
Zenides, The Greeks in America (New York: Doran, 1922),
pp. 89-90.
   21.   Judith R. Kramer, The American Minority Community (New York: Crowell, 1962), pp. 158-59.   These per-
centages were a little higher for the second- and third-
generation ethnic Americans investigated by the author.
   22.   Abdo A. Elkholy, The Arab Moslems in the
United States (New Haven: College and University Press,
1966), p. 30.   H. R. , Polish, third generation, "Autobiographical Report, " April 1971, pp. 7-8, writes that though
his mother grew up in the Polish community of South Boston, she was introduced to non-Polish music at weddings
where one of the partners was an outsider: "When different cultures [sic] began to intermarry at the weddings,
bands played a little Italian, Irish, whatever the other culture's songs were, also. "
   23.   L. P. , Italian, third generation, "Autobiographical Report, " April 1967, p. 7; Neil C. Sandberg, "The
Changing Polish American, " Polish American Studies, 31
(Spring 1974): 11; George J. Prpic, The Croatian Immigrants in America (New York: Philosophical Library,
1971), p. 434.
   24.   I. D. , Jewish, third generation, "Autobiographi-

cal Report, " April 1971, pp. 1-2; W. E. , Italian, second generation, "Autobiographical Report, " April 1976, p. 8; Robert B. Klymasz, The Ukrainian Winter Folksong Cycle in Canada (Ottawa: National Museums of Canada, 1970), p. 9.

25. Pardee Lowe, Father and Glorious Descendant (Boston: Little, Brown, 1943), p. 58.

26. For further discussions of the effect of education, employment, and affluence on ethnic culture see Gordon, Assimilation, pp. 52-53; Jones, American, p. 298; Ware, Greenwich, pp. 84-85; Warner, American, p. 46; Warner and Srole, Social, p. 52; Judith R. Kramer and Seymour Leventman, Children of the Gilded Ghetto (New Haven: Yale University Press, 1961), p. 13; Sandberg, "Changing, " pp. 9-11; Frank Capra, The Name Above the Title, An Autobiography (New York: Macmillan, 1971), pp. 83-84; Wytrwal, America's, pp. 257-58.

27. R. K. , Polish, second generation, Interview, November 1966.

28. Emanuel Carnevali, Autobiography, compiled by Kay Boyle (New York: Horizon, n. d.), pp. 42-43.

29. Sol Liptzin, Eliakum Zunser (New York: Behrman House, 1950), p. 242. Concerning assimilation and the changes in Jewish sacred music, see Ande Manners, Poor Cousins (New York: Coward, McCann & Geoghegan, 1972), p. 152; and Arthur Mann, Yankee Reformers in the Urban Age (New York: Harper & Row, 1966), pp. 52-72.

30. John Foster Carr, Guide for the Immigrant Italian (Garden City, N. Y. : Doubleday, Page, 1911), p. 71.

31. Erik Amfitheatrof, The Children of Columbus (Boston: Little, Brown, 1973), p. 243.

32. See, for example, Leonard Covello with Guido D'Agostino, The Heart Is the Teacher (New York: McGraw-Hill, 1958), p. 34.

33. The author was one of the young attendants.

34. Mary Antin, The Promised Land (Boston: Houghton Mifflin, 1912), p. 267.

35. Jacques L. Gottlieb, "The Music School in the Settlement, " Musical Courier, 12 October 1916, pp. 34-35. Gottlieb at the time was Director of the New York East Side Settlement Music School.

36. Louise Llewellyn, "Boston Orchestra of Wage Earners, " Musical America, 11 May 1912, p. 17. See also Moses Rischin, The Promised City (Cambridge: Harvard University Press, 1962), pp. 101-02.

37. Item on Franz X. Arens and the People's Symphony, in Musical America, 29 October 1910, p. 5; also, "Music School Settlement Concert, " Musical Courier, 21

April 1921, p. 31.

38.   K. S. C., "Bringing Music Home to the Polyglot Population of the East Side," Musical America, 8 June 1912, p. 3.

39.   See Landesman, Brownsville, p. 155; Selig Adler and Thomas C. Connolly, From Ararat to Suburbia (Philadelphia: Jewish Publication Society, 1960), p. 187; Covello, The Heart, pp. 43, 49; Warner and Srole, Social, pp. 144-45.

40.   Ronald Sanders, Reflections on a Teapot (New York: Harper & Row, 1972), p. 132.

41.   Chotzinoff, Lost, pp. 54-55, 68.

42.   Covello, The Heart, p. 27.

43.   This version was sung by the second- and third-grade pupils of the Quincy School, around 1929-30; they puzzled over the identity of this stout John Virgin. Most of the youngsters decided he had to be Greek.

44.   Arthur Mann, La Guardia: A Fighter Against His Times, 1882-1933, Vol. I (Philadelphia: Lippincott, 1951), p. 76.

45.   The author's father and uncle were two who joined up and became citizens. The songs cited are ones the two men continued to sing until their death, though the usual music they enjoyed was Middle Eastern.

46.   B. C., Italian, third generation, "Autobiographical Report," May 1969, p. 4.

47.   S. A., Jewish, third generation, "Autobiographical Report," April 1974, p. 6.

48.   Lowe, Father, p. 43.

49.   B. E., Italian, third generation, "Autobiographical Report," April 1974, p. 1.

50.   Harry Manuel Shulman, Slums of New York (New York: Boni, 1938), p. 22; Halsey Stevens, The Life and Music of Béla Bartók, rev. ed. (New York: Oxford, 1964), p. 93; D. J. Lawless, "Attitudes of Immigrant and Ethnic Societies in Vancouver Towards Integration into Canadian Life," International Migration, 2 (1964): 205; N. M., Spanish-Italian, third generation, "Autobiographical Report," April 1972, pp. 3-4.

51.   See, for example, Xenides, Greeks, p. 149, on the translation of Greek-Orthodox hymns into English. Today almost all of the music in Orthodox churches is sung in English.

52.   Robert E. Park, The Immigrant Press and Its Control (New York: Harper, 1922), pp. 133-34.

53.   Ruth Rubin, "Yiddish Folksongs of Immigration and the Melting Pot," New York Folklore Quarterly, 17 (Autumn 1961): 179.

54. Elizabeth May, "Encounters with Japanese Music in Los Angeles," Western Folklore, 17 (July 1958): 192-93.

55. Bruno Nettl and Ivo Moravcik, "Czech and Slovak Songs Collected in Detroit," Midwest Folklore, 5 (Spring 1955): 37, 40-44.

56. Klymasz, Ukrainian, pp. 10-11.

57. Ibid., pp. 39-40.

58. Ibid., pp. 75-76.

59. Ibid., pp. 73-74, 121-22.

60. Francis J. Brown and Joseph Slabey Roucek, eds., Our Racial and National Minorities (New York: Prentice-Hall, 1939), p. 327.

61. Houston, Farewell, pp. 86-87; Smith, Americans, pp. 246-47.

62. Weiss, Valley, p. 215.

63. Carrie Balaban, Continuous Performance (New York: Balaban Foundation, 1964), p. 30. "Nat' an-for What Are You Waitin'," words and music by James Kendis, was published in 1916; "Cohen Owes Me $97," by Irving Berlin, in 1915.

64. B. C., Italian, third generation, "Autobiographical Report," May 1969, p. 3.

65. Though the author interviewed mostly local Boston musicians, the biographies of performers like Sinatra, Como, and others make clear that these were more than local practices.

66. E. R., Portuguese, second generation, "Autobiographical Report," April 1971, pp. 11-12.

67. Idwal Jones, "Cathay on the Coast," American Mercury, 8 (August 1926): 459; also Jade Snow Wong, Fifth Chinese Daughter (New York: Harper, 1950), pp. 74-75.

68. James Jaffe, The American Jews (New York: Random House, 1968), p. 103.

69. Earlier in this chapter a similar observation was made about Ukrainian music heard in the Christmas season.

70. Kayal, Syrian-Lebanese, pp. 194-95.

71. The author was introduced to this Polish couple by R. K. (see note 27). The old man, a former accordion-player, was born in 1890 and came to America when he was twenty-one years of age. His wife, a former singer, could not remember when she was born, but said that she arrived here, already a young woman, in 1913. They married each other a year after her arrival.

Chapter 5

1. See Judith R. Kramer, The American Minority
Community (New York: Crowell, 1962), pp. 160-61.
2. Virgil Thomson, American Music Since 1910
(New York: Holt, Rinehart & Winston, 1971), p. 16.
3. Maurice R. Davie, "Our Vanishing Minorities,"
in Francis J. Brown and Joseph Slabey Roucek, One World,
rev. ed. (New York: Prentice-Hall, 1945), p. 543.
4. The author has spent, and continues to spend,
time and effort helping to put across now one ethnic festival,
now another. Permanent success remains elusive. The organizers of festas complain that the young refuse and the old
are too feeble to help out. The Boston International Institute's annual "Whole World Celebration" must discover novel
attractions each year in order to keep attendance figures
high.
5. G. C., interviewed on 19 November 1971, was the
owner of an Italian grocery store he had inherited from his
father. Occasionally the father still came down to the store
to help out. G. C. had just been asked about the "extended
family" living in his home.
6. Eugene Stinson writes in the Chicago Daily News,
9 May 1932: "Chicago's music is more than 50 percent de-
pendent upon the foreign-born element of its population"; in
Wasyl Halich, Ukrainians in the United States (Chicago:
University of Chicago Press, 1957), p. 138.
7. See, for example, the comments in John Horace
Mariano, The Second Generation of Italians in New York
City (Boston: Christopher, 1921), p. 259.
8. This is in large part the theme of Louis Adamic,
A Nation of Nations (New York: Harper, 1945).
9. The similarity of blue notes to the pitches produced in cantorial chant is discussed in Isaac Goldberg,
George Gershwin, supplemented by Edith Garson (New York:
Ungar, 1958), p. 40.
10. Over the past ten years students enrolled in the
author's course on American Music have been asked to volunteer for these sessions.
11. Only one group, the descendants of East European Jews, showed a greater curiosity about advanced
twentieth-century musical styles. Some even claimed a
real admiration for the more bizarre compositions.
12. The main sources for the list are Julius Matt-
feld, Variety Music Cavalcade, 1620-1969, 3rd ed. (Englewood Cliffs, N. J.: Prentice-Hall, 1971); David Ewen,
American Popular Songs (New York: Random House, 1966);

and the sheet music itself.

13. Frank Hruby, "Cleveland--A Cultural Enigma, " Musical America (September 1961), p. 17.

14. D. S., Italian, third generation, "Autobiographical Report, " May 1971, pp. 1-6. The writer was a student attending the University of Massachusetts at Boston at the time she submitted the report.

15. Joseph William Carlevale, Americans of Italian Descent in Philadelphia and Vicinity (Philadelphia: Ferguson, 1954), pp. 17, 73-74, 80-81, 111.

16. Louis Adamic, From Many Lands (New York: Harper, 1940), pp. 68-79.

17. Irving Howe, World of Our Fathers (New York: Harcourt Brace Jovanovich, 1976), p. 558.

18. Max Wilk, They're Playing Our Song (New York: Atheneum, 1973), pp. 186-87.

19. Gay Talese, Fame and Obscurity (New York: World, 1970), p. 21.

20. Eddie Cantor, My Life Is In Your Hands, as told to David Freedman (New York: Harper, 1928), p. 80.

21. Cantor, Life, p. 116.

22. Herbert J. Gans, The Urban Villagers (New York: Free Press, 1962), p. 83.

23. Cantor, Life, pp. 100-01.

24. Wladziu Valentino Liberace, An Autobiography (New York: Putnam, 1973), p. 21.

25. George T. Simon, The Big Bands, rev. ed. (New York: Collier, 1974), pp. 321-23, 542.

26. Edward Alsworth Ross, The Old World in the New (New York: Century, 1914), p. 103.

27. Herbert Kupferberg, Those Fabulous Philadelphians (New York: Scribner, 1969), pp. 196-97.

28. Allen H. Eaton, Immigrant Gifts to American Life (New York: Russell Sage Foundation, 1932), p. 16.

29. Cleveland Foreign Language Newspaper Digest, 1937, Vol. IV (Cleveland: W. P. A. in Ohio, 1940), p. 129; George Schiro, Americans by Choice (Utica, N. Y. : N. p. , 1940), pp. 148-49.

30. Cornel Lengyel, ed. , Fifty Local Prodigies, History of Music in San Francisco Series, Vol. V (San Francisco: W. P. A. of California, 1940), p. 89.

31. Lengyel, Fifty, pp. 113-16.

32. Robert Merrill, with Sandford Dody, Once More from the Beginning (New York: Macmillan, 1965), p. 84.

33. Lengyel, Fifty, pp. 109-10.

34. Howe, World, p. 566.

35. Frank Sinatra, in Simon, Bands, p. ix.

36. "How'd You Like to Spoon With Me?"; w. Edward Lasko, m. Jerome Kern (New York: Harms, 1905).

37. "Bimini Bay"; w. Gus Kahn and Raymond Egan, m. Richard Whiting (New York: Remick, 1921).

38. "She's a New Kind of Old-Fashioned Girl"; w. Billy Rose, m. Vincent Rose (New York: Berlin, 1929).

39. Wilk, They're, p. 152-53.

40. Goldberg, Gershwin, pp. 41-42, 104.

41. Macy Nulman, Concise Encyclopedia of Jewish Music (New York: McGraw-Hill, 1975), s. v. "Hassidic Song."

42. "My One and Only"; w. Ira Gershwin, m. George Gershwin (New York: New World Music, 1927).

43. "My Man's Gone Now"; w. Dubose Heyward, m. George Gershwin (New York: Gershwin, 1935).

44. "Fascinating Rhythm"; w. Ira Gershwin, m. George Gershwin (New York: New World, 1924).

45. Goldberg, Gershwin, pp. 39-40.

46. It was first popularized by Columbo's orchestra. Later the song became a staple in the Perry Como repertoire.

47. All are of unknown authorship, except the last, composed by Fassone.

48. "La Capuana" moves into the supertonic minor by means of a flatted seventh. "Se Fossi una Viola, " at the beginning of the tune, moves immediately from I to VI, and later goes toward the flat side by lowering the sixth of the scale.

49. "Sweethearts on Parade"; w. Charles Newman, m. Carmen Lombardo (New York: Mayfair, 1928).

50. "I Only Have Eyes for You"; w. Al Dubin, m. Harry Warren (New York: Remick, 1934).

51. "Moon River"; w. Johnny Mercer, m. Henry Mancini (New York: Famous Music, 1961).

52. See Peter Gammond, One Man's Music (London: Wolfe, 1971), p. 46.

53. David Ewen, ed. American Popular Songs (New York: Random House, 1966), s. v. "Every Little Movement Has a Meaning of Its Own."

54. This first collaboration between the Gershwin brothers was not published for many years. Finally, in 1959, it was issued by the Gershwin Publishing Corporation.

55. Michael Freedland, Irving Berlin (London: Allen, 1974), p. 28; Edward B. Marks, They All Sang (New York: Viking, 1935), p. 174.

56. Freedland, Berlin, pp. 48-49.

57. Marks, They, p. 174.

58. Some of the Jewish contributors to this sort of song are discussed in Harry Golden, The Greatest Jewish City in the World (Garden City, N.Y.: Doubleday, 1972), pp. 26-27.

59. Ewen, American, s.v. "You Made Me Love You."

60. The work was written in 1913 but won extensive recognition only in 1926, when it was employed as the musical theme for the silent movie What Price Glory?

61. See, for example, the list of American composers printed in the Schwann-1 Record and Tape Guide (July 1975), pp. 30-33.

62. The author studied composition under Piston, met Copland during a couple of evening socials at Harvard, where the composer had come to deliver a series of lectures, in 1951-52, and once received a totally unexpected evening visit from Hovhaness that lasted until the early-morning hours.

63. As illustration of one composer's thinking in these matters see Aaron Copland, Music and Imagination (New York: New American Library, 1952); and The New Music, 1900-1960 (New York: Norton, 1968).

64. Gay Talese, New York (New York: Harper, 1961), p. 153.

65. Joseph Machlis, American Composers of Our Time (New York: Crowell, 1963), p. 167.

66. Peter G. Davis, "They Love Him in Seattle," New York Times Magazine, 21 March 1976, p. 46.

67. This praise is found in the David article, p. 42.

68. Ibid., pp. 49-50.

69. Marion Bauer, "Copland," The New Book of Modern Composers, ed. David Ewen (New York: Knopf, 1964), p. 142.

70. Richard Dobrin, Aaron Copland (New York: Crowell, 1967), p. 115.

71. Ibid., Copland, p. 157.

72. The quotations are from Chapter 3 of Copland's Music and Imagination.

73. Dobrin, Copland, p. 195.

74. M.J., Italian, third generation, "Autobiographical Report," May 1973, p. 1.

75. V.M., Jewish, third generation, "Autobiographical Report," April 1969, pp. 1-2.

76. B.PA., Lithuanian, third generation, "Autobiographical Report," April 1969, pp. 9-10.

77. See Michael Novak, The Rise of the Unmeltable Ethnics (New York: Macmillan, 1972), p. 23.

78. L. J., Jewish, third generation, "Autobiographical Report," April 1970, p. 5.
79. S. L., Portuguese, second generation, "Autobiographical Report," April 1970, pp. 7-8.
80. Z. M., Armenian, second generation, "Autobiographical Report," April 1975, pp. 6-7.
81. B. E., Italian, third generation, "Autobiographical Report," April 1974, pp. 1-2.
82. C. T., Italian, third generation, "Autobiographical Report," May 1969, p. 5.
83. D. JA., Italian, third generation, "Autobiographical Report," April 1969, pp. 16-18.
84. B. J., Italian, third generation, "Autobiographical Report," April 1974, pp. 1-2; L. S., Italian, third generation, "Autobiographical Report," April 1976, p. 8.
85. Paul Jacobs and Saul Landau, To Serve the Devil, Vol. II (New York: Random House, 1971), p. 266. See also Christie W. Kiefer, Changing Cultures, Changing Lives (San Francisco: Jossey-Bass, 1974), pp. 3-4, on the solidarity of the Japanese-American group when challenged from the outside.
86. Apparently the song was quasi-improvised. The reproduced text is the one dictated to the author by the singer after the song's completion. It differs in several particulars from what was sung. For example, the sung version of the last line had employed the word "fuck," not "mess." The ethnic's continuing feeling of being discriminated against is discussed by Bill Moyers, in White Ethnics, ed. Joseph Ryan (Englewood Cliffs, N. J.: Prentice-Hall, 1973), p. 69.
87. Kertzer, Today's, p. 239.
88. For the effect of the Middle East conflict on Arab-Americans see Lauree D. Wigle, in Arabic Speaking Communities in American Cities, ed. Barbara C. Aswad (New York: Center for Migration Studies of New York, 1974), pp. 165-66.
89. The shedding of shame over one's background has been a gradual development, as can be seen in Leonard Covello with Guido D'Agostino, The Heart Is the Teacher (New York: McGraw-Hill, 1958), pp. 70-81; and Jacob A. Evanson, "Folksongs of an Industrial City," in Pennsylvania Songs and Legends, ed. George Korson (Baltimore: Johns Hopkins Press, 1949), p. 430.
90. Concerning the Jewish experience with integration see Judith R. Kramer and Seymour Leventman, Children of the Gilded Ghetto (New Haven: Yale University Press, 1961), pp. 10-12; Morris Freedman, "The New Farmers of Lakewood," in Commentary on the American Scene,

ed. Elliot E. Cohen (New York: Knopf, 1953), pp. 127-46;
and Herbert J. Gans, "Park Forest: Birth of a Jewish
Community, " in Commentary on the American Scene, pp.
205-23.
    91. Novak, in White Ethnics, p. 162; Novak, Unmelt-
able, pp. 31-32; Joseph Lopreato, Italian Americans (New
York: Random House, 1970), pp. 84-87, 171; Kertzer, Today's, p. 279; Michael J. Arlen, Passage to Ararat (New
York: Farrar, Straus & Giroux, 1975), pp. 6-7; Colin Greer,
ed., Divided Society (New York: Basic Books, 1974), pp.
17-18.
    92. On the Japanese see Kiefer, Changing, p. 38; the
Croatians, George J. Prpic, The Croatian Immigrants in
America (New York: Philosophical Library, 1971), pp. 385,
430; The New York Times, 9 September 1977, is the source
for the Armenian "One World" fair.
    93. Beverly Gudanowski, "The Best Polish Dancers,"
Boston Sunday Globe, New England Supplement, 11 April
1976, pp. 10-12, 22-23.
    94. The quotations are from Novak, in White Eth-
nics, pp. 160-61; but see also Ludwig Lewisohn, "The Art
of Being a Jew, " Harper's Monthly Magazine, May 1925,
pp. 725-27; Nathan Glazer and Daniel Patrick Moynihan,
Beyond the Melting Pot (Cambridge: M. I. T. and Harvard
University Press, 1963), p. 13; Joseph A. Wytrwal, America's Polish Heritage (Detroit: Endurance, 1961), pp. xx-
xxi, 276, 279-83; Kertzer, Today's, p. 156; Kiefer, Changing, p. 104.
    95. E. R., Armenian, third generation, "Autobio-
graphical Report, " April 1972. The interview took place in
the first week of May.
    96. See Eaton, Immigrant, pp. 29, 53-54; Prpic,
Croatian, pp. 373, 461-62; Alice L. Sickels, Around the
World in St. Paul (Minneapolis: University of Minnesota
Press, 1945). In 1969 a student at the University of Massachusetts at Boston wrote a lengthy study of the Boston
International Music Festival, 1924-1936.
    97. This conversation took place in November 1976,
at a folk festival where the Krakowiak Dancers were appearing.
    98. Members were interviewed in February 1972,
after a performance at the University of Massachusetts at
Boston.
    99. American-Bulgarian Review, 10 (1960): 28-30.
    100. Wytrwal, America's, p. 61; C. Bezalel Sher-
man, The Jew Within American Society (Detroit: Wayne
State University Press, 1961), pp. 53-55; Neil C. Sandberg,

"The Changing Polish American," Polish American Studies, 31 (1974): 11; E. J. Kahn, The American People, the Findings of the 1970 Census (New York: Weybright & Talley, 1974), p. 4.

BIBLIOGRAPHY

●————————————————————

Abbott, Edith. Immigration, Select Documents and Case
Records. Chicago: University of Chicago, 1924.
Accardi, Leonard. Italian Contributions to Albany in the
Nineteenth Century. Albany, N. Y.: La Capitale, 1941.
Adamic, Louis. "The Bohunks." American Mercury 14
(1928): 318-23.
————. Cradle of Life. New York: Harper, 1936.
————. From Many Lands. New York: Harper, 1940.
————. "A Land of Promise." Harper's Magazine, 163
(1931): 618-28.
————. Laughing in the Jungle. New York: Harper,
1932.
————. My America. New York: Harper, 1938.
————. A Nation of Nations. New York: Harper, 1945.
————. "Thirty Million New Americans." Harper's Mag-
azine 169 (1934): 684-94.
————. What's Your Name? New York: Harper, 1942.
Adams, Charlotte. "Italian Life in New York." Harper's
New Monthly Magazine 62 (1881): 676-84.
Adler, Cyrus. I Have Considered the Days. Philadelphia:
Jewish Publication Society, 1941.
Adler, Selig, and Thomas E. Connolly. From Ararat to
Suburbia: The History of the Jewish Community of Buf-
falo. Philadelphia: Jewish Publication Society, 1960.
Alland, Alexander. American Counterpoint. New York:
Day, 1943.
Allen, Frederick Lewis. Only Yesterday. New York:
Harper, 1931.
Alverson, Margaret Blake. Sixty Years of California Song.
Oakland: Author, 1913.
Amfitheatrof, Erik. The Children of Columbus. Boston:
Little, Brown, 1973.
Anderson, Elin L. We Americans. Cambridge: Harvard
University Press, 1937.

Angoff, Charles. Between Day and Dark. New York:
Yoseloff, 1959.
_____. The Bitter Spring. New York: Yoseloff, 1961.
_____. In the Morning Light. New York: Beechhurst,
1952.
_____. Journey to the Dawn. New York: Beechhurst,
1951.
_____. Summer Storm. New York: Yoseloff, 1963.
_____. The Sun at Noon. New York: Beechhurst, 1955.
_____. When I Was a Boy in Boston. New York:
Beechhurst, 1947.
Antin, Mary. The Promised Land. Boston: Houghton
Mifflin, 1912.
_____. They Who Knock at Our Gates. Boston:
Houghton Mifflin, 1914.
Argus, M. K. [Mikhail K. Jeleznov]. Moscow-on-the-
Hudson. New York: Harper, 1951.
Arlen, Michael J. Passage to Ararat. New York: Farrar,
Struas & Giroux, 1975.
Arleo, Joseph. The Grand Street Collector. New York:
Wlaker, 1970.
Aswad, Barbara C. Arabic Speaking Communities in Amer-
ican Cities. New York: Center for Migration Studies of
New York, 1974.
Ausubel, Nathan, ed. A Treasury of Jewish Folklore. New
York: Crown, 1948.
Bagu, S. "Integration of Immigrants." International Migra-
tion, 2 (1964): 40-46.
Balaban, Carrie. Continuous Performance. New York:
Balaban Foundation, 1964.
Barba, Harry. For the Grape Season. New York: Mac-
millan, 1960.
Barron, Milton M., ed. American Minorities. New York:
Knopf, 1962.
Barrows, Esther G. Neighbors All. Boston: Houghton
Mifflin, 1929.
Barry, Griffen. "Where Music Lightens the Toilers' Bur-
dens." Musical America, 22 May 1915, p. 4.
Barth, Gunther. Bitter Strength. Cambridge: Harvard
University Press, 1964.
Barton, Josef J. Peasants and Strangers. Cambridge:
Harvard University Press, 1975.
Beale, Jessie Fremont, and Anne Withington. "Life's
Amenities." In Americans in Process, ed. Robert A.
Woods, pp. 224-53.
Benjamin, Robert Spiers, ed. I Am an American. New
York: Alliance, 1941.

Bercovici, Konrad. Around the World in New York. New York: Century, 1924.
_____. Dust of New York. New York: Boni & Liveright, 1919.
_____. It's the Gypsy in Me. New York: Prentice-Hall, 1941.
_____. On New Shores. New York: Century, 1925.
Berg, Gertrude, and Cherney Berg. Molly and Me. New York: McGraw-Hill, 1961.
Bernard, William S. "Indices of Integration into the American Community." International Migration 11 (1973): 87-101.
Bernheimer, Charles S., ed. The Russian Jew in the United States. Philadelphia: Winston, 1905.
Bertocci, Angelo P. "Memoir of My Mother." Harper's Magazine 175 (1937): 8-19.
Betts, Lillian W. "Child Labor in Shops and Homes." The Outlook 73 (1903): 921-27.
Bianco, Carla. The Two Rosetos. Bloomington: Indiana University Press, 1974.
Bishop, William Henry. "San Francisco." Harper's New Monthly Magazine 66 (1883): 813-32.
Biskin, Miriam. My Life Among the Gentiles. South Brunswick, N. J.: Yoseloff, 1968.
Bisno, Beatrice. Tomorrow's Bread. Philadelphia: Jewish Publication Society, 1938.
Bodnar, John E., ed. The Ethnic Experience in Pennsylvania. Lewisburg: Bucknell University Press, 1973.
Bok, Edward. The Americanization of Edward Bok. New York: Scribner, 1921.
Bolles, Blair. "The Stew in the Melting Pot." Harper's Magazine 186 (1943): 179-86.
Boorstin, Daniel J. The Americans: The Democratic Experience. New York: Random House, 1973.
Bowers, David F., ed. Foreign Influences in American Life. Princeton: Princeton University Press, 1944.
Brandenburg, Broughton. Imported Americans. New York: Stokes, 1904.
Bratush, James D. A Historical Documentary of the Ukrainian Community of Rochester, New York, tr. Anastasia Smerychynska. Rochester: Christopher, 1973.
Bregstone, Philip P. Chicago and Its Jews. Chicago: Author, 1933.
Brewer, Daniel Chauncey. The Conquest of New England by the Immigrant. New York: Putnam, 1926.
Brody, Catharine. "A New York Childhood." American Mercury 14 (1928): 57-66.

Brown, Francis J., and Joseph Slabey Roucek, eds. One World, rev. ed. of Our Racial and National Minorities. New York: Prentice-Hall, 1945.

_____. Our Racial and National Minorities. New York: Prentice-Hall, 1939.

Brown, Lawrence Guy. Immigration. New York: Longmans, Green, 1933.

Burgess, Thomas. Greeks in America. Boston: Sherman, French, 1913.

_____, Charles Kendall Gilbert, and Charles Thorley Bridgeman. Foreigners of Friends. New York: Department of Missions and Church Extension, 1921.

Cachia, Peter. "A 19th Century Arab's Observations on European Music." Ethnomusicology 17 (1973): 41-51.

Cahan, Abraham. The Rise of David Levinsky. New York: Harper, 1917.

Cantor, Eddie. My Life Is in Your Hands, as told to David Freedman. New York: Harper, 1928.

Capek, Thomas. The Czechoslovaks. San Francisco: R. E. Research, 1969.

Capra, Frank. The Name Above the Title, An Autobiography. New York: Macmillan, 1971.

Carlevale, Joseph William. Americans of Italian Descent in Philadelphia and Vicinity. Philadelphia: Ferguson, 1954.

Carnevali, Emanuel. Autobiography, compiled by Kay Boyle. New York: Horizon, n. d.

Carr, John Foster. "The Coming of the Italian." The Outlook 82 (1906): 418-31.

_____. Guide for the Immigrant Italian. Garden City, N. Y.: Doubleday, 1911.

Cautela, Giuseppe. "The Italian Theatre in New York." American Mercury 12 (1927): 106-12.

Chotzinoff, Samuel. Day's at the Morn. New York: Harper & Row, 1964.

_____. A Lost Paradise. New York: Knopf, 1955.

Clark, Dennis. The Ghetto Game. New York: Sheed & Ward, 1962.

Clark, Morris. "America as Cradle of Jewish Music." Musical America, 28 June 1913, p. 25.

Cleveland Foreign Language Newspaper Digest. Hungarian, 1891-1892. Annals of Cleveland Newspaper Series. Cleveland: W. P. A. in Ohio, District Four, 1942.

Cleveland Foreign Language Newspaper Digest, 1937, Vol. IV. Hungarian, Polish. Annals of Cleveland Newspaper Series, W. P. A. Project 1881-C. Cleveland: W. P. A. in Ohio, District Four, 1940.

Cleveland Foreign Language Newspaper Digest, 1938, Vol. I.

Slovak, Roumanian, Carpatho-Russian, Czech. Annals of
Cleveland Newspaper Series. Cleveland: W. P. A. in
Ohio, District Four, 1940.
_____, Vol. III. Jewish. Annals of Cleveland Newspaper
Series. Cleveland: W. P. A. in Ohio, District Four, 1940.
_____, Vol. III. Lithuanian. Annals of Cleveland News-
paper Series. Cleveland: W. P. A. in Ohio, District
Four, 1940.
Coffin, Tristram P., and Hennig Cohen, eds. Folklore in
America. New York: Doubleday, 1966.
Cohen, Elliot E., ed. Commentary on the American Scene.
New York: Knopf, 1953.
Copland, Aaron, "Composer from Brooklyn: An Autobio-
graphical Sketch." In The New Music. New York:
Norton, 1968, pp. 151-68.
Cordasco, Francesco, and Eugene Bucchioni. The Italians.
Clifton, N. J.: Kelley, 1974.
Corsel, Ralph. Up There the Stars. New York: Citadel,
1968.
Corsi, Edward. In the Shadow of Liberty. New York:
Macmillan, 1935.
Covello, Leonard. The Social Background of the Italo-
American School Child. Leiden, Netherlands: Brill,
1967.
_____, with Guido D'Agostino. The Heart Is the Teacher.
New York: McGraw-Hill, 1958.
D'Agostino, Guido. Olives On the Apple Tree. New York:
Doubleday, Doran, 1940.
D'Angelo. Lou. What the Ancients Said. Garden City,
N. Y.: Doubleday, 1971.
D'Angelo, Pascal. Son of Italy. New York: Macmillan,
1924.
Davenport, William E. "The Italian Immigrant in America."
The Outlook 73 (1903): 28-37.
Davie, Maurice R. World Immigration. New York: Mac-
millan, 1936.
Davis, Jerome. The Russian Immigrant. New York:
Macmillan, 1922.
_____. The Russians and Ruthenians in America. New
York: Doran, 1922.
Davis, Peter G. "They Love Him in Seattle." The New
York Times Magazine, 21 March 1976, pp. 42-52.
DeCapite, Raymond. The Coming of Fabrizze. New York:
McKay, 1960.
DiDonato, Pietro di. Christ in Concrete. Indianapolis:
Bobbs-Merrill, 1939.
_____. Naked Author. New York: Phaedra, 1970.

242 ● A Sound of Strangers

_____. Three Circles of Light. New York: Messner, 1960.

Dobrin, Arnold. Aaron Copland: His Life and Times. New York: Crowell, 1967.

Eaton, Allen H. Immigrant Gifts to American Life. New York: Russell Sage Foundation, 1932.

Elkholy, Abdo A. The Arab Moslems in the United States. New Haven: College & University Press, 1966.

Ets, Marie Hall. Rosa, the Life of an Italian Immigrant. Minneapolis: University of Minnesota Press, 1970.

Evanson, Jacob A. "Folk Songs of an Industrial City." In Pennsylvania Songs and Legends, ed. George Korson. Baltimore: Johns Hopkins Press, 1949.

Ewen, David. American Popular Songs. New York: Random, 1966.

_____, comp. and ed. Composers Since 1900. New York: Wilson, 1969.

_____. A Journey to Greatness. New York: Holt, 1956.

_____. Leonard Bernstein. London: Allen, 1967.

Fairchild, Henry Pratt. Greek Immigration to the United States. New Haven: Yale University Press, 1911.

_____. Immigrant Backgrounds. New York: Wiley, 1927.

_____. The Melting-Pot Mistake. Boston: Little, Brown, 1926.

Fante, John. Dago Red. New York: Viking, 1940.

_____. Full of Life. Boston: Little, Brown, 1952.

_____. Wait Until Spring, Bandini. New York: Stackpole, 1938.

"Festa." The New Yorker, 5 October 1957, pp. 34-36.

Fisher, Renee B. Musical Prodigies. New York: Associated Press, 1973.

Foley, Rolla. Song of the Arab. New York: Macmillan, 1953.

Fowler, Gene. Schnozzola. New York: Viking, 1951.

Fox, Paul. The Poles in America. New York: Doran, 1922.

Freedland, Michael. Irving Berlin. London: Allen, 1974.

_____. Jolson. New York: Stein & Day, 1972.

Friedman, Theodore, and Robert Gordis, eds. Jewish Life in America. New York: Horizon, 1955.

Frye, Ellen. The Marble Threshing Floor. Austin: University of Texas, 1973.

Fumento, Rocco. Devil by the Tail. New York: McGraw-Hill, 1954.

_____. Tree of Dark Reflection. New York: Knopf, 1962.

Gale, Zona. "Robin Hood in Jones Street." The Outlook 92 (1909): 439-46.

Galitzi, Christine Avghi. A Study of Assimilation Among the Roumanians in the United States. 1929; rpt. New York: AMS, 1968.

Gallo, Patrick J., Ethnic-Alienation, The Italian-Americans. Rutherford, N. J.: Fairleigh Dickinson University Press, 1974.

Gallop, Rodney. "The Fado (The Portuguese Song of Fate)." Musical Quarterly 19 (1933): 199-213.

Gambino, Richard. Blood of My Blood, The Dilemma of the Italian-Americans. Garden City, N. Y.: Doubleday, 1974.

Gammond, Peter. One Man's Music. London: Wolfe, 1971.

Gans, Herbert J. Popular Culture and High Culture. New York: Basic Books, 1974.

_____. The Urban Villagers. New York: Free Press, 1962.

Gayton, A. H. "The 'Festa da Serreta' at Gustine." Western Folklore 7 (1948): 251-65.

Gigli, Beniamino. Memoirs, tr. Darina Silone. London: Cassell, 1957.

Ginzberg, Eli, and Hyman Berman. The American Worker in the Twentieth Century. New York: Free Press, 1963.

Glanz, Dr. Rudolf. Jew and Italian. New York: N. p., 1971.

Glazer, Nathan, and Daniel Patrick Moynihan. Beyond the Melting Pot. Cambridge: M. I. T. and Harvard University Press, 1963.

Gold, Michael. "East Side Memories." American Mercury 18 (1929): 95-101.

_____. "Reb Samuel." American Mercury 19 (1930): 176-80.

Goldberg, Isaac. George Gershwin, supplemented by Edith Garson. New York: Ungar, 1958.

Golden, Harry. The Greatest Jewish City in the World. Garden City, N. Y.: Doubleday, 1972.

Gor Yun, Leong. Chinatown Inside Out. New York: Barrows Mussey, 1936.

Gordon, Albert I. Jews in Transition. Minneapolis: University of Minnesota Press, 1949.

Gordon, Milton M. Assimilation in American Life. New York: Oxford University Press, 1964.

Gottlieb, Jacques L. "The Music School in the Settlement." Musical Courier, 12 October 1916, pp. 34-35.

Govorchin, Gerald Gilbert. Americans from Yugoslavia. Gainesville: University of Florida Press, 1961.

Graham, Stephen. "The Bowery Under Prohibition."

Harper's Magazine 154 (1927): 335-341.
_____. With Poor Immigrants to America. New York:
Macmillan, 1914.
Greer, Colin, ed. Divided Society. New York: Basic
Books, 1974.
Grose, Howard B. Aliens or Americans. New York: Mis-
sionary Education Movement of the U.S. and Canada,
1912.
Grossman, Ronald P. The Italians in America. Minneapo-
lis: Lerner, 1966.
Gudanowski, Beverly. "The Best Polish Dancers." Boston
Sunday Globe, 11 April 1976, pp. 10-12, 22-23.
Gunda, Bela. "The Investigation of the Culture of Different
Generations in Ethnology and Folklore." Midwest Folk-
lore 1 (1951): 85-90.
Hagopian, Elain C., and Ann Paden, eds. The Arab-
Americans. Wilmette, Ill.: Medina University, 1969.
Halich, Wasyl. Ukrainians in the United States. Chicago:
University of Chicago, 1937.
Handlin, Oscar. Boston's Immigrants, rev. ed. Cam-
bridge: Harvard University Press, 1959.
_____, ed. Children of the Uprooted. New York:
Braziller, 1966.
_____. Immigration as a Factor in American History.
Englewood Cliffs, N.J.: Prentice-Hall, 1959.
_____. Race and Nationality in American Life. Boston:
Little, Brown, 1957.
_____. The Uprooted. New York: Grosset & Dunlap,
1951.
Hansen, Marcus Lee. The Immigrant in American History,
ed. Arthur M. Schlesinger. Cambridge: Harvard Uni-
versity Press, 1940.
Hapgood, Hutchins. The Spirit of the Ghetto, ed. Moses
Rischin. Cambridge: Harvard University Press, 1967.
_____. Types from City Streets. New York: Funk &
Wagnalls, 1910.
Hare, Maude Cuney. "Portuguese Folk-Songs from Prov-
incetown, Cape God, Mass." Musical Quarterly 14
(1928): 35-53.
Harrington, Michael. The Other America. Baltimore:
Penguin, 1963.
Hartmann, Edward George. The Movement to Americanize
the Immigrant. New York: Columbia University Press,
1948.
Haskin, Frederic J. The Immigrant. New York: Revell,
1913.
Herlihy, Elisabeth, ed. and comp. Fifty Years of Boston.

Boston: Subcommittee on Memorial History of the Boston Tercentenary Committee, 1932.

Herndon, Booton. The Sweetest Music This Side of Heaven, The Guy Lombardo Story. New York: McGraw-Hill, 1964.

Higham, John. Strangers in the Land, 2nd ed. New York: Atheneum, 1973.

Hindus, Maurice. Green Worlds. New York: Doubleday, 1938.

Hitti, Philip K. The Syrians in America. New York: Doran, 1924.

Holde, Artur. Jews in Music. New York: Philosophical Library, 1959.

Holmes, Ralph. "Mark Twain and Music." The Century, 104 (1922): 844-50.

Holt, Hamilton, ed. The Life Stories of Undistinguished Americans. New York: Pott, 1906.

Hosokawa, Bill. Nisei, the Quiet Americans. New York: Morrow, 1969.

Houston, Jeanne Wakatsuki, and James D. Houston. Farewell to Manzanar. Boston: Houghton Mifflin, 1973.

Howe, Irving. World of Our Fathers. New York: Harcourt Brace Jovanovich, 1976.

Hoy, William J. "Chinatown Devises Its Own Street Names." California Folklore Quarterly 2 (1943): 71-75.

_____. "Native Festivals of the California Chinese." Western Folklore 7 (1948): 240-50.

Hruby, Frank. "Cleveland--A Cultural Enigma." Musical America, September 1961, pp. 16-19, 47, 49.

Hsu, Francis L. K. Americans and Chinese. Garden City, N. Y.: Doubleday, 1970.

Hull, Eleanor. Suddenly the Sun. New York: Friendship, 1957.

Ichihashi, Yamato. Japanese in the United States. Stanford: Stanford University Press, 1932.

Idelsohn, A. Z. Jewish Music. New York: Holt, 1929.

The Immigrant Jew in America, ed. Edward J. James. New York: Buck, 1907.

Italians in the City. New York: Arno, 1975.

Ito, Kazuo. Issei, A History of Japanese Immigrants in North America, tr. Shimichiro Nakamura and Jean S. Gerard. Seattle: Japanese Community Service, 1973.

Jacobs, Paul, and Saul Landau. To Serve the Devil, Vol. II. New York: Random House, 1971.

Jansen, Clifford J. "Leadership in the Toronto Italian Ethnic Group." International Migration 4 (1969): 25-43.

Jellinek, George. Callas. London: Gibbs & Phillips, 1961.

Jenks, Jeremiah W., and W. Jett Lanck. The Immigration
Problem, 6th ed. rev. Rufus D. Smith. New York:
Funk & Wagnalls, 1926.
Johnston, Ruth. "Immigrant's Search for Cultural Identity."
International Migration 6 (1968): 216-19.
Jones, Idwal. "Cathay on the Coast." American Mercury
8 (1926): 453-60.
Jones, Maldwyn Allen. American Immigration. Chicago:
University of Chicago Press, 1960.
Jordan, Emil L. Americans. New York: Norton, 1939.
Joseph, Suad. "Where the Twain Shall Meet--Lebanese in
Cortland County." New York Folklore Quarterly 20
(1964): 175-91.
K. S. C. "Bringing Music Home to the Polyglot Population of
the East Side." Musical America, 8 June 1912, p. 3.
Kahn, E. J., Jr., The American People, The Findings of
the 1970 Census. New York: Weybright & Talley, 1974.
Kayal, Philip M., and Joseph M. Kayal. The Syrian-
Lebanese in America. Boston: Twayne, 1975.
Kaye, Evelyn. "Thursday the Rabbi Explained." Boston
Sunday Globe, "New England," 27 February 1977, pp. 12-
15.
Kazin, Alfred. A Walker in the City. New York: Har-
court, Brace & World, 1951.
Kelly, Myra. Little Aliens. New York: Scribner, 1910.
_____. Little Citizens. New York: Doubleday, Page,
1904.
_____. Words of Liberty. New York: McClure, 1907.
Kertzer, Morris N. Today's American Jew. New York:
McGraw-Hill, 1967.
Kiefer, Christie W. Changing Cultures, Changing Lives.
San Francisco: Jossey-Bass, 1974.
Klutznick, Philip M. No Easy Answers. New York: Far-
rar, Straus & Cudahy, 1961.
Klymasz, Robert B. The Ukrainian Winter Folksong Cycle
in Canada. Ottawa: National Museums of Canada, 1970.
Kolehmainen, John I., and George W. Hill. Haven in the
Woods. Madison: State Historical Society of Wisconsin,
1951.
Konnyu, Leslie. Hungarians in the U. S. A. St. Louis:
American Hungarian Review, 1967.
Korson, George, ed. Pennsylvania Songs and Legends.
Baltimore: Johns Hopkins Press, 1949.
Kramer, Judith R. The American Minority Community.
New York: Crowell, 1962.
_____, and Seymour Leventman. Children of the Gilded
Ghetto. New Haven: Yale University Press, 1961.

Kupferberg, Herbert. Those Fabulous Philadelphians. New York: Scribner, 1969.

Kuropas, Myron B. The Ukrainians in America. Minneapolis: Lerner, 1972.

Kutak, Robert I. The Story of a Bohemian-American Village. Louisville, Ky.: Standard Printing, 1933.

La Guardia, Fiorello H. The Making of an Insurgent. Philadelphia: Lippincott, 1948.

LaGumina, Salvatore J., ed. Wop! San Francisco: Straight Arrow, 1973.

Landesman, Alter F. Brownsville. New York: Bloch, 1969.

Lantz, Herman R. People of Coal Town. New York: Columbia University Press, 1958.

LaPinna, G. The Italians in Milwaukee, Wisconsin. Milwaukee: N. p., 1915.

Lawless, D. J. "Attitudes of Leaders of Immigrant and Ethnic Societies in Vancouver Towards Integration into Canadian Life." International Migration 2 (1964): 201-11.

Lee, Calvin. Chinatown, U. S. A. New York: Doubleday, 1965.

Lee, Rose Hum. The Chinese in the United States. Hong Kong: Hong Kong University, 1960.

Lengyel, Cornel, ed. Fifty Local Prodigies. History of Music in San Francisco Series, Vol. V. San Francisco: W. P. A. of California, 1940.

Lengyel, Emil. Americans from Hungary. Philadelphia: Lippincott, 1948.

Leslie, Gerald R. The Family in Social Context, 3rd ed. New York: Oxford University Press, 1976.

Leupp, Constance D. "Climbing Out Through Music." The Outlook 102 (1912): 403-09.

Levant, Oscar. A Smattering of Ignorance. Garden City, N. Y.: Doubleday, 1959.

Levy, Harriet Lane. 920 O'Farrell Street. Garden City, N. Y.: Doubleday, 1947.

Levy, Lester. Flashes of Merriment. Norman: University of Oklahoma Press, 1971.

Lewisohn, Ludwig. "The Art of Being a Jew." Harper's Monthly Magazine 150 (1925): 725-29.

Leyburn, James G. "The Problem of Ethnic and National Impact from a Sociological Point of View." In Foreign Influences in American Life, ed. David F. Bowers. Princeton: Princeton University Press, 1944, pp. 57-66.

Liberace, Wladziu Valentino. An Autobiography. New York: Putnam, 1973.

Lifson, David S. The Yiddish Theatre in America. New

York: Yoseloff, 1965.

Liptzin, Sol. Eliakum Zunser. New York: Behrman House, 1950.

Llewellyn, Louise. "Boston Orchestra of Wage Earners." Musical America, 11 May 1912, p. 17.

Lopreato, Joseph. Italian Americans. New York: Random House, 1970.

Lord, Eliot, John J. D. Trenor, and Samuel J. Barrows. The Italian in America. 1905; rpt. Freeport, N. Y.: Books for Libraries, 1970.

Lowe, Pardee. Father and Glorious Descendant. Boston: Little, Brown, 1943.

Lui, Garding. Inside Los Angeles Chinatown. Los Angeles: N. p., 1948.

[McCulloch, Rhoda E.] And Who Is My Neighbor?, 2nd ed. New York: Association Press, 1928.

McLaughlen, Virginia Yans. "Like the Fingers of the Hand: The Family and Community Life of First-Generation Italian-Americans in Buffalo, New York, 1880-1930." Ph. D. diss., State University of New York at Buffalo, 1970.

McLellan, Mary B., and Albert V. DeBonis, eds. Within Our Gates. New York: Harper, 1940.

McWilliams, Carey. Brothers Under the Skin, rev. ed. Boston: Little, Brown, 1951.

Makar, János. The Story of an Immigrant Group in Franklin, New Jersey, tr. August J. Molnár. Franklin: Author, 1969.

Mangano, Antonio. "The Italian Colonies of New York City." In Italians in the City. New York: Arno, 1975, pp. 1-57.

_____. Sons of Italy. New York: Missionary Education Movement of the United States and Canada, 1917.

Mangione, Jerre. Mount Allegro. New York: Knopf, 1952.

Mann, Arthur. La Guardia: A Fighter Against His Times, 1882-1933. Philadelphia: Lippincott, 1959.

_____. Yankee Reformers in the Urban Age. New York: Harper & Row, 1966.

Manners, Ande. Poor Cousins. New York: Coward, McCann & Geoghegan, 1972.

Marchello, Maurice R. Crossing the Tracks. New York: Vantage, 1969.

Marden, Charles F., and Gladys Meyer. Minorities in American Society, 3rd ed. New York: Van Nostrand Reinhold, 1968.

Mariano, John Horace. The Italian Contribution to American Democracy. Boston: Christopher, 1921.

_____. The Second Generation of Italians in New York

City. Boston: Christopher, 1921.
Marinacci, Barbara. They Came from Italy. New York: Dodd, Mead, 1967.
Marks, Edward B. They All Sang. New York: Viking, 1935.
May, Elizabeth. "Encounters with Japanese Music in Los Angeles." Western Folklore 17 (1958): 192-95.
Mele, Frank. Polpetto. New York: Crown, 1973.
Melendy, H. Brett. The Oriental Americans. New York: Twayne, 1972.
Meller, Sidney. Home Is Here. New York: Macmillan, 1941.
_____. Roots in the Sky. New York: Macmillan, 1938.
Mellish, Mary. Sometimes I Reminisce. New York: Putnam, 1941.
Merrill, Robert, with Sandford Dody. Once More from the Beginning. New York: Macmillan, 1965.
Mighels, Philip Verrill. "A Music-School Settlement." Harper's Monthly Magazine 111 (1905): 832-41.
Militello, Pietro. Italians in America. Philadelphia: Franklin, 1973.
Miller, Kenneth D. The Czecho-Slovaks in America. New York: Doran, 1922.
Miller, Lucius Hopkins. Our Syrian Population. San Francisco: R. & E. Associates, 1969.
Miller, Maxine Adams. Ali, A Persian Yankee. Caldwell, Ida.: Caxton, 1965.
Monticelli, Giuseppe Lucrezio. "Italian Emigration." In The Italian Experience in the United States, ed. Silvano M. Tomasi and Madeline H. Engel. Staten Island, N. Y.: Center for Migration Studies, 1970, pp. 3-22.
Moquin, Wayne, and Charles Van Doren, eds. A Documentary History of the Italian Americans. New York: Praeger, 1974.
Musmanno, Michael A. The Story of the Italians in America. New York: Doubleday, 1965.
Nagata, Judith A. "Adaptation and Integration of Greek Working Class Immigrants in the City of Toronto, Canada, A Situational Approach." International Migration 4 (1969): 44-70.
Narodny, Ivan. "Laying Cornerstone for Upbuilding of Italian Music." Musical America, 31 May 1913, p. 13.
_____. "Music of the Balkan Nations." Musical America, 7 June 1913, p. 21.
_____. "Music of the Poles in America." Musical America, 3 May 1913, p. 27.
_____. "Musical Spices from the Orient." Musical

America, 9 August 1913, p. 19.
_____. "Two of Hungary's Leading Composers Now in
America." 17 May 1913, p. 13.
Nelli, Humbert S. Italians in Chicago, 1880-1930. New
York: Oxford University Press, 1970.
_____. "Italians in Urban America." In Urban America
in Historical Perspective, ed. Raymond A. Mohl and Neil
Betten. New York: Weybright & Talley, 1970.
Nettl, Bruno, and Ivo Moravcik. "Czech and Slovak Songs
Collected in Detroit." Midwest Folklore 5 (1955): 37-49.
Nettl, Paul. National Anthems, 2nd ed., tr. Alexander
Gade. New York: Ungar, 1967.
Novak, Michael. The Rise of the Unmeltable Ethnics. New
York: Macmillan, 1972.
Nulman, Macy. Concise Encyclopedia of Jewish Music.
New York: McGraw-Hill, 1975.
Okimoto, Daniel I. American in Disguise. New York:
Weatherhill, 1971.
[Ornitz, Samuel.] Haunch, Paunch and Jowl, An Anonymous
Autobiography. New York: Boni & Liveright, 1923.
Pagano, Jo. The Condemned. New York: Prentice-Hall,
1947.
_____. Golden Wedding. New York: Random House,
1943.
Panunzio, Constantine. Immigration Crossroads. New
York: Macmillan, 1927.
_____. The Soul of an Immigrant. New York: Mac-
millan, 1921.
Papashvily, George, and Helen Waite Papashvily. Anything
Can Happen. New York: Harper, 1945.
Park, No-Yong. Chinaman's Chance. Boston: Meador,
1940.
Park. Robert E. The Immigrant Press and Its Control.
New York: Harper, 1922.
_____, and Herbert A. Miller. Old World Traits Trans-
planted. New York: Harper, 1921.
Pawlowski, Harriet M., collector and ed. Merrily We Sing,
105 Polish Folksongs, analysis of music by Grace L.
Engel. Detroit: Wayne State University Press, 1961.
Peacock, Kenneth. Twenty Ethnic Songs from Western
Canada. Ottawa: National Museums of Canada, 1966.
Peeler, Claire P. "Where Music Moulds the Future Citi-
zen." Musical America, 24 July 1915, p. 15.
Pellegrini, Angelo M. Americans by Choice. New York:
Macmillan, 1956.
_____. Immigrant's Return. New York: Macmillan,
1952.

Perry, George Sessions. Families of America. New York: Whittlesey, 1949.
Petrakis, Harry Mark. Lion at My Heart. Boston: Little, Brown, 1959.
_____. The Odyssey of Kostas Volakis. New York: McKay, 1963.
_____. Pericles on 31st Street. Chicago: Quadrangle, 1965.
_____. Stelmark: A Family Recollection. New York: McKay, 1970.
_____. The Waves of Night and Other Stories. New York: McKay, 1959.
The Poles of Chicago, 1837-1937. Chicago: Polish Pageant, 1937.
Popkin, Zelda F. "The Changing East Side." American Mercury 10 (1927): 168-75.
Pozzetta, G. E. "The Italians of New York City, 1890-1914." Ph. D. diss., University of North Carolina at Chapel Hill, 1971.
Pribichevick, Stoyan. "In an American Factory." Harper's Magazine 177 (1938): 362-73.
Prisland, Marie. From Slovenia--To America. Chicago: Slovenian Women's Union of America, 1968.
The Problem of Immigration in Massachusetts. Report of the Commission on Immigration, Bernard J. Rothwell, chairman. Boston: 1914.
Prpic, George J. The Croatian Immigrants in America. New York: Philosophical Library, 1971.
Pupin, Michael. From Immigrant to Inventor. New York: Scribner, 1924.
Purcell, Joanne B. "Traditional Ballads Among the Portuguese in California." Western Folklore 28 (1969): 1-19.
Puzo, Mario. "Choosing a Dream." In The Immigrant Experience, ed. Thomas C. Wheeler. New York: Dial, 1971, pp. 35-49.
_____. The Fortunate Pilgrim. New York: Atheneum, 1965.
Radin, Paul. "The Italians of San Francisco." Abstract from the SERA project 2-F2-98 (3-F2-145): Cultural Autobiography. July 1935.
Ravage, M. E. An American in the Making. New York: Harper, 1917.
Rihbany, Abraham Mitrie. A Far Journey. Boston: Houghton Mifflin, 1914.
Riis, Jacob A. The Battle with the Slum. New York: Macmillan, 1902.
_____. The Children of the Poor. New York: Scribner,

1892.
_____. How the Other Half Lives, ed. Sam Bass Warner,
Jr. Cambridge: Belknap Press of Harvard University
Press, 1970.
_____. The Making of an American. New York: Mac-
millan, 1903.
_____. Out of Mulberry Street. New York: Century,
1898.
Rischin, Moses. The Promised City. Cambridge: Har-
vard University Press, 1962.
Rizk, Salom. Syrian Yankee. Garden City, N. Y.: Double-
day, 1943.
Roberts, Peter. Anthracite Coal Communities. New York:
Macmillan, 1904.
_____. The New Immigration. New York: Macmillan,
1912.
Rolle, Andrew F. The American Italians. Belmont, Calif.:
Wadsworth, 1972.
_____. The Immigrant Upraised. Norman: University
of Oklahoma Press, 1968.
Roots: An Asian American Reader, eds. Amy Tachiki, Ed-
die Wong, Franklin Odo, and Buck Wong. Los Angeles:
University of California Press, 1971.
Rose, Philip M. The Italians in America. New York:
Doran, 1922.
Rosenblatt, Samuel. Yossele Rosenblatt. New York: Far-
rar, Straus & Young, 1954.
Roskolenko, Harry. "America, the Thief." In The Immi-
grant Experience, ed. Thomas C. Wheeler. New York:
Dial, 1971, pp. 153-78.
Ross, Edward Alsworth. The Old World in the New. New
York: Century, 1914.
Rubin, Ruth. A Treasury of Jewish Folksong. New York:
Schocken, 1950.
_____. Voices of a People. New York: Yoseloff, 1963.
_____. "Yiddish Folksongs of Immigration and the Melt-
ing Pot." New York Folklore 17 (1961): 173-82.
Ryan, Joseph, ed. White Ethnics. Englewood Cliffs, N.J.:
Prentice-Hall, 1973.
Saloutos, Theodore. The Greeks in America. New York:
Teachers College Press, Columbia University, 1967.
_____. The Greeks in the United States. Cambridge:
Harvard University Press, 1964.
Sandberg, Neil C. "The Changing Polish American." Polish
American Studies 31 (1974): 5-13.
Sanders, Ronald. The Downtown Jews. New York: Harper
& Row, 1969.

_____. Reflections on a Teapot. New York: Harper & Row, 1972.

Santoro, Daniel, and John A. Rollo. Italians--Past and Present. Staten Island, N. Y.: Italian Historical Society, n. d. ["Foreword, " 1955].

Saroyan, William. My Name Is Aram. New York: Harcourt, Brace, 1940.

_____. The Saroyan Special. New York: Harcourt, Brace, 1948.

Sartorio, Rev. Enrico C. Social and Religious Life of Italians in America. Boston: Christopher, 1918.

Schaffer, Alan. Vito Marcantonio, Radical in Congress. Syracuse, N. Y.: Syracuse University Press, 1966.

Schermerhorn, R. A. These Our People. Boston: Heath, 1949.

Schiavo, Giovanni Ermenegildo. Italian-American History. New York: Vigo, 1947.

Schiro, George. Americans by Choice. Utica, N. Y.: N. p., 1940.

Schoener, Allan. Portal to America. New York: Holt, Rinehart & Winston, 1967.

Scott, John Anthony. The Ballad of America. New York: Bantam, 1966.

Seabrook, William. These Foreigners. New York: Harcourt, Brace, 1938.

Shaw, Arnold. Sinatra. New York: Holt, Rinehart & Winston, 1968.

Sherman, Allan. A Gift of Laughter. New York: Atheneum, 1965.

Sherman, C. Bezalel. The Jew Within American Society. Detroit: Wayne State University Press, 1961.

Shulman, Harry Manuel. Slums of New York. New York: Boni, 1938.

Sickels, Alice L. Around the World in St. Paul. Minneapolis: University of Minnesota Press, 1945.

Silber, Irwin. Songs America Voted By. Harrisburg, Pa.: Stackpole, 1971.

Simirenko, Alex. Pilgrims, Colonists, and Frontiersmen. London: Free Press of Glencoe, 1964.

Simon, George T. The Big Bands, rev. and enl. ed. New York: Collier, 1974.

Singer, Caroline. "An Italian Saturday. " The Century 101 (1921): 591-600.

Sklare, Marshall. America's Jews. New York: Random House, 1971.

Smith, Julia. Aaron Copland. New York: Dutton, 1955.

Smith, Richmond Mayo. Emigration and Immigration. New

York: Scribner, 1890.
Smith, William Carlson. Americans in Process. Ann Arbor, Mich.: Edwards, 1937.
Sone, Monica. Nisei Daughter. Boston: Little, Brown, 1953.
Sorrentino, Joseph N. Up from Never. Englewood Cliffs, N. J.: Prentice-Hall, 1971.
Souders, D. A. The Magyars in America. 1922; rpt. New York: Doran, 1969.
Spadoni, Adriana. "Cecco Remains." The Century 102 (1921): 880-88.
Spanuth, August. "Nationality and Virtuosity." Musical America, 29 October 1898, p. 11.
Speranza, Gino. Race or Nation. Indianapolis: Bobbs-Merrill, 1925.
Speroni, Charles. "The Development of the Columbus Day Pageant of San Francisco." Western Folklore 7 (1948): 325-35.
Spicer, Dorothy Gladys. Folk Festivals and the Foreign Community. New York: Woman's Press, 1923.
Stearn, E. G. My Mother and I. New York: Macmillan, 1918.
Steiner, Edward A. "The Hungarian Immigrant." The Outlook 74 (1903): 1040-44.
_____. The Immigrant Tide, Its Ebb and Flow, 2nd ed. New York: Revell, 1909.
_____. On the Trail of the Immigrant. New York: Revell, 1906.
Stevens, Halsey. The Life and Music of Béla Bartók, rev. ed. New York: Oxford University Press, 1964.
Straus, Henrietta. "Music Students in New York." The Century 108 (1924): 26-34.
Sullivan, Margaret J. L. P. "Hyphenism in St. Louis, 1900-1921: The View from the Outside." Ph. D. diss., St. Louis University, 1968.
Sutherland, Anne. Gypsies, the Hidden Americans. London: Tavistock, 1975.
Taft, Donald R. "Two Portuguese Communities in New England." Studies in History, Economics, and Public Law, ed. Faculty of Political Science of Columbia University, 118, Number 241 (1923).
Tait, Joseph Wilfrid. Some Aspects of the Effect of the Dominant American Culture Upon Children of Italian-Born Parents. New York: Teachers College Press, Columbia University, 1942.
Talese, Gay. Fame and Obscurity. New York: World, 1970.

_____. New York. New York: Harper, 1961.
Taylor, Philip. The Distant Magnet. London: Eyre & Spottiswoode, 1971.
Thomas, William I., and Florian Znaniecki. The Polish Peasant in Europe and America, 2 vols., 2nd ed. New York: Knopf, 1927.
Thomson, Virgil. American Music Since 1910. New York: Holt, Rinehart & Winston, 1971.
Toffler, Alvin. The Culture Consumers. Baltimore: Penguin, 1965.
Tomasi, Lydio F. The Italian American Family. Staten Island, N. Y.: Center for Migration Studies, 1972.
_____, ed. The Italian in America: The Progressive View, 1891-1914. Staten Island, N. Y.: Center for Migration Studies, 1972.
Tomasi, Mario. Like Lesser Gods. Milwaukee: Bruce, 1949.
Tomasi, Silvano M. Piety and Power. Staten Island, N. Y.: Center for Migration Studies, 1975.
_____, and Madeline H. Engel, eds. The Italian Experience in the United States. Staten Island: Center for Migration Studies, 1970.
Torrielli, Andrew J. Italian Opinion on America. Cambridge: Harvard University Press, 1941.
Valletta, Clement Lawrence. A Study of Americanization in Carneta. New York: Arno, 1975. [Reprint of Ph. D. diss., University of Pennsylvania, 1968]
Vaz, August Mark. The Portuguese in California. Oakland: I. D. E. S. Supreme Council, 1965.
Vecoli, Rudolph J. The People of New Jersey. Princeton: Van Nostrand, 1965.
Vlachos, Evangelos C. The Assimilation of Greeks in the United States. Athens, Greece: National Centre of Social Researches, 1968.
Vorse, Mary Heaton. A Footnote to Folly. New York: Farrar & Rinehart, 1935.
_____. Time and the Town, A Provincetown Chronicle. New York: Dial, 1942.
Vujnovich, Milos M. Yugoslavs in Louisiana. Gretna, La.: Pelican, 1974.
Ware, Caroline F. Greenwich Village, 1920-1930. Boston: Houghton Mifflin, 1935.
Ware, Helen. "The American-Hungarian Folk-Song." Musical Quarterly 2 (1916): 434-41.
Wargelin, John. The Americanization of the Finns. Hancock, Mich.: Finnish Lutheran Book Concern, 1924.
Warner, Frank M. "A Salute and a Sampling of Songs."

New York Folklore 14 (1958): 202-23.
Warner, W. Lloyd. American Life, Dream and Reality,
  rev. ed. Chicago: University of Chicago Press, 1962.
_____, and Leo Srole. The Social Systems of American
  Ethnic Groups. New Haven: Yale University Press,
  1945.
Wasastjerna, Hans R., ed. The History of the Finns in
  Minnesota, tr. Toivo Rosvall. Duluth: Minnesota
  Finnish-American Historical Society, 1957.
Weiss, Milford S. Valley City, A Chinese Community in
  America. Cambridge: Schenkman, 1974.
Weld, Ralph Foster. Brooklyn Is America. New York:
  Columbia University Press, 1950.
Wheeler, Thomas C., ed. The Immigrant Experience.
  New York: Dial, 1971.
Whyte, William Foote. Street Corner Society, 2nd ed.
  Chicago: University of Chicago Press, 1955.
Wilk, Max. They're Playing Our Song. New York:
  Atheneum, 1973.
Williams, Phyllis H. South Italian Folkways in Europe and
  America. New York: Russell & Russell, 1938.
Williams, Robin M., Jr. American Society, 2nd ed. New
  York: Knopf, 1967.
Wittke, Carl. We Who Built America. Cleveland: Western
  Reserve University, 1939.
Wong, Jade Snow. Fifth Chinese Daughter. New York:
  Harper, 1950.
_____. No Chinese Stranger. New York: Harper &
  Row, 1975.
Wood, Arthur Evans. Hamtramck, Then and Now. New
  York: Bookman, 1955.
Woods, Robert A., ed. Americans in Process. Boston:
  Houghton Mifflin, 1903.
Woods, Sister Frances Jerome. Cultural Values of Ameri-
  can Ethnic Groups. New York: Harper, 1956.
Wu, Cheng-Tsu. "Chink!" New York: World, 1972.
Wytrwal, Joseph A. America's Polish Heritage. Detroit:
  Endurance, 1961.
Xenides, J. P. The Greeks in America. New York:
  Doran, 1922.
Yaffe, James. The American Jews. New York: Random
  House, 1968.
Yezierska, Anzia. Red Ribbon on a White Horse. New
  York: Scribner, 1950.
Yutang, Lin. Chinatown Family. New York: Day, 1948.

AUTOBIOGRAPHICAL REPORTS EMPLOYED IN THIS STUDY

A. C., Jewish, second generation, May 1973.
A. J., Italian, first generation, April 1970.
A. J., Lebanese, first generation, November 1949.
A. R., Albanian, second generation, January 1969.
A. V., Italian, second generation, April 1972.
B. B., Italian, third generation, May 1972.
B. C., Italian, third generation, May 1969.
B. E., Italian, third generation, April 1974.
B. EA., Jewish, third generation, April 1971.
B. J., Italian, third generation, April 1974.
B. P., Greek, third generation, April 1967.
B. PA., Lithuanian, third generation, April 1969.
B. R., Lithuanian, third generation, May 1969.
B. RA., Jewish, third generation, May 1974.
B. S., Jewish, third generation, May 1974.
C. A., Chinese, first generation, November 1973.
C. B., Italian, second generation, May 1969.
C. M., Syrian, first generation, December 1949.
C. MA., Jewish, third generation, April 1977.
C. MB., Italian, third generation, April 1977.
C. T., Italian, third generation, May 1969.
D. C., Italian, third generation, May 1972.
D. CA., Italian, third generation, May 1974.
D. D., Greek, third generation, May 1974.
D. J., Italian, third generation, May 1973.
D. JA., Italian, third generation, April 1969.
D. JB., Italian, third generation, May 1973.
D. L., Italian, third generation, April 1970.
D. M., Albanian, third generation, April 1970.
D. P., Italian, third generation, April 1972.
D. S., Italian, third generation, May 1971.
D. S., Jewish, third generation, April 1976.
D. SI., Italian, third generation, May 1971.
D. V., Greek, first generation, December 1949.
E. B., Lithuanian, second generation, April 1972.
E. C., Italian, third generation, January 1969.
E. R., Portuguese, second generation, April 1971.
E. S., Syrian, first generation, November 1974.
F. S., Polish, third generation, January 1969.
G. C., Italian, second generation, November 1972.
G. F., Italian, third generation, April 1977.
G. P., Italian, third generation, April 1975.
G. R., Italian, third generation, April 1971.
G. RA., Italian, third generation, April 1970.
G. S., Jewish, third generation, April 1977.

G. SA., Jewish, third generation, May 1972.
H. A., Armenian, second generation, April 1977.
H. C., American, May 1972.
H. J., Armenian, first generation, December 1949.
H. R., Polish, third generation, April 1971.
H. RA., Armenian, second generation, April 1972.
I. D., Jewish, third generation, April 1971.
J. H., Greek, first generation, January 1950.
K. C., Jewish-Italian, third generation, May 1972.
K. D., Greek, third generation, May 1972.
K. K., Armenian, third generation, April 1970.
K. L., Czech, third generation, April 1975.
K. LA., Polish, third generation, January 1969.
K. M., Lebanese, second generation, April 1969.
K. MA., Lithuanian, third generation, May 1974.
K. V., Armenian, first generation, May 1976.
L. B., Italian, third generation, May 1974.
L. D., Jewish, third generation, January 1969.
L. J., Jewish, third generation, April 1970.
L. JA., Korean, first generation, April 1976.
L. M., Polish, first generation, May 1969.
L. P., Italian, third generation, April 1967.
L. PA., Jewish, third generation, May 1972.
L. S., Italian, third generation, April 1976.
M. A., Jewish, third generation, January 1969.
M. D., Italian, third generation, January 1969.
M. J., Italian, third generation, May 1973.
M. JA., Jewish, third generation, April 1970.
M. M., Italian, second generation, April 1976.
M. P., Italian, third generation, May 1972.
M. R., Hungarian, third generation, May 1974.
M. S., Greek, second generation, October 1971.
N. M., Spanish-Italian, third generation, April 1972.
O. V., Italian, third generation, May 1969.
P. A., Polish, third generation, May 1969.
P. B., Czech, third generation, April 1972.
P. M., Polish, second generation, April 1977.
P. P., Italian, third generation, April 1975.
P. R., Jewish, third generation, May 1971.
R. A., Italian, third generation, May 1972.
R. D., Polish, third generation, January 1969.
R. E., Greek, third generation, April 1970.
R. K., Polish, second generation, November 1966.
R. L., Italian, third generation, May 1972.
R. M., Portuguese, second generation, May 1973.
R. R., Italian, third generation, May 1973.
R. S., Italian, third generation, May 1971.

R. SA., Italian, third generation, May 1972.
R. T., Syrian, second generation, July 1969.
R. V., Armenian, second generation, April 1969.
P. W., Polish, third generation, May 1973.
S. A., Jewish, third generation, April 1974.
S. AB., Italian, third generation, May 1973.
S. C., Jewish, third generation, January 1969.
S. C., Polish, third generation, January 1969.
S. F., Italian, third generation, April 1975.
S. G., Ukrainian, first generation, October 1971.
S. H., Italian, third generation, April 1977.
S. I., Jewish, second generation, June 1971.
S. K., Ceylon, first generation, April 1975.
S. L., Portuguese, second generation, April 1970.
S. M., Armenian, third generation, April 1972.
S. N., Italian, third generation, April 1969.
S. S., Armenian, third generation, April 1976.
S. V., Hungarian, third generation, April 1972.
S. W., Chinese, second generation, November 1973.
T. C., Italian, third generation, May 1971.
T. J., Greek-Syrian, third generation, May 1972.
T. M., Polish, third generation, December 1965.
V. M., Jewish, third generation, April 1969.
V. S., Armenian, first generation, November 1976.
W. E., Italian, second generation, April 1976.
W. L., Jewish, third generation, April 1977.
Y. D., Armenian, third generation, April 1975.
Y. M., Japanese, second generation, November 1973.
Z. A., Jewish, third generation, May 1972.
Z. M., Armenian, second generation, April 1975.

MUSICAL EXAMPLES

Example 1. HUNGARIAN FLOWER-LOVE SONG

Ha kimegyek én a rétre kaszálni,
Nem tudok a virágtól rendet vágni,
Mert a virág elakasztja kaszámat,
Más öleli, az én kedves babámat.
Más öleli, más is ül az ölébe,
Más kacsintgat fekete két szemébe.

I am going to the meadow to mow grass,
I can't cut the flowers, around them I pass,
Every flower reminds me of my sweetheart,
Whom I still love, although we are now apart,
Someone else kisses her, sitting in her lap,
Winking in her eyes, I am therefore sad.

Trans. by Abigel Krajick

263

Example 2. HUNGARIAN MARCHING SONG

Hármat füttyentett a gözös masina,
Meghozta a levelemet a posta,
Az van irva gyász levelem lapjára,
Be köl rukkolni huszonhatodikára.

Be köl rukkolni huszonhatodikára,
Itt köl hagyni a jó édesanyámat,
Itt köl hagyni testvérjeim, szeretöm,
Jaj Istenem, ki lesz a gondviselöm?

Thrice the engine whistled as the train rolled by,
As I saw my mail, my head began to feel awry.
In my grief bearing letter it was written,
That I had to report to my regiment.

On the twenty-sixth I will have to report,
To my dear mother's aid I will not resort.
I will have to leave my brothers and my love;
Who will guard me, O Lord of heaven above?

Trans. by Abigel Krajick

Example 3.   NEAPOLITAN SONG: CARMÈ

Fuori mura ci stauna picciotta,
Fra le spine s'è fatta una casa:
Sul le foglie riposa la notte
Una rosa più bella non v'è.
Dormi, Carmè, Il più bel della vita è dormir!
Sogna di me, Su nel Cielo con te vo' salir!

Out beyond the gray walls lives a maiden;
Mid the rosebushes nestles her cottage;
On the leaves rests the night shadow laden:
No rose with her face can compare.
Slumber, Carmè! For to sleep is life's dearest delight!
Dream of me there! Up to heav'n we should both take our
    flight!

Trans. by Nathan Haskell
Dole

265

Example 4.   NEAPOLITAN SONG: IL GRANATELLO

Rita, sù svegliati, scendi bel bello,
Il Granatello lo vedi, è là,
Con questo tremulo mare d'argento,
Con questo vento a vol s'andrà!
Gli aranci olezzano dai bei giardini,
Ninfe e zerbini stanno a danzar:
Resina e Portici avremo allato,
Luogo più grato non puoi trovar!

Rita, my beauty, arise from thy pillow,
Il Granatello beckons away!
Silver the tremulous glittering billow,
Th'air soft and mellow, jocund the bay!

Oranges make all the gardens entrancing
Gayly are dancing Lovers rosecrowned,
Beautiful villages give us their greeting!
Lovelier meeting place cannot be found!

Trans. by Nathan Haskell
Dole

Example 5. GREEK IMMIGRATION SONG

Fevgo, glikia, fevgo, glikia, fevgo, glikia manula mu, Ah!
Fevgo, glikia, manula mu, mi varianastenazis;
Ke ti ftochi, ke ti ftochi kardula mu, Ah!
Ke ti ftochi kardula mu mi mu ti kommatiassis.

Tha pago stin, tha pago stin Ameriki, Ah!
Tha pago stin Ameriki, grigora na plutisso;
Ta dakria sou, ta dakria sou, mana mu, Ah!
Ta dakria sou, mana mu, ego na ta sfonghisso.

Ti m'ofeli, ti m'ofeki i Ameriki, Ah!
Ti m'ofeli i Ameriki ke ola ta kala tis,
Pu marane, pu marane tis manas mu, Ah!
Pu marane tis manas mu ta filla tis kardias tis?

I leave, sweet, I leave, sweet mother of mine,
Ah, I leave, sweet mother of mine, don't sigh painfully.
And poor, and poor heart of mine,
Ah, poor heart of mine, don't break.

I will go, I will go to America,
Ah, I will go to America soon to get rich;
Those tears of yours, those tears of yours, mother of mine,
Ah, those tears of yours, mother of mine, wipe them away.

Of what benefit is America,
Ah, of what benefit is America and all her wealth;

268

After I have withered, after I have withered,
Ah, after I have withered the leaves of my mother's heart?

Trans. by Vardoulis and
Rudolph Agraphiotis

Example 6.   SYRIAN IMMIGRATION SONG

Thelenna be rass'l babor w'nzilna,
W' d'moo il im rah mu'na,
Nihna baludna dushernaha
W'bi Boston abina mu suhoobina.

Ya Souria shifthek dum'ee ala chudoodee.
Rohithna dushernaha wurrana.
W'aimthain b'shoofek, ya uchthee,
Allah b'yufreh; ah, ya dounya.

We climbed to the top of the ship and descended,
And the tears of our mothers went with us;
We have departed from our homeland,
And remain in Boston with our friends.

O Syria, I picture you with tears on my cheeks.
Our souls we have left behind us.
And when I will see you again, my sister,
God only knows; ah, such is fate.

Trans. by the author

Example 7.   PORTUGUESE SAILOR SONG

Triste vida é do mariyo,
Qual d'ellas a mais cançada
Que pela trista solda de passa?
Tormentos, tormentos, Bom, Bom!

A sad life is that of a sailor.
What life is more tiresome?
Whose life is poorly compensated
And tormented, tormented, Bom, Bom!

Example 8. SLOVAK SONG

Ej Božemoj cotej Ameriki! Idze doňej narod preveliki,
Ija pojdzem, sak som mladi ešče. Dami Panboh tam dajake
sčesce.

Jaše vracim kecme nezabije, lem ti čekaj odomňe novinu.
Jak ot domne novinu dostaneš, šicko sebe doporjatku prines,
Sama šedneš navraneho koňa, atak pridzeš draha dušo moja.

Ajak vona do McKeesport prišla, to uš muža živoho nenašla;
Lem totu krev co znoho kapkala atak nadnu, prehorko plakala.

"Ej mužumoj co žeši ucinil, zesi tote dzeci osirocil!"
"Provic ženo tej mojej siroce, žeja lezim utej Americe;
Povic ženo najme nečekaju, boja ležim v Americkim kraju."

Ah, my God, what's in America? Very many people are going over there.
I will also go, for I am still young; God, the Lord, grant
me good luck there.

I'll return if I don't get killed, but you wait for news from
me.
Put everything in order, mount a raven-black horse, and
come to me, dear soul of mine.

But when she came to McKeesport, she did not find her
husband alive;
Only his blood did she find, and over it bitterly she cried.

"Ah, my husband, what did you do, orphaned these children

271

of ours?"
"To these orphans of mine, my wife, say that I lie in
America.
Tell them, wife of mine, not to wait for me, for I lie in
the American land. "

Example 9. LEBANESE LOVE SONG

Uh, bihoobek, wurde min il leile;
Uh, bishofthek, rah'l u'lath wi chere.
Smu'ee min ashab wurakee,
Smu'ee min il ashab, il ashab, il ashab wurakee, uh--
Uh, bihoobek, wurde min il leile;
Uh, bishofthek, rah'l u'lath wi chere.

Ah, from my love for you, flower of night;
Ah, from looking at you, I lost my mind and carefreeness.
Listen to your friends who are around you,
Listen to your friends, your friends, your friends who are
around you, ah--
Ah, from my love for you, flower of night;
Ah, from looking at you, I have lost my mind and carefree-
ness.

Trans. by the author

Example 10.   CHINESE LOVE SONG: THE MAID IN LOVE

Streamlet running by his window
Bears the sorrow and the pain;
In her heart, the maiden crying,
Puts her hand into the water,
Sends her longing down to him.

Paraphrased by the author

Example 11. HUNGARIAN CAROL

Pasztorok pasztorok orvendezve,
Sietnek Jezushoz Bethlehembe;
Koszontest mondanak a kis dednek,
Ki valtsagot hozott az embernek.

Angyalok szozata minket is hiv,
Ertse meg ezt tehat minden hu sziv;
A kisdid Jezuskat mi is aldjuk
Mint a hiv pasztorok magasztaljuk.

Zsasskovzky Enektar (The
Hymnal), 1855

The Shepherds, the shepherds are rejoicing,
To Bethlehem to Jesus they're going;
They bring greetings to the newly born child,
Who is the good Saviour of all mankind.

The songs of the angels to us calling too,
We hear this, understand and now so do,
The little child Jesus humbly to praise
Same way as the shepherds in the old days.

Trans. by Abigel Krajick

Example 12.   ITALIAN POPULAR SONG: CIRIBIRIBIN

275

(Example 12 cont.)

Su finiscila coi baci
Bel moruccio biricchin,
Ma non vedi tu la luna
Che dal ciel fa capolin?
Lascia pur la luna spii
Noi lasciamola spiar;
Anzi, il pallido suo raggio
Ci consiglia a seguitar!
Ma poi chisà? Cosa dirà? E via dirà, Quel che vorrà.
Aha? Aha? Ciribiribin, Ciribiribin, Ciribiribin.
Ciribiribin, che bel faccin,
Che sguardo dolce d'assassin.
Ciribiribin, che bel nasin,
Che bei dentin, che bel bocchin!
Ciribiribin, che bel faccin,
Che sguardo dolce d'assassin.
Ciribiribin, Ciribiribin, Ciribiribin, che bel faccin.

When the moon is brightly shining
On a lovely night like this,
Ev'ry maiden's heart is pining
For a sweetheart's tender kiss.
'Tis the song of sweet romancing
Filling hearts with love's desire;
'Tis a melody entrancing
Setting each maiden's heart afire!
Now from afar, hear the guitar; oh hear it played, sweet
    serenade.
Aha? Aha? Ciribiribin, Ciribiribin, Ciribiribin.
Ciribiribin, I love you and
Do cherish you with all my heart.
Ciribiribin, I hope and pray
Each day that we will never part!
Ciribiribin, if you would only
Say your love will never die.
Ciribiribin, Ciribiribin, Ciribiribin, I love you so.

Example 13a. PORTUGUESE SONG FOR THE JANEIRAS: SANTOS REIS

Example 13b.

Escutae, oh nobre gente,
Escutae e ouvireis,
Que da partedo Oriente
São chegados as treis Reis.

Listen, oh noble people,
Listen and you shall hear
That from the Orient
The three Kings do appear.

Example 14.   PORTUGUESE DANCE-SONG

Dancae, moças, esta noite,
Se do vosso gosto é,
Cheriam bem todas as hervas
Onde vos pondes o pe.

Dance, maidens, this night
If it is to your liking.
All the grass will smell the sweeter,
Where you place your feet.

Example 15. NEAPOLITAN SONG: FENESTA CHE LUCIVE

Fenesta che lucive mo non luce,
Segn'e che nenna mia stace ammalata,
S'affaccia la sorella e me lo dice:
"Nennella toja è morta e sotterrata.
Piangeva sempe ca dormeva sola, ah!
Mo dorme co li muorte accompagnata!
Mo dorme co li muorte accompagnata!"

"Va nella chiesa e scuopre lo tavuto,
Vide nennella toja comm'e tornata,
Da chella vocca che n'asceano sciure,
Mo n'escono le vierme, oh che pietate!
Zi Parrocchiano mio abbice cura, ah!
'Na lampa sempe tienece allumata!
'Na lampa sempe tienece allumata!"

That window once so bright, a curtain veiling,
A gloomy presage through my heart sent creeping,
"All grief," her sister said, "is unavailing,
In vain for her a loving watch you're keeping.
Your darling now is gone and left us wailing, ah!
And with the silent dead, alas, is sleeping!
Now with the silent dead, alas, is sleeping!"

"Go seek the church where Nina now reposes,
Beside her tomb thy faithful vigil keeping,
There lay the earliest violet that uncloses,
And lilies pale as she who there is sleeping.
And strew with loving hand her tomb with roses, ah!
And burn a lamp where our poor darling's sleeping!
And burn a lamp where our poor darling's sleeping!"

Trans. by Maria X. Hayes

Example 16. JAPANESE SONG: CHOCHAI BUSHI

Oeado neehon bashi,
Nanatsu Dashi,
Hatsunobori.
Guyoretsu soroeete
Ahrewaysainosa,
Chosha Takanawa yoache no,
Choshin chesu, Chochai, Chochai.

From the bridge of Yedo
Starts the endless file,
In the morning light
People are slowly coming.
They're seen moving everywhere,
Lanterns dim at Takanawara
As the sun emerges, Chochai, Chochai.

Paraphrase by the author

281

Example 17. <u>KOL NIDRE</u>

Example 18. YIDDISH SACRED SONG: <u>ELI, ELI</u>

Eli, Eli lomo azavtoni? Eli, Eli lomo azavtoni?
In feier un flam hut men uns gebrent,
Iberal gemacht tzu shand un shpot,
Doch optzuvenden hut uns keiner nit gekent
Fun dir, mine Gott, mit dine hayliger Toireh, un dine gebut.
Eli, Eli lomo azavtoni? Eli, Eli lomo azavtoni?
Tog un nacht, nor ich tracht fun mine Gott.
Ich heat mit moi-reh up dine Toireh, dine gebut.
Rete meech, rete meech fun gefar
Vee amol d'ovos fun bayzen gzar!
Hair mine gebait un mine gevane,
Helfen kenst du nor Gott alane,
Sh'ma Yisroel Adonoy eloheynu Adonoy echod.

Oh God, my God, why have You forsaken me? Oh God, my
    God, why have You forsaken me?
In fire and in flame they burned us,
Everywhere they dishonored and mocked us,
Yet they could not turn us away
From You, my God, from Your holy Torah, and from Your
    commandments.
Oh God, my God, why have You forsaken me? Oh God, my
    God, why have You forsaken me?
Night and day, I think only of my God.
Fearfully I guard Your Torah and Your commandments.
Deliver me, deliver me from danger
And from evil decree as You once did our forefathers!
Hear my prayer and my weeping,
Only You alone, God, can succor me!
Hear, O Lord, the Lord our God, the Lord is One!

Example 19a. FRAGMENT OF A VIOLIN TUNE

Example 19b. HASSIDIC DANCE

Example 20. MAGYAR NATIONAL ANTHEM: HIMNUSZ

Isten, áldd meg a magyart,
Jó kedvvel, bőséggel,
Njúts feléje védő kard,
Ha küzd ellenséggel.
Balsors akit régen tép,
Hozz réá vig esztendőt,
Megbünhödte már a nép
A multat 's jövendőt.

Gracious God, bless the Magyar,
With good cheer, prosperity,
In the ravages of war,
Shield her from adversity,
Whom from old ill fate has torn,
Bring her to a happy morn.
Long have we atoned and mourn
For the past and years unborn.

Trans. by Julianna C. Toth

Example 21. GREEK TRADITIONAL DANCE-SONG:
A <u>KALAMATIANOS</u>

Alas, my fine young friend
Has gone insane with love.
Oh, nothing stops his rushing to get wed
And tragic leap into the marriage bed.
(Refrain)
Drink to him, the poor lad;
Ah, drink to him and be glad
That she snagged him, and
We continue free,
Foiling other women's plans.

Trans. by M. S.

Example 22.   HUNGARIAN BRIDAL SONG

Megkötöttek nékem a koszorút,
Zöldlevele a kötömbe hűllott;
Hűllj le, hűllj le koszorúm levele,
Ugy sem teszlek többet a fejemre.

As they put the bridal wreath on my head
In my white apron the green leaves fluttered;
Fall down, fall down leaves of my bridal wreath,
I shall never wear one until my death.

Trans. by Abigel Krajick

Example 23a.   ITALIAN FUNERAL MARCH

Example 23b.   CHINESE FUNERAL MARCH

Example 24. GREEK EULOGY: ENKOMION

Hai geneai pasai
Hymnon tê taphê sou
Pro spherousi, Khriste mou.

1
All Thy people coming
To Thy tomb are singing
Eulogies, dear Christ, to
  Thee.

2
All Thy creation comes
Singing lamentations
And praises to Thee, O Lord.

3
He who in death hath life,
We have anointed now
In devotion, God, to Thee.

4
O Thou, who granteth life,
Glory be to Thy might,
That hath chained the power
  of hell.

5
Thee, we mourn with dirges
As did Thy Mother once,
When Thou, our Christ,
  wast murder'd.

6
Death by Thy death hast Thou,
O God, slain with the
  strength
Of the mighty Trinity.

7
Father, Son, and Holy
Spirit have mercy now
Upon Thy sinful people.

8
Through the Resurrection
Of Thy Son, O Mother
Of God, grant eternal life.

Example 25a.   HUNGARIAN SONG: DON'T BE SURPRISED

Don't be surprised, dear friend, that you find me so pale.
Alas, nine years have I been grinding
Steel in Albers' great shops.
I grind and grind and grind the steel plows for the American
   farmers.

Example 25b.   HUNGARIAN SONG: WHY DID I COME?

Why did I come, if not for cursed gold!
No judge's sentence compelled me to flee,
Nor was it an evil saying that pursued me;
Just gold, shining gold did I want to see.

Example 26.   JAPANESE MELODY

Example 27a.   CZECH MELODY 1

Example 27b.   CZECH MELODY 2

Example 27c.   CZECH MELODY 3

Example 27d. CZECH MELODY 4

Example 28. UKRAINIAN CAROL, THE GREEN APPLE
             TREE

(Refrain)

A green, green apple tree bore red apples.
[This line also recurs as a refrain, following each of the
following lines:]
A gracious maiden was caring for it.
Her mother came to her and asked,
"O my daughter, Marusja, pluck an apple for me!"
"I cannot, for I am keeping them all for my beloved."
Her beloved came to her,
"O my sweetheart! Pluck an apple for me!"
"O I shall, I shall! I've been keeping them for you!"

And for this carol give us a barrel of beer.
And for this entertainment--a quart of whisky!

Sung by Mrs. Doris
Uhrynjuk Plumas, Manitoba,
1964

Example 29.   UKRAINIAN CAROL, A WONDROUS EVENT

A wondrous event occurred this day in Bethlehem:
The Blessed Virgin gave birth to a son!
Swaddled and in a manger among the calves,
The Lord was resting on the hay, alone.
   [Repeat second line]

And now the cherubs are singing glory!
Angelic choirs greet the Master!
The poor shepherd brings what ever he can
In order to present a gift to the child of God!

And a bright star announces to the world:
The Messiah brings joy and happiness!
Let everyone hurry today to Bethlehem
To greet the Lord in a poor stable!

Sung by a member of the
collector's family, Toronto,
Ontario, 1961

Example 30a.   UKRAINIAN CAROL, <u>GOD ETERNAL WAS</u>
                                <u>THRASHING PEAS</u>

God eternal was thrashing peas--
Some for grits, some for groats--
I sure love your young daughter:
I think I'll marry her!

                    Sung by Tony Myk
                    Ashville, Manitoba, 1963

Example 30b.   UKRAINIAN CAROL, <u>GOD ETERNAL IS BORN</u>

God eternal is born!
He came this day from the heavens
To save all mankind
And he rejoiced!

                    Sung by members of the
                    collector's family,
                    Toronto, Ontario, 1961